Essay Index

THE COLLECTED ESSAYS & ADDRESSES

OF THE

Rt. Hon. AUGUSTINE BIRRELL

THE COLLECTED
ESSAYS & ADDRESSES
OF THE RT. HON.
AUGUSTINE BIRRELL
1880-1920

VOL. THREE

Essay Index Reprint Series

 BOOKS FOR LIBRARIES PRESS
FREEPORT, NEW YORK

First Published 1922
Reprinted 1968

LIBRARY OF CONGRESS CATALOG CARD NUMBER:

68-24844

PRINTED IN THE UNITED STATES OF AMERICA

CONTENTS

vi   CONTENTS

TRUTH-HUNTING

1884

IT is common knowledge that the distinguishing characteristic of the day is the zeal displayed by us all in hunting after Truth. A really not inconsiderable portion of whatever time we are able to spare from making or losing money or reputation, is devoted to this sport, whilst both reading and conversation are largely impressed into the same service.

Nor are there wanting those who avow themselves anxious to see this, their favourite pursuit, raised to the dignity of a national institution. They would have Truth-hunting established and endowed.

Mr. Carlyle has somewhere described with great humour the " dreadfully painful " manner in which Kepler made his celebrated calculations and discoveries; but our young men of talent fail to see the joke, and take no pleasure in such anecdotes. Truth, they feel, is not to be had from them on any such terms. And why should it be? Is it not notorious that all who are lucky enough to supply wants grow rapidly and enormously rich; and is not Truth a now recognised want in ten thousand homes—wherever, indeed, persons are to be found wealthy enough to pay Mr. Mudie a guinea and so far literate as to be able to read? What, save the modesty, is there surprising in the demand now made on behalf of some young people, whose means are incommensurate with their talents, that they should be allowed, as a reward for doling out monthly or quarterly portions of truth, to live in houses rent free, have their meals for nothing, and a trifle of money besides? Would Bass consent to supply us with beer in return for board and lodging, we of course defraying the actual cost of his brewery, and allowing him some £300 a year for himself? Who, as he read about *Sun-spots*, or *Fresh Facts for Darwin*, or the *True History of Modesty or Veracity*, showing how it came about that these high-sounding virtues are held in their present somewhat general esteem, would find it in his heart to grudge the admirable authors their freedom from petty cares?

But, whether Truth-hunting be ever established or not, no one can doubt that it is a most fashionable pastime, and one which is being pursued with great vigour.

All hunting is so far alike as to lead one to believe that there must sometimes occur in Truth-hunting, just as much as in fox-hunting, long pauses, whilst the covers are being drawn in search of the game, and when thoughts are free to range at will in pursuit of far other objects than those giving their name to the sport. If it should chance to any Truth-hunter, during some " lull in his hot chase," whilst, for example, he is waiting for the second volume of an *Analysis of Religion*, or for the last thing out on the Fourth Gospel, to take up this book, and open it at this page, we should like to press him for an answer to the following question : " Are you sure that it is a good thing for you to spend so much time in speculating about matters outside your daily life and walk?"

Curiosity is no doubt an excellent quality. In a critic it is especially excellent. To want to know all about a thing, and not merely one man's account or version of it; to see all around it, or, at any rate, as far round as is possible; not to be lazy or indifferent, or easily put off, or scared away—all this is really very excellent. Sir FitzJames Stephen professes great regret that we have not got Pilate's account of the events immediately preceding the Crucifixion. He thinks it would throw great light upon the subject; and no doubt, if it had occurred to the Evangelists to adopt in their narratives the method which long afterwards recommended itself to the author of *The Ring and the Book*, we should now be in possession of a mass of very curious information. But, excellent as all this is in the realm of criticism, the question remains, How does a restless habit of mind tell upon conduct?

John Mill was not one from whose lips the advice " *Stare super antiquas vias* " was often heard to proceed, and he was by profession a speculator, yet in that significant book, the *Autobiography*, he describes this age of Truth-hunters as one " of weak convictions, paralysed intellects, and growing laxity of opinions."

Is Truth-hunting one of those active mental habits which, as Bishop Butler tells us, intensify their effects by constant use ; and are weak convictions, paralysed intellects, and laxity of opinions amongst the effects of Truth-hunting on the majority of minds? These are not unimportant questions.

Let us consider briefly the probable effects of speculative habits on conduct.

The discussion of a question of conduct has the great charm of justifying, if indeed not requiring, personal illustration; and this particular question is well illustrated by instituting a comparison between the life and character of Charles Lamb and those of some of his distinguished friends.

Personal illustration, especially when it proceeds by way of comparison, is always dangerous, and the dangers are doubled when the subjects illustrated and compared are favourite authors. It behoves us to proceed warily in this matter. A dispute as to the respective merits of Gray and Collins has been known to result in a visit to an attorney and the revocation of a will. An avowed inability to see anything in Miss Austen's novels is reported to have proved destructive of an otherwise good chance of an Indian judgeship. I believe, however, I run no great risk in asserting that, of all English authors, Charles Lamb is the one loved most warmly and emotionally by his admirers, amongst whom I reckon only those who are as familiar with the four volumes of his *Life and Letters* as with *Elia*.

But how does he illustrate the particular question now engaging our attention?

Speaking of his sister Mary, who, as everyone knows, throughout *Elia* is called his Cousin Bridget, he says:

It has been the lot of my cousin, oftener, perhaps, than I could have wished, to have had for her associates and mine freethinkers, leaders and disciples of novel philosophies and systems, but she neither wrangles with nor accepts their opinions.

Nor did her brother. He lived his life cracking his little jokes and reading his great folios, neither wrangling with nor accepting the opinions of the friends he loved to see around him. To a contemporary stranger it might well have appeared as if his life were a frivolous and useless one as compared with those of these philosophers and thinkers. *They* discussed their great schemes and affected to probe deep mysteries, and were constantly asking, " What is Truth? " *He* sipped his glass, shuffled his cards, and was content with the humbler inquiry, " What are Trumps? " But to us, looking back upon that little group, and knowing what we now do about each member of it, no such mistake is possible. To us it is plain beyond all question that, judged by whatever standard of excellence it is possible for any reasonable human being to take, Lamb stands head and shoulders a better man than any of them. No need to stop to compare him with Godwin, or Hazlitt, or Lloyd; let us boldly put him in the scales with one whose fame is in all the churches—with Samuel Taylor Coleridge, " logician, metaphysician, bard."

There are some men whom to abuse is pleasant. Coleridge is not one of them. How gladly we would love the author of *Christabel* if we could! But the thing is flatly impossible. His was an unlovely character. The sentence passed upon him by Mr. Matthew Arnold (parenthetically, in one of the *Essays in Criticism*)—" Coleridge had no morals" —is no less just than pitiless. As we gather information about him from numerous quarters, we find it impossible to resist the conclusion that he was a man neglectful of restraint, irresponsive

to the claims of those who had every claim upon
him, willing to receive, slow to give.

In early manhood Coleridge planned a Panti-
socracy where all the virtues were to thrive. Lamb
did something far more difficult: he played crib-
bage every night with his imbecile father, whose
constant stream of querulous talk and fault-finding
might well have goaded a far stronger man into
practising and justifying neglect.

That Lamb, with all his admiration for Coleridge,
was well aware of the dangerous tendencies in his
character, is made apparent by many letters,
notably by one written in 1796, in which he says:

> O my friend, cultivate the filial feelings! and let no man
> think himself released from the kind charities of relationship:
> these shall give him peace at the last; these are the best
> foundation for every species of benevolence. I rejoice to hear
> that you are reconciled with all your relations.

This surely is as valuable an " aid to reflection "
as any supplied by the Highgate seer.

Lamb gave but little thought to the wonderful
difference between the " reason " and the " understanding." He preferred old plays—an odd diet,
some may think, on which to feed the virtues;
but, however that may be, the noble fact remains,
that he, poor, frail boy! (for he was no more when
trouble first assailed him) stooped down and, without a sigh or sign, took upon his own shoulders the
whole burden of a life-long sorrow.

Coleridge married. Lamb, at the bidding of
duty, remained single, wedding himself to the sad
fortunes of his father and sister. Shall we pity
him? No; he had his reward—the surpassing
reward that is only within the power of literature

to bestow. It was Lamb, and not Coleridge, who wrote *Dream-Children: a Reverie*:

Then I told how for seven long years, in hope sometimes, sometimes in despair, yet persisting ever, I courted the fair Alice W——n; and as much as children could understand, I explained to them what coyness and difficulty and denial meant in maidens—when, suddenly turning to Alice, the soul of the first Alice looked out at her eyes with such a reality of representment that I became in doubt which of them stood before me, or whose that bright hair was; and while I stood gazing, both the children gradually grew fainter to my view, receding and still receding, till nothing at last but two mournful features were seen in the uttermost distance, which, without speech, strangely impressed upon me the effects of speech. " We are not of Alice nor of thee, nor are we children at all. The children of Alice call Bartrum father. We are nothing, less than nothing, and dreams. We are only *what might have been.*"

Godwin! Hazlitt! Coleridge! Where now are their " novel philosophies and systems "? Bottled moonshine, which does *not* improve by keeping.

Only the actions of the just
Smell sweet and blossom in their dust.

Were we disposed to admit that Lamb would in all probability have been as good a man as everyone agrees he was—as kind to his father, as full of self-sacrifice for the sake of his sister, as loving and ready a friend—even though he had paid more heed to current speculations, it is yet not without use in a time like this, when so much stress is laid upon anxious inquiry into the mysteries of soul and body, to point out how this man attained to a moral excellence denied to his speculative contemporaries; performed duties from which they, good men as they were, would one and all have shrunk; how, in short, he contrived to achieve what no one of his friends, not even the immaculate Wordsworth or the precise Southey, achieved—the living of a life, the records of which are inspiriting to read, and are indeed " the presence of a good diffused "; and managed to do it all without either " wrangling with or accepting " the opinions that " hurtled in the air " about him.

But *was* there no relation between his unspeculative habit of mind and his honest, unwavering service of duty, whose voice he ever obeyed as the ship the rudder? It would be difficult to name anyone more unlike Lamb, in many aspects of character, than Dr. Johnson, for whom he had (mistakenly) no warm regard; but they closely resemble one another in their indifference to mere speculation about things—if things they can be called—outside our human walk; in their hearty love of honest earthly life, in their devotion to their friends, their kindness to dependents, and in their obedience to duty. What caused each of them the most pain was the recollection of a past unkindness. The poignancy of Dr. Johnson's grief on one such recollection is historical; and amongst Lamb's letters are to be found several in which, with vast depths of feeling, he bitterly upbraids himself for neglect of old friends.

Nothing so much tends to blur moral distinctions, and to obliterate plain duties, as the free indulgence of speculative habits. We must all know many a sorry scrub who has fairly talked himself into the belief that nothing but his intellectual difficulties prevents him from being another St. Francis. We think we could suggest a few score of other obstacles.

Would it not be better for most people, if,

instead of stuffing their heads with controversy, they were to devote their scanty leisure to reading books, such as, to name one only, Kaye's *History of the Sepoy War*, which are crammed full of activities and heroisms, and which force upon the reader's mind the healthy conviction that, after all, whatever mysteries may appertain to mind and matter, and notwithstanding grave doubts as to the authenticity of the Fourth Gospel, it is bravery, truth and honour, loyalty and hard work, each man at his post, which make this planet inhabitable?

In these days of champagne and shoddy, of display of teacups and rotten foundations— especially, too, now that the *nexus* of "cash payment," which was to bind man to man in the bonds of a common pecuniary interest, is hopelessly broken—it becomes plain that the real wants of the age are not analyses of religious belief, nor discussions as to whether " Person " or " Stream of Tendency " are the apter words to describe God by; but a steady supply of honest, plain-sailing men who can be safely trusted with small sums, and to do what in them lies to maintain the honour of the various professions, and to restore the credit of English workmanship. We want Lambs, not Coleridges. The verdict to be striven for is not " Well guessed," but " Well done."

All our remarks are confined to the realm of opinion. Faith may be well left alone, for she is, to give her her due, our largest manufacturer of good works, and whenever her furnaces are blown out, morality suffers.

But speculation has nothing to do with faith.

The region of speculation is the region of opinion, and a hazy, lazy, delightful region it is; good to talk in, good to smoke in, peopled with pleasant fancies and charming ideas, strange analogies and killing jests. How quickly the time passes there! how well it seems spent! The Philistines are all outside; everyone is reasonable and tolerant, and good-tempered; you think and scheme and talk, and look at everything in a hundred ways and from all possible points of view; and it is not till the company breaks up and the lights are blown out, and you are left alone with silence, that the doubt occurs to you, What is the good of it all?

Where is the actuary who can appraise the value of a man's opinions? "When we speak of a man's opinions," says Dr. Newman, "what do we mean but the collection of notions he happens to have?" Happens to have! How did he come by them? It is the knowledge we all possess of the sorts of ways in which men get their opinions that makes us so little affected in our own minds by those of men for whose characters and intellects we may have great admiration. A sturdy Nonconformist minister, who thinks Mr. Gladstone the ablest and most honest man, as well as the ripest scholar within the three kingdoms, is no whit shaken in his Nonconformity by knowing that his idol has written in defence of the Apostolical Succession, and believes in special sacramental graces. Mr. Gladstone may have been a great student of Church history, whilst Nonconformist reading under that head usually begins with Luther's Theses—but what of that? Is it not all explained by the fact that Mr. Gladstone was at Oxford in 1831? So at least the Nonconformist minister will think.

The admission frankly made, that these remarks are confined to the realms of opinion, prevents me from urging on everyone my prescription, but, with the two exceptions to be immediately named, I believe it would be found generally useful. It may be made up thus:

> As much reticence as is consistent with good-breeding upon, and a wisely tempered indifference to, the various speculative questions now agitated in our midst.

This prescription would be found to liberate the mind from all kinds of cloudy vapours which obscure the mental vision and conceal from men their real position, and would also set free a great deal of time which might be profitably spent in quite other directions.

The first of the two exceptions I have alluded to is of those who possess—whether honestly come by or not we cannot stop to inquire—strong convictions upon these very questions. These convictions they must be allowed to iterate and reiterate, and to proclaim that in them is to be found the secret of all this (otherwise) unintelligible world.

The second exception is of those who pursue Truth as by a divine compulsion, and who can be likened only to the nympholepts of old; those unfortunates who, whilst carelessly strolling amidst sylvan shades, caught a hasty glimpse of the flowing robes or even of the gracious countenance of some spiritual inmate of the woods, in whose pursuit their whole lives were ever afterwards fruitlessly spent.

The nympholepts of Truth are profoundly interesting figures in the world's history, but their lives are melancholy reading, and seldom fail to raise a crop of gloomy thoughts. Their finely touched spirits are not indeed liable to succumb to the ordinary temptations of life, and they thus escape the evils which usually follow in the wake of speculation; but what is their labour's reward?

Readers of Dr. Newman will remember, and will thank me for recalling it to mind, an exquisite passage, too long to be quoted, in which speaking as a Catholic to his late Anglican associates, he reminds them how he once participated in their pleasures and shared their hopes, and thus concludes:

When, too, shall I not feel the soothing recollection of those dear years which I spent in retirement, in preparation for my deliverance from Egypt, asking for light, and by degrees getting it, with less of temptation in my heart and sin on my conscience than ever before?

But the passage is sad as well as exquisite, showing to us, as it does, one who from his earliest days has rejoiced in a faith in God, intense, unwavering, constant; harassed by distressing doubts, he carries them all, in the devotion of his faith, the warmth of his heart, and the purity of his life, to the throne where Truth sits in state; living, he tells us, in retirement, and spending great portions of every day on his knees; and yet—we ask the question with all reverence—what did Dr. Newman get in exchange for his prayers?

I think it impossible to withstand the evidence which is brought for the liquefaction of the blood of St. Januarius at Naples, or for the motion of the eyes of the pictures of the Madonna in the Roman States. I see no reason to doubt the

material of the Lombard Cross at Monza, and I do not see
why the Holy Coat at Trèves may not have been what it professes to be. I firmly believe that portions of the True Cross
are at Rome and elsewhere, that the Crib of Bethlehem is at
Rome, and the bodies of St. Peter and St. Paul; also I firmly
believe that the relics of the Saints are doing innumerable
miracles and graces daily. I firmly believe that before now
Saints have raised the dead to life, crossed the seas without
vessels, multiplied grain and bread, cured incurable diseases,
and stopped the operations of the laws of the universe in a
multitude of ways.

So writes Dr. Newman, with that candour, that
love of putting the case most strongly against
himself, which is only one of the lovely characteristics of the man whose long life has been a
miracle of beauty and grace, and who has contrived
to instil into his very controversies more of the
spirit of Christ than most men can find room for
in their prayers. But the dilemma is an awkward
one. Does the Madonna wink, or is Heaven deaf?

Oh, Spirit of Truth, where wert thou when the
remorseless deep of superstition closed over the
head of John Henry Newman, who surely deserved
to be thy best-loved son?

But this is a digression. With the nympholepts
of Truth we have nought to do. They must be
allowed to pursue their lonely and devious paths,
and though the records of their wanderings, their
conflicting conclusions, and their widely-parted
resting-places may fill us with despair, still they
are witnesses whose testimony we could ill afford
to lose.

But there are not many nympholepts. The
symptoms of the great majority of our modern
Truth-hunters are very different, as they will,
with their frank candour, be the first to admit.
They are free " to drop their swords and daggers "

whenever so commanded, and it is high time they did.

With these two exceptions I think my prescription will be found of general utility, and likely to promote a healthy flow of good works.

I had intended to say something as to the effect of speculative habits upon the intellect, but cannot now do so. The following shrewd remark of Mr. Latham's in his interesting book on the *Action of Examinations* may, however, be quoted; its bearing will be at once seen, and its truth recognised by many:

A man who has been thus provided with views and acute observations may have destroyed in himself the germs of that power which he simulates. He might have had a thought or two now and then it he had been let alone, but if he is made first to aim at a standard of thought above his years, and then finds he can get the sort of thoughts he wants without thinking, he is in a fair way to be spoiled.

THE CHRISTIAN EVIDENCES

1901

I T is one of Bishop Butler's tremendous sayings, so resonant with the sincerity of his character, that religion is nothing unless it is true. I do not think this is the general belief. Gibbon's famous sneer about philosophers, magistrates, and mobs has not yet lost its point, and there are still many well-credited citizens who would not scruple to say that the Christian religion, which is the only one that makes any demands upon the Western World, is so closely bound up with our admirable Common Law, is so intimately associated with our educational system, so admirably well-adapted (in the opinion of the rich) to make the poor contented with their lot, affords so safe an outlet for the enthusiasm latent in many breasts, that, whether it be true or false, so far from being *nothing*, it is one of the most valuable bulwarks of society.

Such an opinion, however, is obviously not personal, and it may be that Butler was thinking of the individual man and what religion is to him in the dark watches of the night, and not what he may imagine it to be to others whose passions or predatory instincts he may very reasonably desire to control.

The assent of the mind to a proposition or to a series of propositions is never hypothetical. You cannot repeat the Apostles' Creed with faith, on the footing that if it happens to be untrue you are none the worse off for having believed it, whilst if it turns out to be true in substance and in fact, you are all the better for having given it the credit to which it proves entitled. You may sway backwards and forwards, from belief to unbelief, but you cannot at any one moment of time be in both states of mind.

Christianity being, so far as its confessions of faith are concerned, a modern religion, has from the first been subjected to hostile criticism. There have always been those who, though they had a fair chance of believing in its divine authority, refused to do so. The Gospels record instances of sceptics. In the correspondence of the Christian Fathers, who lived in the times, so near, in many respects, to our own, when the New Faith was partly crushing out and partly raking in the half-smoking embers of paganism, you may read the arguments and apprehend the frame of mind of educated men and women of lofty life and noble aim, who found it impossible to accept Christianity even when presented to them with fascinating friendliness and unfailing urbanity in the private letters of St. Augustine and St. Jerome.

From those times downwards we grow accustomed to a dreary, though important, section of literature—Christian Apologetics, the Defence of Faith, sometimes compendiously called the Christian Evidences.

Evidence is one of the great words of humanity. We all want it. Without it we do not willingly act in any matter of personal importance, yet what it is and how it should be brought home to the mind

are questions which have taken courts of justice
centuries to unravel. Our English law of evidence,
which has largely coloured men's minds, has been
called " the child of the jury." As soon as juries
ceased to be themselves witnesses, and became
judges of the facts in dispute, the King's judges
began with one accord to frame rules of exclusion,
which should prevent the untutored lay mind from
jumping to conclusions, and our so-called Law of
Evidence became nothing but a list of things that
might not be said and of witnesses who could not
be called. It was a long time being built up, and
it has taken just a century to pull it all down. It
is hardly too much to say that nothing is left of
our so-called Law of Evidence but the rule pro-
hibiting hearsay. The jury still must not be told
what the soldier said, for unless the soldier is there
to go into the box, what he said " is not evidence."

The law will not help us in this matter; it will
rather hinder us by suggesting false analogies and
filling our minds with misleading memories.

But the question of evidence remains. All are
agreed that the Christian religion has an historical
basis. Something happened in Judæa, and because
something happened there, our assent is invited
to a number of assertions purporting to be a revelation from heaven, which are in themselves incapable
of demonstration, and, indeed, of exact expression
in words. " A Revelation," says Dr. Mozley, " is,
properly speaking, such only by virtue of telling us
something which we could not know without it.
But how do we know that that communication of
what is undiscoverable by human reason is true? "

The clear-headed, if prosaic, Paley has his answer

ready: Miracles, nothing but miracles. And for long the controversy raged over the multiplication of loaves and the miraculous draught of fishes. Prove the Gospel miracles, and then you have simply *got* to believe in the whole cycle of Christian doctrine. You cannot help it. You may believe and tremble, as do the devils, or you may believe and rejoice, as do the saints, but believe you must. On the other hand, shake the Gospel miracles, any one of them, and down topple to their fall all the means of grace and the hope of glory.

It was a clear issue on paper, though really quite outside the human heart. It was contested on both sides here in England during the eighteenth century with great polemical vigour. A favourable example is Bishop Sherlock's *Trial of the Witnesses of the Resurrection,* published in 1729. This lively piece takes the agreeable form of a mock trial conducted, after a little preliminary buffoonery, by some gentlemen of the Inns of Court. Two counsel were appointed to argue for and against the Resurrection, and a fortnight was allowed them to get the case up, for, as the free-thinking advocate said pleasantly of his orthodox opponent, " Consider, sir, the gentleman is not to argue out of Littleton, Plowden, or Coke, authors to him well known; but he must have his authorities from Matthew, Mark, Luke and John, and a fortnight is time little enough of all conscience to gain a familiarity with a new acquaintance." And, turning to the gentleman, he said: " I will call upon you before the fortnight is out, to see how reverend an appearance you make behind Hammond on the New Testament, a Concordance on the one hand, and a folio Bible with references on the other." His opponent replied good-humouredly to this banter, and then, " Upon this we parted, all pleased with the appointment made except the two gentlemen who were to provide the *entertainment.*"

The entertainment consisted in first calling upon Counsel to prove the accusation that the evidence of the Resurrection is false. Says the Judge in a fine parody of the judicial manner of the day:

> Look ye, the evidence of the resurrection of Jesus is before the Court recorded by Matthew, Mark, and others. You must take it as it is, you can neither make it better or worse. These witnesses are accused of giving false evidence. Come to the point, and let us hear what you have to offer to prove the accusation.

On this business footing the argument proceeds and does not call for much remark, except that Dr. Sherlock puts into the mouth of the prosecuting counsel the argument usually associated with the name of Hume:

> That in common affairs where nothing is asserted but what is probable and possible and according to the usual course of nature, a reasonable degree of evidence ought to determine every man; for the very probability or possibility of the thing is a support to the evidence, and in such cases we have no doubt but a man's senses qualify him to be a witness. But when the thing testified is contrary to the order of nature, and at first sight at least impossible, what evidence can be sufficient to overturn the constant evidence of Nature which she gives us in the constant and regular method of her operations. If a man tells me he has been in France, I ought to give a reason for not believing him; but if he tells me he comes from the grave, what reason can he give why I should believe him?

However, the Judge sums up on the orthodox side, and the jury after consultation return their verdict, that the Apostles are not guilty of giving false evidence in the case of the resurrection of

Jesus; and thereupon the Judge jumps down from the bench, and is at once offered a fee if he will undertake to argue Lazarus's case, which is to come on next.

Anything more essentially irreligious, more defiling to the mysteries of the faith Dr. Sherlock was honestly defending, can hardly be imagined. Nor is there from first to last in this once famous tract any real appreciation of the nature of strict proof of an event alleged to have taken place seventeen hundred years before. You have no right to appeal unto Cæsar and then to disregard the rules of Cæsar's court. To parody a Court of Justice, and a trial by jury in England of a disputed fact, and then to produce out of the library four old books in print without any evidence of their authorship, authority, or date, or of the circumstances of their compilation, and to treat the several statements contained in them as uncontradicted evidence, is, of course, childish. A religion may be none the worse for not being able to prove its supernatural origin before a British judge and jury, but to allege that it can do so is now impossible.

When, in 1825, Dr. Newman sat down to write his first essay on miracles, his temper and frame of mind were very different from Dr. Sherlock's, and yet in one respect they did not differ; for Newman does not in that essay bestow any attention on the documents which record the Scripture miracles. He simply takes them for granted, but for all that he is not prepared to rest with his whole weight upon miracles. He sees much that was hid from the old Bishop of London. Miracles have become but *a branch* of the Evidences. Newman, in 1825, recognised how previous apologists have first used the miracles to attest the doctrine, and then cited the doctrine to make you credit the miracle; and he also clearly saw how, apart from an antecedent belief in a good and omnipotent God, miracles can be no evidence of the *morality* of a revelation. And he bluntly remarks what one now hears on all sides, that if the single fact of the Resurrection be established, quite enough will be proved to justify a belief in all the miracles of Scripture, and (he might have added, though he did not) to render belief in the other miracles a matter of indifference.

Since 1825 the oversight of Dr. Sherlock and Dr. Newman has indeed been cured, and the documents of Christianity have been rigorously, and sometimes almost vindictively, criticised and examined. It would be unwise for any plain man who has his living to make in a workaday world to pin his faith too tightly to any school of Biblical criticism. Romance, imagination, predilection, passion, prejudice, personal aversion, are at least as likely to be found inhabiting the studies of biblical students as infecting the laboratories of rival biologists or the offices of party politicians. A wholesome truth is quickly expanded into an exaggeration; exaggerated statements provoke a reaction which easily becomes retrogression. Still, despite the ebb and flow, the growth of reputations, and then the ruthless lopping of them down to the ground, progress of some kind is made; and in the matter of Christian apologetics, though proof by miracle has not been formally abandoned, Paleyism is as dead as Queen Anne. In 1870, when Dr. Newman came to publish the *Grammar of Assent*, his dislike of Paleyism, observable enough in 1825 in the *Essay on Miracles*, bursts forth in unmistakable sincerity and warmth of expression:

> I confess to much suspicion of legal proceedings and legal arguments when used in questions whether of religion or of philosophy. . . . Why am I to begin with taking up a position not my own, and unclothing my mind of that large outfit of existing thoughts, principles, likings, desires and hopes which make me what I am? If I am asked to use Paley's argument for my own conversion, I say plainly I do not want to be converted by a smart syllogism; if I am asked to convert others by it, I say plainly I do not care to overcome their reason without touching their hearts. I wish to deal not with controversialists, but with inquirers.

This is very spirited, but it is to give up a great part of the case. " I do not want to be converted by a smart syllogism "; or, in plain English, Dr. Newman will not be converted by the force of mere argument addressed to his reason. But is there no such thing as mental compulsion? Has a man *never* been convinced of anything against his wish? Is it to be assumed that for the future nobody will become a Christian unless he is mysteriously predisposed so to do? If this be so, whence comes this predisposition? Soul of Jonathan Edwards, art thou about to be justified after all these years?

The passage just quoted from the *Grammar of Assent* indicates the remarkable shifting of ground that has taken place during the last three decades.

A quarter of a century ago the ordinary Christian apologist had not completely shed his Paleyism, and still maintained the arguments, though he might cease to read the treatises of John Locke and Bishop Sherlock and Archdeacon Paley, whilst, to quote the language of the learned author of *Supernatural Religion* (1874):

The prevalent characteristic of popular theology in England at this time may be said to be a tendency to eliminate from Christianity with thoughtless dexterity every supernatural element which does not quite accord with current opinion, and yet to ignore the fact that in so doing ecclesiastical Christianity has practically been altogether abandoned.

To lighten the burden of faith, to maintain a rational Christianity, free from dogmas that cannot be verified historically, was the aim of the Broad Church party in the Church of England in 1874. Where is that party now? Its almost total disappearance is a remarkable and noteworthy fact. Broad Churchmen are all either dead or dumb.

Yet never was there a time when religion was more discussed. Young men and maidens are not so tongue-tied about it as it was the fashion to be thirty years ago. At the Universities, at the public schools, great changes are noticeable in this important respect. There is much fervour, not wholly unlike the manifestations that used to be called Evangelical. All around us we see proofs of energy and zeal and determination and self-sacrifice frequently associated with a devotion—albeit sometimes a hazy devotion—to the services of the Anglican Church.

Now, as it is not possible to dissociate Christianity from evidence of some kind or other, and as Paleyism is dead, and the Broad Church party which dispensed with dogma is silenced, it is interesting to inquire, How are men's minds reconciled to the Christian Faith at this present moment?

The ground has shifted. About that there is no

doubt. Canon Scott Holland, who is always frank, puts it thus:

> If this be the relation of faith to reason, we see the explanation of what seems at first sight to the philosopher to be the most irritating and hypocritical characteristic of faith. It is always shifting its intellectual defences. It adopts this or that fashion of philosophical apology, and then when this is shattered by some novel scientific generalisation of faith, probably after a passionate struggle to retain the old position, suddenly and gaily abandons it, and takes up the new formula, just as if nothing had happened. It discovers that the new formula is admirably adapted for its purposes, and is, in fact, what it always meant, only it has unfortunately omitted to mention it. So it goes on, again and again; and no wonder that the philosophers growl at those humbugs the clergy (*Lux Mundi*, 15th ed., 25).

Happily, there is never any real necessity for philosophers to growl at the clergy, unless, indeed, the philosophers are tied to the stake. Things run their destined course, but what that course is may without offence be made the subject-matter of inquiry.

One great change is easily noticed. It is the growing disposition to approach the central dogmas of Christianity by the avenues of Ritual. Dogma, said the Jewish Rationalist Bernez, is a source of disunion, but ancient ritual observances preserve a common *esprit de corps*.[1] Atmosphere is a great word just now. To deny the existence of atmosphere in the realm of thought is, in my opinion, proof of blunted susceptibilities. Not only does it exist, but its effect can hardly be exaggerated. The opponents of an Irish University with a Catholic atmosphere often point to Oxford and Cambridge as they now are, and ask triumphantly

[1] I borrow this quotation from a remarkable article that lately appeared in the *Quarterly Review*, entitled " The Ethics of Religious Conformity."

whether youthful members of dissenting house-
holds do not annually proceed to those seats of
learning from whence all religious tests (or nearly
all) have been banished. Why should not the
Catholic youth of Ireland be content with Trinity
College, Dublin, which throws open her famous
doors to all ingenuous souls, regardless of religious
opinions? But atmosphere can only be tested by
results, and one would like to know what percent-
age of the Nonconformist undergraduates who
have proceeded to their degrees at Oxford and
Cambridge during the last thirty-five years have
successfully resisted the *genius loci*, have become
ministers, deacons, and elders of their family
chapels, and are now to be seen on Sunday morn-
ings and evenings conducting a retinue of young
schismatics into the family pew. I should like to
have the figures. Atmosphere, I repeat, is a great
word and a great thing, and ritual tends to breed
it and to promote a dreamy acquiescence in hazy
mysteries. I think those clergy who attach importance to incense in church services show more
knowledge of human nature and of the strange
forces of association than do those who laugh and
sneer at fumigation. I know an old man who has
admitted to me that he can never discern a tan-
yard by its smell without profound emotion, so
instantly is he reminded of his first home, and the
shadowy outlines and tender impressiveness of a
mother who died when he was but five years old.
His father, I should guess, was a tanner.

It is obvious that a man who does not wish to
break with Christianity, yet finds it out of the
question to believe in any downright honest sense

in the creed of Christendom, can find no shelter
more convenient, less jarring and disagreeable,
than an ancient, time-worn ritual, which gives
dim expression to ghostly ideas, shadowy, sym-
bolical, sacramental notions of sin, sacrifice and
atonement, ideas which possess the advantage of
never coming into contact with the so-called
realities of history, and elude as gracefully as a
wreath of white smoke the grasp of proof.

It is now thought, and even felt, to be indelicate
to drag dogmas down into the arena of strife. I
frankly shudder at the spectacle of Bishop Sherlock's Templars bandying about arguments for and
against the Resurrection, and their discussions as
to whether Christ was an enthusiast or a rogue or
God Himself make me sick. Yet an undogmatic
Christianity is an empty pretence. I remember
Dr. Wallace in the House of Commons pointing
out in his unrivalled manner the intensely dogmatic character of " Board School Christianity,"
which is based upon two stupendous dogmas—
the existence of God and the revelation in the
New Testament.

Dogma cannot be dispensed with, but if it is
introduced to your notice through the sensuous
medium of Ritual and the observances of the
Church, it is, so to speak, banished from the
realms of day, from the fierce light that beats
upon argument, to an emotional region, where it is
so easy to assume whatever it is pleasant to believe
or unprofitable to deny. The Christian apologist
of the future will be more like Mr. Pater than
Mr. Paley.

This frame of mind has been fostered by the

undoubted force with which certain fashionable thinkers, themselves trained in the schools of sceptical thought, but personally indisposed for a variety of reasons, some good, some (it may be) not quite so good, to abandon Christianised notions and their relations (all of an easy nature) with the Christian Church, have carried and planted in the middle of the field of physical science the very agnostical flag which forty years ago the men of science had so triumphantly waved over the field of revealed religion.

Assumptions incapable of logical proof, once thought to be the peculiar weakness of dogmatic religion, are shown to lie about the very foundations of science. It does seem impossible out of the individual experiences of our poor limping senses to construct a theory of causation or of anything else. The world has very soon grown weary of the rhetoric of natural philosophers. The great Sir Robert Peel was probably the last man of real eminence who could with gravity assure a company of his fellow-sinners that physical science imparts pleasure and consolation on a death-bed, nor would Lord Brougham to-day find a sympathetic audience ready to cheer his self-satisfied statement that one of the most gratifying *treats* which science affords us is the knowledge of the *extraordinary* powers with which the human mind is endowed. To-day we are not a little disenchanted. These treats and consolations turn our stomachs. The spectacle of Lord Brougham's extraordinary powers no longer pleases. We are in a mood ripe for an indolent reaction. We could almost revile the Moses who led us out of the land of Egypt. The flesh-pots were pleasant, and it is with a malicious pleasure that we learn that Science has no better logical foundation for its syntheticism than our poor old friend Religion has for hers.

The Christian apologists look on with a bland smile. They can have no objection to an enlargement of the area of the scepticism of the natural man. Philosophic [1] doubt is no bad site for a Christian temple, and, after all, every religious man feels, though in bygone days he did not think it wise to say so, that a religion which cannot prove itself cannot be proved *ab extra*. Stories about strange occurrences in remote places, of which different versions have travelled down the ages, will no longer convince, if they ever did convince, a single free intelligence; but, on the other hand, no man is going to be put off his faith in God on account of the Gadarene swine.

This predisposition to believe is now, with an almost amazing frankness, taken as the starting-point in the race for faith.

You believe in Conscience, " the aboriginal vicar of Christ, a prophet in its informations, a monarch in its peremptoriness, a priest in its blessings "; but Conscience not only makes cowards of us all, but theists of a good many. Whence came this love of justice " dwelling between the endless jar of right and wrong " ? From believing in Conscience you come to believe in God. Believing in God, you chance one day to recognise in the reported words of Jesus the notes of Deity. Never man spoke like this Man. You believe Christ to be

[1] " To despair of philosophy has become the first basis of theology."
—RENAN: *The Future of Science.*

Divine. Believing Him to be Divine, it is impossible to believe that

> Far hence He lies
> In the lone Syrian town,
> And on His grave with shining eyes
> The Syrian stars look down.

No; He rose from the dead, not because to rise from the dead is a convincing thing to do, but because, being Divine, He could not do otherwise. Had he not risen, He would not have been God. Having risen, it seems to follow, as the night the day, that the spirit of God should remain upon the earth God had visited, to work upon the hearts of men all down the ages. The mission of the Comforter is as inevitable after the Ascension as was the Resurrection after the death upon the Cross. If you are so minded, and find as a matter of daily experience that the Spirit of God is conveyed to you through sacramental channels, attested by the authority of the Church, who can say you nay?

What has evidence, in any ordinary sense of the word, got to do with this?

By the term " evidence " [says Jeremy Bentham], considered according to the most extended application that is ever given to it, may be, and seems in general to be, understood any matter of fact the effect, tendency, or design of which, when presented to the mind, is to produce a persuasion concerning the existence of some other matter of fact, a persuasion either affirmative or disaffirmative of its existence. The first question in natural religion is no more than a question of evidence. From the several facts that have come under my senses relative to the several beings that have come under my senses, have I or have I not sufficient ground to be persuaded of the existence of a being distinct from all these beings, a being whose agency is the cause of the existence of all these, but whose separate existence has never at any time by any perceptible impressions presented itself, as that of other beings has done, to the cognisance of the senses? (*Rationale of Judicial Evidence*, vol. i.)

Whenever a man writes like that about such a
subject as Religion, whether he calls it natural or
revealed, you know he has made up his mind
beforehand. The most powerful teacher of the
spirituality of things religious in England during
the last century was Carlyle, who, writing in the
year 1829, said of Novalis:

> He belongs to that class of persons who do not recognise
> the syllogistic method as the chief organ for investigating
> truth, or feel themselves bound to stop short where its light
> fails them. Many of his opinions he would despair of proving
> in the most patient court of law, and would remain well
> content that they should be disbelieved there.

This is very much Dr. Newman's attitude.

It would, however, be premature to say that
Christian apologists have thrown all the Christian
evidences as they used to be understood to the
winds. They may still be found resting their case
on the historical fact of the Resurrection, and this
not so much because it is or is not an historical
fact—for that in itself is felt to be somewhat of
an objection to it—but because unless Christ rose
from the dead, the Incarnation is conceived to be
impossible, and the Incarnation is the basis of
Christian dogma.

This is the way in which Mr. Moberley handles
the subject in *Lux Mundi* (15th Ed., 171):

> Upon the historical truth or falsehood of the Resurrection
> hangs the whole question of the nature and work of Jesus
> Christ, the whole doctrine of Incarnation and Atonement.
> But in saying this it is necessary to guard our proper meaning.
> If we admit the fact of the Resurrection to be cardinal, what
> is the fact of the Resurrection which is in question? It is
> as far as possible from being simply a question whether " a
> man " could or could not, did or did not, reappear after death
> in life. . . . However much Christians may have at times
> to argue about the simple evidence for the " yes " or " no "

of the Resurrection of Jesus as if it were the alleged resurrection of any other man that was in question, neither the question itself nor the evidence about it can possibly be, in fact, of the same nature or upon the same level as the evidence about another. No amount of conviction of the reappearance in life of any other man would have any similar meaning or carry any similar consequences. The inherent character of Him who rose and the necessary connection between what He was and had said and claimed for Himself on the one hand, and on the other His rising out of death; this is an essential part of that fact of the Resurrection which comes up for proof or disproof. The fact that Jesus Christ, *being what He was*, the climax and fulfilment of a thousand converging lines—nay, of all the antecedent history of mankind —rose from the dead, and by that fact of Resurrection illuminated and explained for the first time all that had before seemed enigmatical or contradictory in what He was, and, indeed, in all humanity; this is the real fact of the Resurrection which confronts us. It is this vast fact which is either true or false. The Resurrection of the crucified Jesus cannot possibly be a bare or simple fact. When viewed as material manifestation of the moment only, it is at least misunderstood; it may be unintelligible. It is, no doubt, an event in history, and yet it confronts us even there in its place and witness in history, not simply as a finite historical event, but as an eternal counsel and infinite act of God.

This lofty vein would have puzzled good Bishop Sherlock, and been altogether beyond the powers of the young gentleman who got up his brief for the Resurrection in a fortnight, but it is a perfectly fair way of treating so tremendous a theme. Nobody ever became a Christian as the result of studying the Gospel accounts of the appearances of Christ after the Crucifixion. The Resurrection itself is nowhere described; it is assumed. Nor did, so we are now assured, the Lord appear to His disciples in the Body which had hung upon the Cross. "This fact," says Bishop Westcott, "seems to me to involve the essence of the whole revelation of the risen Christ " (*The Revelation of the Risen Lord*). But if it was not a natural objective Body what was it? Sometimes the Gospel narrative tells us of a ghostly presence—a phantom—liberated from the laws of matter; sometimes of a presence so materialised as to appear to exhibit the *stigmata* of the Cross.

The Bishop of Durham finds it necessary to discuss the problems of personality and identity, and to employ language not understanded of the common people. The Apostle John uses the remarkable words, " For as yet they knew not the Scripture that He *must* rise from the dead." After this it is almost absurd to talk about evidence. Christianity presents itself to the mind imperatively or not at all. If Christ were God He rose from the dead according to the Scriptures. A Christian believes in the Resurrection because he believes in the Incarnation, of all mysteries the most mysterious, the most ineffable, the farthest removed from the ken of man, and yet the one mystery which has been popularised and day after day presented to the people in the great drama of the Mass.

Readers of Dr. Newman's story, *Loss and Gain*, have not forgotten the famous passage Dean Stanley could never read without horror, describing in language of breathless rapidity and prodigious excitement the advent of God upon the Altar. The Miracle of the Mass flows from the Miracle of Calvary, and it is through the Mass that our present Christian apologists would have us approach the Incarnation.

Evidence is here out of place. We seem to be approaching a time in England when sceptics and divines may shake limp hands. The divine need no longer assert that he can compel belief or prove anything except, experimentally, upon the sad heart of man, whilst the sceptic may as well at once admit that he has disproved nothing. The finest philosophical poem of last century is Robert Browning's *Bishop Blougram*. Furthermore, the divine, if gently handled, may not be indisposed to admit that the central dogma of the Incarnation cannot yet be stated in language of finality but only in words of adumbration and mystical symbolism, whilst no sceptic can have any objection to make the most hackneyed of all Shakespearean quotations. The divine may then array himself in the robes of ancient sacrifice, and approach the altar, leaving the sceptic to conceal himself behind a pillar in the nave until the service is over. But when next they meet they should avoid the subject of *Church Discipline*. On that rock their friendship is destined to founder.

THE MUSE OF HISTORY

1887

TWO distinguished men of letters, each an admirable representative of his University —Mr. John Morley and Professor Seeley— have lately published opinions on the subject of history, which, though very likely to prove right, deserve to be carefully considered before assent is bestowed upon them.

Mr. Morley, when President of the Midland Institute, and speaking in the Town Hall of Birmingham, said: " I do not in the least want to know what happened in the past, except as it enables me to see my way more clearly through what is happening to-day," and this same indifference is professed, though certainly nowhere displayed, in other parts of Mr. Morley's writings.[1]

Professor Seeley never makes his point quite so sharp as this, and probably would hesitate to do so, but in *The Expansion of England* he expounds a theory of history largely based upon an indifference like that which Mr. Morley professed at Birmingham. His book opens thus:

It is a favourite maxim of mine that history, while it should be scientific in its method, should pursue a practical object —that is, it should not merely gratify the reader's curiosity about the past, but modify his view of the present and his forecast of the future. Now, if this maxim be sound, the history of England ought to end with something that might be called a moral.

[1] *Critical Miscellanies*, vol. iii., p. 9.

This, it must be admitted, is a large order. The task of the historian, as here explained, is not merely to tell us the story of the past, and thus gratify our curiosity, but, pursuing a practical object, to seek to modify our views of the present and help us in our forecasts of the future; and this the historian is to do, not unconsciously and incidentally, but deliberately and of set purpose. One can well understand how history, so written, will usually begin with a maxim, and invariably end with a moral.

What we are afterwards told in the same book follows in logical sequence upon our first quotation —namely, that " history fades into *mere literature* (the italics are ours) when it loses sight of its relation to practical politics." In this grim sentence we read the dethronement of Clio. The poor thing must forswear her father's house, her tuneful sisters, the invocation of the poet, the worship of the dramatist, and keep her terms at the University, where, if she is really studious and steady, and avoids literary companions (which ought not to be difficult), she may hope some day to be received into the Royal Society as a second-rate science. The people who do not usually go to the Royal Society will miss their old playmate from her accustomed slopes, but, even were they to succeed in tracing her to her new home, access would be denied them; for Professor Seeley, that stern custodian, has his answer ready for all such seekers.

If you want recreation, you must find it in Poetry, particularly Lyrical Poetry. Try Shelley. We can no longer allow you to disport yourselves in the Fields of History as if they were a mere playground. Clio is enclosed.

At present, however, this is not quite the case;

for the old literary traditions are still alive, and
prove somewhat irritating to Professor Seeley, who,
though one of the most even-tempered of writers,
is to be found on p. 173 almost angry with Thackeray, a charming person, who, as we all know, had,
after his lazy literary fashion, made an especial
study of Queen Anne's time, and who cherished
the pleasant fancy that a man might lie in the
heather with a pipe in his mouth, and yet, if he
had only an odd volume of the *Spectator* or the
Tatler in his hand, be learning history all the time.
" As we read in these delightful pages," says the
author of *Esmond*, " the past age returns; the
England of our ancestors is revivified; the May-
pole rises in the Strand; the beaux are gathering in
the coffee houses "; and so on, in the style we all
know and love so well, and none better, we may
rest assured, than Professor Seeley himself, if only
he were not tortured by the thought that people
were taking this to be a specimen of the science of
which he is a Regius Professor. His comment on
this passage of Thackeray's is almost a groan.
" What is this but the old literary groove, leading
to no trustworthy knowledge? " and certainly no
one of us, from letting his fancy gaze on the May-
pole in the Strand, could ever have foretold the
Griffin. On the same page he cries: " Break the
drowsy spell of narrative. Ask yourself questions,
set yourself problems; your mind will at once
take up a new attitude. Now modern English
history breaks up into two grand problems—the
problem of the Colonies and the problem of India."
The Cambridge School of History with a vengeance.
    In a paper read at the South Kensington Museum

in 1884, Professor Seeley observes: " The essential point is this, that we should recognise that to study history is to study not merely a narrative, but *at the same time* certain theoretical studies." He then proceeds to name them: Political philosophy, the comparative study of legal institutions, political economy, and international law.

These passages are, I think, adequate to give a fair view of Professor Seeley's position. History is a science, to be written scientifically and to be studied scientifically in conjunction with other studies. It should pursue a practical object and be read with direct reference to practical politics—using the latter word, no doubt, in an enlightened sense. History is not a narrative of all sorts of facts—biographical, moral, political, but of such facts as a scientific diagnosis has ascertained to be historically interesting. In fine, history, if her study is to be profitable and not a mere pastime, less exhausting than skittles and cheaper than horse exercise, must be dominated by some theory capable of verification by reference to certain ascertained facts belonging to a particular class.

Is this the right way of looking upon history? The dictionaries tell us that history and story are the same word, and are derived from a Greek source, signifying information obtained by inquiry. The natural definition of history, therefore, surely is the story of man upon earth, and the historian is he who tells us any chapter or fragment of that story. All things that on earth do dwell have, no doubt, their history as well as man; but when a member, however humble, of the human race speaks of history without any explanatory context, he may be presumed to be alluding to his own family records, to the story of humanity during its passage across the earth's surface.

"A talent for history "—I am quoting from an author whose style, let those mock at it who may, will reveal him—" may be said to be born with us as our chief inheritance. History has been written with quipo-threads, with feather pictures, with wampum belts, still oftener with earth-mounds and monumental stone-heaps, whether as pyramid or cairn; for the Celt and the Copt, the red man as well as the white, lives between two eternities, and warring against oblivion, he would fain unite himself in clear, conscious relation, as in dim unconscious relation he is already united, with the whole future and the whole past."

To keep the past alive for us is the pious function of the historian. Our curiosity is endless, his the task of gratifying it. We want to know what happened long ago. Performance of this task is only proximately possible; but none the less it must be attempted, for the demand for it is born afresh with every infant's cry. History is a pageant and not a philosophy.

Poets, no less than professors, occasionally say good things even in prose, and the following oracular utterance of Shelley is not pure nonsense:

History is the cyclic poem written by Time upon the memories of men. The past, like an inspired rhapsodist, fills the theatre of everlasting generations with her harmony.

If this be thought a little too fanciful, let me adorn this page with a passage from one of the great masters of English prose—Walter Savage Landor. Would that the pious labour of transcription could confer the tiniest measure of the gift! In that bundle of imaginary letters Landor called *Pericles and Aspasia*, we find Aspasia writing to her friend Cleone as follows:

To-day there came to visit us a writer who is not yet an author: his name is Thucydides. We understand that he has been these several years engaged in preparation for a history. Pericles invited him to meet Herodotus, when that wonderful man had returned to our country, and was about to sail from Athens. Until then it was believed by the intimate friends of Thucydides that he would devote his life to poetry, and, such is his vigour both of thought and expression, that he would have been the rival of Pindar. Even now he is fonder of talking on poetry than on any other subject, and blushed when history was mentioned. By degrees, however, he warmed, and listened with deep interest to the discourse of Pericles on the duties of a historian.

"May our first Athenian historian not be the greatest," said he, "as the first of our dramatists has been, in the opinion of many. We are growing too loquacious, both on the stage and off. We make disquisitions which render us only more and more dim-sighted, and excursions that only consume our stores. If some among us who have acquired celebrity by their compositions, calm, candid, contemplative men, were to undertake the history of Athens from the invasion of Xerxes, I should expect a fair and full criticism on the orations of Antiphon, and experience no disappointment at their forgetting the battle of Salamis. History, when she has lost her Muse, will lose her dignity, her occupation, her character, her name. She will wander about the Agora; she will start, she will stop, she will look wild, she will look stupid, she will take languidly to her bosom doubts, queries, essays, dissertations, some of which ought to go before her, some to follow, and all to stand apart. The field of history should not merely be well tilled, but well peopled. None is delightful to me or interesting in which I find not as many illustrious names as have a right to enter it. We might as well in a drama place the actors behind the scenes, and listen to the dialogue there, as in a history push valiant men back and protrude ourselves with husky disputations. Show me rather how great projects were executed, great advantages gained, and great calamities averted. Show me the generals and the statesmen who stood foremost, that I may bend to them in reverence; tell me their names, that I may repeat them to my children. Teach me whence laws were introduced, upon what foundation laid, by what custody guarded, in what inner keep preserved.

Let the books of the treasury lie closed as religiously as the
Sibyl's; leave weights and measures in the market-place,
Commerce in the harbour, the Arts in the light they love,
Philosophy in the shade; place History on her rightful throne,
and at the sides of her Eloquence and War."

This is, doubtless, a somewhat full-dress view of
history. Landor was not one of our modern dress-
ing-gown-and-slippers kind of authors. He always
took pains to be splendid, and preferred stately
magnificence to chatty familiarity.   But, after
allowing for this, is not the passage I have quoted
infused with a great deal of the true spirit which
should animate the historian, and does it not seem
to take us by the hand, and lead us very far away
from Professor Seeley's maxims and morals, his
theoretical studies, his political philosophy, his
political economy, and his desire to break the
drowsy spell of narrative, and to set us all problems ?
I ask this question in no spirit of enmity towards
these theoretical studies, nor do I doubt for one
moment that the student of history proper, who
has a turn in their directions, will find his pursuit
made only the more fascinating the more he studies
them—just as a little botany is said to add to the
charm of a country walk; but—and surely the
assertion is not necessarily paradoxical—these
studies ought not to be allowed to disfigure the
free-flowing outline of the historical Muse, or to
thicken her clear utterance, which in her higher
moods chants an epic, and in her ordinary moods
recites a narrative which need not be drowsy.

As for maxims, we all of us have our "little
hoard of maxims " wherewith to preach down our
hearts and justify anything shabby we may have
done; but the less we import their cheap wisdom

into history the better. The author of *The Expansion of England* will probably agree with Burke in thinking that " a great empire and little minds go ill together," and so, surely, *a fortiori*, must a mighty universe and any possible maxim. There have been plenty of brave historical maxims before Professor Seeley's, though only Lord Bolingbroke's has had the good luck to become itself historical.[1] And as for theories, Professor Flint, a very learned writer, has been at the pains to enumerate fourteen French and thirteen German philosophies of history current (though some, I expect, never ran either fast or far) since the revival of learning.

We are (are we not?) in these days in no little danger of being philosophy-ridden, and of losing our love for facts simply as facts. So long as Carlyle lived, the concrete had a representative, the strength of whose epithets sufficed, if not to keep the philosophers in awe, at least to supply their opponents with stones. But now it is different. Carlyle is no more a model historian than is Shakespeare a model dramatist. The merest tyro can count the faults of either on his clumsy fingers. That born critic, the late Sir George Lewis, had barely completed his tenth year before he was able, in a letter to his mother, to point out to her the essentially faulty structure of *Hamlet*, and many a duller wit, a decade or two later in his existence, has come to the conclusion that *Frederick the Great* is far too long. But whatever were Carlyle's faults, his historical method was superbly naturalistic.

---

[1] " I will answer you by quoting what I have read somewhere or other, in Dionysius Halicarnassensis I think, that history is philosophy teaching by examples." See Lord Bolingbroke's *Second Letter on the Study and Use of History*.

Have we a historian left us so honestly possessed
as he was with the genuine historical instinct, the
true enthusiasm to know what happened; or one
half so fond of a story for its own sake, or so in
love with things, not for what they were, but
simply because they were? " What wonderful
things are events," wrote Lord Beaconsfield in
Coningsby; " the least are of greater importance
than the most sublime and comprehensive speculations." To say this is to go perhaps too far; certainly it is to go farther than Carlyle, who none
the less was in sympathy with the remark; for he
also worshipped events, believing as he did that
but for the breath of God's mouth they never
would have been events at all. We thus find him
always treating even comparatively insignificant
facts with a measure of reverence, and handling
them lovingly, as does a book-hunter the shabbiest
pamphlet in his collection. We have only to think
of Carlyle's essay on *The Diamond Necklace* to fill
our minds with his qualifications for the proud
office of the historian. Were that inimitable piece
of workmanship to be submitted to the criticisms
of the new scientific school, we doubt whether it
would be so much as classed, whilst the celebrated
description of the night before the battle of Dunbar
in *Cromwell*, or any hundred scenes from *The French
Revolution*, would, we expect, be catalogued as
good examples of that degrading process whereby
history fades into mere literature.

This is not a question, be it observed, of style.
What is called a picturesque style is generally a
great trial. Who was it who called Professor
Masson's style Carlyle on wooden legs? What can

be drearier than when a plain matter-of-fact writer attempts to be animated, and tries to make his characters live by the easy but futile expedient of writing about them in the present tense? What is wanted is a passion for facts; the style may be left to take care of itself. Let me name a historian who detested fine writing, and who never said to himself, " Go to, I will make a description," and who yet was dominated by a love for facts, whose one desire always was to know what happened, to dispel illusion, and establish the true account— Dr. S. R. Maitland, of the Lambeth Library, whose volumes entitled *The Dark Ages* and *The Reformation* are to history what Milton's *Lycidas* is said to be to poetry: if they do not interest you, your tastes are not historical.

The difference, we repeat, is not of style, but of aim. Is history a pageant or a philosophy? That eminent historian, Lord Macaulay, whose passion for letters and for " mere literature " ennobled his whole life, has expressed himself in some places, I need scarcely add in a most forcible manner, in the same sense as Mr. Morley. In his well-known essay on history, contributed to the *Edinburgh Review* in 1828, we find him writing as follows: " Facts are the mere dross of history. It is from the abstract truth which interpenetrates them, and lies latent amongst them like gold in the ore, that the mass derives its whole value." And again: " No past event has any intrinsic importance. The knowledge of it is valuable only as it leads us to form just calculations with respect to the future." These are strong passages; but Lord Macaulay was a royal eclectic, and was quite out of sympathy

with the majority of that brotherhood who are
content to tone down their contradictories to the
dull level of ineptitudes. Macaulay never toned
down his contradictories, but, heightening everything all round, went on his sublime way, rejoicing
like a strong man to run a race, and well knowing
that he could give anybody five yards in fifty and
win easily. It is, therefore, no surprise to find him,
in the very essay in which he speaks so contemp-
tuously of facts, laying on with his vigorous brush
a celebrated purple patch I would gladly transfer
to my own dull page were it not too long and too
well known. A line or two taken at random will
give its purport:

A truly great historian would reclaim those materials the
novelist has appropriated. We should not then have to look
for the wars and votes of the Puritans in Clarendon and for
their phraseology in *Old Mortality*, for one half of King James
in Hume and for the other half in *The Fortunes of Nigel.* . . .
Society would be shown from the highest to the lowest, from
the royal cloth of state to the den of the outlaw, from the
throne of the legate to the chimney-corner where the beg-
ging friar regaled himself. Palmers, minstrels, crusaders, the
stately monastery with the good cheer in its refectory, and
the tournament with the heralds and ladies, the trumpets
and the cloth of gold, would give truth and life to the
representation.

It is difficult to see what abstract truth interpenetrates the cheer of the refectory, or what just
calculations with respect to the future even an
upholsterer could draw from a cloth, either of
state or of gold; whilst most people will admit
that, when the brilliant essayist a few years later
set himself to compose his own magnificent history,
so far as he interpenetrated it with the abstract
truths of Whiggism, and calculated that the future

would be satisfied with the first Reform Bill, he did ill and guessed wrong.

To reconcile Macaulay's utterances on this subject is beyond my powers, but of two things I am satisfied: the first is that, were he to come to life again, a good many of us would be more careful than we are how we write about him; and the second is that, on the happening of the same event, he would be found protesting against the threatened domination of all things by scientific theory. A Western American, who was once compelled to spend some days in Boston, was accustomed in after-life to describe that seat of polite learning to his horrified companions in California as a city in whose streets Respectability stalked unchecked. This is just what philosophical theories are doing amongst us, and a decent person can hardly venture abroad without one, though it does not much matter which one. Everybody is expected to have " a system of philosophy with principles coherent, interdependent, subordinate, and derivative," and to be able to account for everything, even for things it used not to be thought sensible to believe in, like ghosts and haunted houses. Keats remarks in one of his letters with great admiration upon what he christens Shakespeare's " negative capability," meaning thereby Shakespeare's habit of complaisant observation from outside of theory, and his keen enjoyment of the unexplained facts of life. He did not pour himself out in every strife. We have but little of this negative capability. The ruddy qualities of delightfulness, of pleasantness, are all " sicklied o'er with the

pale cast of thought." The varied elements of
life—the

> Murmur of living,
> Stir of existence,
> Soul of the world!

seem to be fading from literature. Pure literary
enthusiasm sheds but few rays. To be lively is
to be flippant, and epigram is dubbed paradox.

That many people appear to like a drab-coloured
world hung round with dusky shreds of philosophy
is sufficiently obvious. These persons find any
relaxation they may require from a too severe
course of theories, religious, political, social, or
now, alas! historical, in the novels of Mr. W. D.
Howells, an American gentleman who has not been
allowed to forget that he once asserted of fiction
what Professor Seeley would be glad to be able to
assert of history, that the drowsy spell of narrative
has been broken. We are to look for no more Sir
Walters, no more Thackerays, no more Dickenses.
The stories have all been told. Plots are exploded.
Incident is over. In moods of dejection these
dark sayings seemed only too true. Shakespeare's
saddest of sad lines rose to one's lips:

> My grief lies onward and my joy behind.

Behind us are *Ivanhoe* and *Guy Mannering*, *Pen-
dennis* and *The Virginians*, Pecksniff and Micawber.
In front of us stretch a never-ending series, a dreary
vista of *Foregone Conclusions*, *Counterfeit Present-
ments*, and *Undiscovered Countries*. But the darkest
watch of the night is the one before the dawn, and
relief is often nearest us when we least expect it.
All this gloomy nonsense was suddenly dispelled,
and the fact that really and truly, and behind this

philosophical arras, we were all inwardly ravening
for stories was most satisfactorily established by
the incontinent manner in which we flung ourselves
into the arms of Mr. Robert Louis Stevenson, to
whom we could almost have raised a statue in the
market-place for having written *Treasure Island*.

But to return to history. The interests of our
poor human life, which seems to become duller
every day, require that the fields of history should
be kept for ever unenclosed, and be a free breath-
ing-place for a pallid population well-nigh stifled
with the fumes of philosophy.

Were we, imaginatively, to propel ourselves
forward to the middle of the next century, and
to fancy a well-equipped historian armed with the
digested learning of Gibbon, endowed with the
eye of Carlyle, and say one-fifteenth of his humour
(even then a dangerous allotment in a dull world),
the moral gravity of Dr. Arnold, the critical sympathy of Sainte-Beuve, and the style of Dr. Newman, approaching the period through which we
have lived, should we desire this talented mortal
to encumber himself with a theory into which to
thrust all our doings as we toss clothes into a
portmanteau; to set himself to extract the essence
of some new political philosophy, capable of being
applied to the practical politics of his own day, or
to busy himself with problems or economics? To
us personally, of course, it is a matter of indifference how the historians of the twentieth century
conduct themselves, but ought not our altruism
to bear the strain of a hope that at least one of the
band may avoid all these things, and, leaving
political philosophy to the political philosopher

and political economy to the political economist,
remember that the first, if not the last, duty of the
historian is to narrate, to supply the text not the
comment, the subject not the sermon, and proceed
to tell our grandchildren and remoter issue the
story of our lives? The clash of arms will resound
through his pages as musically as ever it does
through those of the elder historians as he tells
of the encounter between the Northern and
Southern States of America, in which Right and
Might, those great twin-brethren, fought side by
side; but Romance, that ancient parasite, clung
affectionately with her tendril-hands to the mouldering walls of an ancient wrong, thus enabling
the historian, whilst awarding the victor's palm
to General Grant, to write kindly of the lost cause,
dear to the heart of a nobler and more chivalrous
man, General Lee, of the Virginian Army. And
again, is it not almost possible to envy the historian
to whom will belong the task of writing with full
information, and all the advantage of the true
historic distance, the history of that series of
struggles and heroisms, of plots and counter-plots,
of crimes and counter-crimes, resulting in the
freedom of Italy, and of telling to a world, eager
to listen, the life-story of Joseph Mazzini?

> Of God nor man was ever this thing said,
>   That he could give
> Life back to her who gave him, whence his dead
>   Mother might live.
> But this man found his mother dead and slain,
>   With fast sealed eyes,
> And bade the dead rise up and live again,
>   And she did rise.

Nor will our imaginary historian be unmindful of

Cavour, or fail to thrill his readers by telling them how, when the great Italian statesman, with many sins upon his conscience, lay in the very grasp of death, he interrupted the priests, busy at their work of intercession, almost roughly, with the exclamation, " Pray not for me. Pray for Italy! " whilst if he be one who has a turn for that ironical pastime, the dissection of a king, the curious character, and muddle of motives, calling itself Carlo Alberto will afford him material for at least two paragraphs of subtle interest. Lastly, if our historian is ambitious of a larger canvas and of deeper colours, what is there to prevent him, bracing himself to the task,

> As when some mighty painter dips
> His pencil in the hues of earthquake and eclipse,

from writing the epitaph of the Napoleonic legend?

But all this time I hear Professor Seeley whispering in my ear, " What is this but the old literary groove leading to no trustworthy knowledge? " If by trustworthy knowledge is meant demonstrable conclusions, capable of being expressed in terms at once exact and final, trustworthy knowledge is not to be gained from the witness of history, whose testimony none the less must be received, weighed, and taken into account. Truly observes Carlyle: " If history is philosophy teaching by examples, the writer fitted to compose history is hitherto an unknown man. Better were it that mere earthly historians should lower such pretensions, and, aiming only at some picture of the thing acted, which picture itself will be but a poor approximation, leave the inscrutable purport of them an acknowledged secret. Some picture of the thing acted." Here we behold the task of the historian; nor is it an idle, fruitless task. Science is not the only, or the chief source of knowledge. The *Iliad*, Shakespeare's plays, have taught the world more than the *Politics* of Aristotle or the *Novum Organum* of Bacon.

Facts are not the dross of history, but the true metal, and the historian is a worker in that metal. He has nothing to do with abstract truth, or with practical politics, or with forecasts of the future. A worker in metal he is, and has certainly plenty of what Lord Bacon used to call " stuff " to work upon; but if he is to be a great historian, and not a mere chronicler, he must be an artist as well as an artisan, and have something of the spirit which animated such a man as Francesco Francia of Bologna, now only famous as a painter, but in his own day equally celebrated as a worker in gold, and whose practice it was to sign his pictures with the word Goldsmith after his name, whilst he engraved Painter on his golden crucifixes.

The true historian, therefore, seeking to compose a true picture of the thing acted, must collect facts, select facts, and combine facts. Methods will differ, styles will differ. Nobody ever does anything exactly like anybody else; but the end in view is generally the same, and the historian's end is truthful narration. Maxims he will have, if he is wise, never a one; and as for a moral, if he tell his story well, it will need none; if he tell it ill, it will deserve none.

The stream of narrative flowing swiftly, as it does, over the jagged rocks of human destiny must often be turbulent and tossed; it is, therefore, all the more the duty of every good citizen to keep it as undefiled as possible, and to do what in him lies to prevent peripatetic philosophers on the banks from throwing their theories into it, either dead ones to decay, or living ones to drown. Let the philosophers ventilate their theories, construct their blow-holes, extract their essences, discuss their maxims, and point their morals as much as they will; but let them do so apart. History must not lose her Muse, or " take to her bosom doubts, queries, essays, dissertations, some of which ought to go before her, some to follow, and all to stand apart." Let us at all events secure our narrative first—sermons and philosophy the day after.

THE OFFICE OF LITERATURE

1887

DR. JOHN BROWN'S pleasant story has
become well known, of the countryman
who, being asked to account for the gravity
of his dog, replied, " Oh, sir! life is full of sairious-
ness to him—he can just never get eneugh o'
fechtin'." Something of the spirit of this saddened
dog seems lately to have entered into the very
people who ought to be freest from it—our men of
letters. They are all very serious and very quarrel-
some. To some of them it is dangerous even to
allude. Many are wedded to a theory or period,
and are the most uxorious of husbands—ever ready
to resent an affront to their lady. This devotion
makes them very grave, and possibly very happy
after a pedantic fashion. One remembers what
Hazlitt, who was neither happy nor pedantic, has
said about pedantry:

> The power of attaching an interest to the most trifling
> or painful pursuits is one of the greatest happinesses of our
> nature. The common soldier mounts the breach with joy,
> the miser deliberately starves himself to death, the mathe-
> matician sets about extracting the cube-root with a feeling
> of enthusiasm, and the lawyer sheds tears of delight over
> *Coke upon Littleton*. He who is not in some measure a pedant,
> though he may be a wise cannot be a very happy man.

Possibly not; but then we are surely not content
that our authors should be pedants in order that
they may be happy and devoted. As one of the
great class for whose sole use and behalf literature

52

exists—the class of readers—I protest that it is to me a matter of indifference whether an author is happy or not. I want him to make me happy. That is his office. Let him discharge it.

I recognise in this connection the corresponding truth of what Sydney Smith makes his Peter Plymley say about the private virtues of Mr. Perceval, the Prime Minister:

> You spend a great deal of ink about the character of the present Prime Minister. Grant all that you write—I say, I fear that he will ruin Ireland, and pursue a line of policy destructive to the true interests of his country; and then you tell me that he is faithful to Mrs. Perceval, and kind to the Master Percevals. I should prefer that he whipped his boys and saved his country.

We should never confuse functions or apply wrong tests. What can books do for us? Dr. Johnson, the least pedantic of men, put the whole matter into a nutshell (a cocoa-nut shell, if you will—Heaven forbid that I should seek to compress the great Doctor within any narrower limits than my metaphor requires!), when he wrote that a book should teach us either to enjoy life or endure it. " Give us enjoyment! " " Teach us endurance! " Hearken to the ceaseless demand and the perpetual prayer of an ever unsatisfied and always suffering humanity!

How is a book to answer the ceaseless demand?

Self-forgetfulness is of the essence of enjoyment, and the author who would confer pleasure must possess the art, or know the trick, of destroying for the time the reader's own personality. Undoubtedly the easiest way of doing this is by the creation of a host of rival personalities—hence the number and the popularity of novels. Whenever a novelist fails his book is said to flag; that is, the reader suddenly (as in skating) comes bump down upon his own personality, and curses the unskilful author. No lack of characters and continual motion is the easiest recipe for a novel, which, like a beggar, should always be kept " moving on." Nobody knew this better than Fielding, whose novels, like most good ones, are full of inns.

When those who are addicted to what is called " improving reading " inquire of you petulantly why you cannot find change of company and scene in books of travel, you should answer cautiously that when books of travel are full of inns, atmosphere, and motion, they are as good as any novel; nor is there any reason in the nature of things why they should not always be so, though experience proves the contrary.

The truth or falsehood of a book is immaterial. George Borrow's *Bible in Spain* is, I suppose, true; though now that I come to think of it, in what is to me a new light, one remembers that it contains some odd things. But was not Borrow the accredited agent of the British and Foreign Bible Society? Did he not travel (and he had a free hand) at their charges? Was he not befriended by our minister at Madrid, Mr. Villiers, subsequently Earl of Clarendon in the peerage of England? It must be true; and yet at this moment I would as lief read a chapter of *The Bible in Spain* as I would *Gil Blas*; nay, I positively would give the preference to Señor Giorgio.

Nobody can sit down to read Borrow's books without as completely forgetting himself as if he were a boy in the forest with Gurth and Wamba.

Borrow is provoking and has his full share of faults, and, though the owner of a style, is capable of excruciating offences. His habitual use of the odious word " individual " as a noun-substantive (seven times in three pages of *The Romany Rye*) elicits the frequent groan, and he is certainly once guilty of calling fish the " finny tribe." He believed himself to be animated by an intense hatred of the Church of Rome, and disfigures many of his pages by Lawrence-Boythorn-like tirades against that institution; but no Catholic of sense need on this account deny himself the pleasure of reading Borrow, whose one dominating passion was *camaraderie*, and who hob-a-nobbed in the friendliest spirit with priest and gipsy in a fashion as far beyond praise as it is beyond description by any pen other than his own. Hail to thee, George Borrow! Cervantes himself, Gil Blas, do not more effectually carry their readers into the land of the Cid than does this miraculous agent of the Bible Society, by favour of whose pleasantness we can, any hour of the week, enter Villafranca by night, or ride into Galicia on an Andalusian stallion (which proved to be a foolish thing to do), without costing anybody a *peseta*, and at no risk whatever to our necks—be they long or short.

Cooks, warriors, and authors must be judged by the effects they produce: toothsome dishes, glorious victories, pleasant books—these are our demands. We have nothing to do with ingredients, tactics, or methods. We have no desire to be admitted into the kitchen, the council, or the study. The cook may clean her saucepans how she pleases— the warrior place his men as he likes—the author handle his material or weave his plot as best he can—when the dish is served we only ask, Is it good? when the battle has been fought, Who won? when the book comes out, Does it read?

Authors ought not to be above being reminded that it is their first duty to write agreeably—some very disagreeable men have succeeded in doing so, and there is therefore no need for anyone to despair. Every author, be he grave or gay, should try to make his book as ingratiating as possible. Reading is not a duty, and has consequently no business to be made disagreeable. Nobody is under any obligation to read any other man's book.

Literature exists to please—to lighten the burden of men's lives; to make them for a short while forget their sorrows and their sins, their silenced hearths, their disappointed hopes, their grim futures—and those men of letters are the best loved who have best performed literature's truest office. Their name is happily legion, and I will conclude these disjointed remarks by quoting from one of them, as honest a parson as ever took tithe or voted for the Tory candidate, the Rev. George Crabbe. Hear him in *The Frank Courtship*:

> " I must be loved "; said Sybil; " I must see
> The man in terrors, who aspires to me:
> At my forbidding frown his heart must ache,
> His tongue must falter, and his frame must shake;
> And if I grant him at my feet to kneel,
> What trembling fearful pleasure must he feel:
> Nay, such the rapture that my smiles inspire
> That reason's self must for a time retire."
> " Alas! for good Josiah," said the dame,
> " These wicked thoughts would fill his soul with shame;
> He kneel and tremble at a thing of dust!
> He cannot, child ":—the child replied, " He must."

Were an office to be opened for the insurance of

literary reputations, no critic at all likely to be in the society's service would refuse the life of a poet who could write like Crabbe. Cardinal Newman, Mr. Leslie Stephen, Mr. Swinburne, are not always of the same way of thinking, but all three hold the one true faith about Crabbe.

But even were Crabbe now left unread, which is very far from being the case, his would be an enviable fame—for was he not one of the favourite poets of Walter Scott, and whenever the closing scene of the great magician's life is read in the pages of Lockhart, must not Crabbe's name be brought upon the reader's quivering lip?

To soothe the sorrow of the soothers of sorrow, to bring tears to the eyes and smiles to the cheeks of the lords of human smiles and tears, is no mean ministry, and it is Crabbe's.

WORN-OUT TYPES

1887

IT is now a complaint of quite respectable
antiquity that the types in which humanity
was originally set up by a humour-loving
Providence are worn out and require recasting.
The surface of society has become smooth. It
ought to be a bas-relief—it is a plane. Even a
Chaucer (so it is said) could make nothing of us
as we wend our way to Brighton. We have tempers,
it is true—bad ones for the most part; but no
humours to be in or out of. We are all far too
much alike; we do not group well; we only mix.
All this, and more, is alleged against us. A cheer-
fully disposed person might perhaps think that,
assuming the prevailing type to be a good, plain,
readable one, this uniformity need not necessarily
be a bad thing; but had he the courage to give
expression to this opinion he would most certainly
be at once told, with that mixture of asperity and
contempt so properly reserved for those who take
cheerful views of anything, that without well-
defined types of character there can be neither
national comedy nor whimsical novel; and as it
is impossible to imagine any person sufficiently
cheerful to carry the argument further by inquiring
ingenuously, " And how would that matter? " the
position of things becomes serious, and demands
a few minutes' investigation.

As we said at the beginning, the complaint is an old one—most complaints are. When Montaigne was in Rome in 1580 he complained bitterly that he was always knocking up against his own country-men, and might as well have been in Paris. And yet some people would have you believe that this curse of the Continent is quite new. More than seventy years ago that most quotable of English authors, Hazlitt, wrote as follows:

It is, indeed, the evident tendency of all literature to generalise and dissipate character by giving men the same artificial education and the same common stock of ideas; so that we see all objects from the same point of view, and through the same reflected medium; we learn to exist not in ourselves, but in books; all men become alike, mere readers —spectators, not actors, in the scene, and lose all proper personal identity. The templar,—the wit,—the man of pleasure and the man of fashion, the courtier and the citizen, the knight and the squire, the lover and the miser—Love-lace, Lothario, Will Honeycomb and Sir Roger de Coverley, Sparkish and Lord Foppington, Western and Tom Jones, my Father and my Uncle Toby, Millamant and Sir Sampson Legend, Don Quixote and Sancho, Gil Blas and Guzman d'Alfarache, Count Fathom and Joseph Surface,—have all met and exchanged commonplaces on the barren plains of the *haute littérature,*—toil slowly on to the Temple of Science, seen a long way off upon a level, and end in one dull compound of politics, criticism, chemistry, and metaphysics.

Very pretty writing, certainly; [1] nor can it be disputed that uniformity of surroundings puts a tax upon originality. To make bricks and find your own straw are terms of bondage. Modern char-acters, like modern houses, are possibly built too

---

[1] Yet in his essay *On Londoners and Country People* we find Hazlitt writing, " London is the only place in which the child grows completely up into the man. I have known characters of this kind, which, in the way of childish ignorance and self-pleasing delusion, exceeded anything to be met with in Shakespeare or Ben Jonson, or the Old Comedy."

much on the same lines. Dickens's description of Coketown is not easily forgotten:

All the public inscriptions in the town were painted alike, in severe characters of black and white. The jail might have been the infirmary, the infirmary might have been the jail, the town hall might have been either, or both, or anything else, for anything that appeared to the contrary in the graces of their construction.

And the inhabitants of Coketown are exposed to the same objection as their buildings. Everyone sinks all traces of what he vulgarly calls " the shop " (that is, his lawful calling), and busily pretends to be nothing. Distinctions of dress are found irksome. A barrister of feeling hates to be seen in his robes save when actually engaged in a case. An officer wears his uniform only when obliged. Doctors have long since shed all outward signs of their healing art. Court dress excites a smile. A countess in her jewels is reckoned indecent by the British workman, who, all unemployed, puffs his tobacco smoke against the window-pane of the carriage that is conveying her ladyship to a drawing-room; and a West-end clergyman is with difficulty restrained from telling his congregation what he had been told the British workman said on that occasion. Had he but had the courage to repeat those stirring words, his hearers (so he said) could hardly have failed to have felt their force—so unusual in such a place; but he had not the courage, and that sermon of the pavement remains unpreached. The toe of the peasant is indeed kibing the heel of the courtier. The passion for equality in externals cannot be denied. We are all woven strangely in the same piece, and so it comes about that, though our modern society has invented new callings, those callings have not created new types. Stockbrokers, directors, official liquidators, philanthropists, secretaries,—not of State, but of companies,—speculative builders, are a new kind of people known to many, indeed playing a great part among us, but who, for all that, have not enriched the stage with a single character. Were they to disappear tomorrow, to be blown dancing away like the leaves before Shelley's west wind, where in reading or play-going would posterity encounter them? Alone amongst the children of men, the pale student of the law, burning the midnight oil in some one of the "high lonely towers" recently built by the Benchers of the Middle Temple (in the Italian taste), would, whilst losing his youth over that interminable series, *The Law Reports*, every now and again strike across the old track, once so noisy with the bayings of the well-paid hounds of justice, and, pushing his way along it, trace the history of the bogus company, from the acclamations attendant upon its illegitimate birth to the hour of disgrace when it dies by strangulation at the hands of the professional wrecker. The pale student will not be a wholly unsympathetic reader. Great swindles have ere now made great reputations, and lawyers may surely be permitted to take a pensive interest in such matters.

> Not one except the Attorney was amused—
> He, like Achilles, faithful to the tomb,
> So there were quarrels, cared not for the cause,
> Knowing they must be settled by the laws.

But our elder dramatists would not have let any of these characters swim out of their ken.

A glance over Ben Jonson, Massinger, Beaumont and Fletcher, is enough to reveal their frank and easy method. Their characters, like an apothecary's drugs, wear labels round their necks. Mr. Justice Clement and Mr. Justice Greedy; Master Matthew, the town gull; Sir Giles Overreach, Sir Epicure Mammon, Mr. Plenty, Sir John Frugal, need no explanatory context. Are our dramatists to blame for withholding from us the heroes of our modern society? Ought we to have

> Sir Moses, Sir Aaron, Sir Jamramagee,
> Two stock-jobbing Jews, and a shuffling Parsee?

Baron Contango, the Hon. Mr. Guinea-Pig, poor Miss Impulsia Allottee, Mr. Jeremiah Builder— Rare Old Ben, who was fond of the city, would have given us them all and many more; but though we may well wish he were here to do it, we ought, I think, to confess, that the humour of these typical persons who so swell the *dramatis personæ* of an Elizabethan is, to say the least of it, far to seek. There is a certain warm-hearted tradition about their very names which makes disrespect painful. It seems a churl's part not to laugh, as did our fathers before us, at the humours of the conventional parasite or impossible servingman; but we laugh because we will, and not because we must.

Genuine comedy—the true tickling scene, exquisite absurdity, soul-rejoicing incongruity—has really nothing to do with types, prevailing fashions, and such like vulgarities. Sir Andrew Aguecheek is not a typical fool; he *is* a fool, seised in fee simple of his folly.

Humour lies not in generalisations, but in the

individual; not in his hat nor in his hose, even though the latter be " cross-gartered "; but in the deep heart of him, in his high-flying vanities, his low-lying oddities—what we call his " ways " —nay, in the very motions of his back as he crosses the road. These stir our laughter whilst he lives and our tears when he dies, for in mourning over him we know full well we are taking part in our own obsequies. " But indeed," wrote Charles Lamb, "we die many deaths before we die, and I am almost sick when I think that such a hold as I had of you is gone."

Literature is but the reflex of life, and the humour of it lies in the portrayal of the individual, not the type; and though the young man in *Locksley Hall* no doubt observes that the " individual withers," we have but to take down George Meredith's novels to find the fact is otherwise, and that we have still one amongst us who takes notes, and against the battery of whose quick wits even the costly raiment of Poole is no protection. We are forced as we read to exclaim with Petruchio, " Thou hast hit it; come sit on me." No doubt the task of the modern humorist is not so easy as it was. The surface ore has been mostly picked up. In order to win the precious metal you must now work with in-stroke and out-stroke after the most approved methods. Sometimes one would enjoy it a little more if we did not hear quite so distinctly the snorting of the engine, and the groaning and the creaking of the gear as it painfully winds up its prize: but what would you? Methods, no less than men, must have the defects of their qualities.

If, therefore, it be the fact that our national comedy is in a decline, we must look for some other reasons for it than those suggested by Hazlitt in 1817. When Mr. Chadband inquired, " Why can we not fly, my friends ? " Mr. Snagsby ventured to observe, " in a cheerful and rather knowing tone, ' No wings! ' " but he was immediately frowned down by Mrs. Snagsby. We lack courage to suggest that the somewhat heavy-footed movements of our recent dramatists are in any way due to their not being provided with those twin adjuncts indispensable for the genius who would soar.

CAMBRIDGE AND THE POETS
1887

WHY all the English poets, with a barely decent number of exceptions, have been Cambridge men, has always struck me, as did the abstinence of the Greeks from malt Mr. Calverley, " as extremely curious." But in this age of detail, one must, however reluctantly, submit to prove one's facts, and I, therefore, propose to institute a " Modest Inquiry " into this subject. Imaginatively, I shall don proctorial robes, and, armed with a duster, saunter up and down the library, putting to each poet as I meet him the once dreaded question, " Sir, are you a member of this University ? "

But whilst I am arranging myself for this function, let me utilise the time by making two preliminary observations—the first one being that, as to-day is Sunday, only such free libraries are open as may happen to be attached to public-houses, and I am consequently confined to my own poor shelves, and must be forgiven even though I make some palpable omissions. The second is that I exclude from my survey living authors. I must do so; their very names would excite controversy about a subject which, when wisely handled, admits of none.

I now pursue my inquiry. That Chaucer was a Cambridge man cannot be proved. It is the better opinion that he was (how else should he have known anything about the Trumpington Road ?), but it is only an opinion, and as no one has ever been found reckless enough to assert that he was an Oxford man, he must be content to " sit out " this inquiry along with Shakespeare, Webster, Ford, Pope, Cowper, Burns, and Keats, no one of whom ever kept his terms at either University. Spenser is, of course, the glory of the Cambridge Pembroke, though were the fellowships of that College made to depend upon passing a yearly examination in *The Faerie Queene*, to be conducted by Dean Church, there would be wailing and lamentation within her rubicund walls. Sir Thomas Wyatt was at St. John's, Fulke Greville Lord Brooke at Jesus, Giles and Phineas Fletcher were at King's, Herrick was first at St. John's, but migrated to the Hall, where he is still reckoned very pretty reading, even by boating men. Cowley, most precocious of poets, and Suckling were at Trinity, Waller at King's, Francis Quarles was of Christ's. The Herbert family were divided, some going to Oxford and some to Cambridge, George, of course, falling to the lot of Cambridge. John Milton's name alone would deify the University where he pursued his almost sacred studies. Andrew Marvell, a pleasant poet and savage satirist, was of Trinity. The author of *Hudibras* is frequently attributed to Cambridge, but, on being interrogated, he declined to name his college —always a suspicious circumstance.

I must not forget Richard Crashaw, of Peterhouse. Willingly would I relieve the intolerable tedium of this dry inquiry by transcribing a few lines of his now beneath my eye. But I forbear, and "steer right on."

Of dramatists we find Marlowe (untimelier death

than his was never any) at Corpus; Greene (I do not lay much stress on Greene) was both at St. John's and Clare. Ben Jonson was at St. John's, so was Nash. John Fletcher (whose claims to be considered the senior partner in his well-known firm are simply paramount) was at Corpus. James Shirley, the author of *The Maids' Revenge* and of the beatiuful lyric beginning "The glories of our birth andstate," in the innocence of his heart first went to St. John's College, Oxford, from whence he was speedily sent down, for reasons which the delightful author of *Athenæ Oxonienses* must really be allowed to state for himself. " At the same time (1612) Dr. William Laud presiding at that house, he had a very great affection for Shirley, especially for the pregnant parts that were visible in him, but then having a broad or large mole upon his left cheek, which some esteemed a deformity, that worthy doctor would often tell him that he was an unfit person to take the sacred function upon him, and should never have his consent to do so." Thus treated, Shirley left Oxford, that " home of lost causes," but not apparently of large moles, and came to Cambridge, and entered at St. Catharine's Hall, where, either because the authorities were not amongst those who esteemed a broad or large mole upon the left cheek to be a deformity, or because a mole, more or less, made no sort of difference in the personal appearance of the college, or for other good and sufficient reasons, Shirley was allowed, without, I trust, being often told of his mole, to proceed to his degree and to Holy orders.

Starting off again, we find John Dryden, whose very name is a tower of strength (were he to come

to life again he would, like Mr. Brown of Calaveras,
" clean out half the town "), at Trinity. In this
poet's later life he said he liked Oxford better. His
lines on this subject are well-known:

> Oxford to him a dearer name shall be
> Than his own Mother-University.
> Thebes did his rude, unknowing youth engage,
> He chooses Athens in his riper age.

But idle preferences of this sort are beyond the
scope of my present inquiry. After Dryden we
find Garth at Peterhouse and charming Matthew
Prior at John's. Then comes the great name of
Gray. Perhaps I ought not to mention Christopher Smart, who was a Fellow of Pembroke,
and yet the author of *David*, under happier circumstances, might have conferred additional poetic
lustre, even upon the college of Spenser.[1]

In the present century, we find Byron and his
bear at Trinity, Coleridge at Jesus, and Wordsworth at St. John's. The last named poet was
fully alive to the honour of belonging to the same
University as Milton. In language not unworthy
of Mr. Trumbull, the well-known auctioneer in
Middlemarch, he has recorded as follows:

> Among the band of my compeers was one
> Whom chance had stationed in the very room
> Honoured by Milton's name. O temperate Bard!
> Be it confest that for the first time seated
> Within thy innocent lodge and oratory,
> One of a festive circle, I poured out
> Libations, to thy memory drank, till pride
> And gratitude grew dizzy in a brain
> Never excited by the fumes of wine
> Before that hour or since.[2]

---

[1] This passage was written before Mr. Browning's *Parleyings* had
appeared. Christopher is now " a person of importance," and needs
no apology.

[2] *The Prelude*, p. 55.

I know of no more amiable trait in the character of Cambridge men than their willingness to admit having been drunk *once*.

After the great name of Wordsworth any other must seem small, but I must, before concluding, place on record Praed, Macaulay, Kingsley, and Calverley.

A glorious Roll-call indeed!

> Earth shows to Heaven the names by thousands told
> That crown her fame.

So may Cambridge.

Oxford leads off with one I could find it in my heart to grudge her, beautiful as she is—Sir Philip Sidney. Why, I wonder, did he not accompany his friend and future biographer, Fulke Greville, to Cambridge? As Dr. Johnson once said to Boswell, " Sir, you *may* wonder! " Sidney most indisputably was at Christ Church. Old George Chapman, who I suppose was young once, was (I believe) at Oxford, though I have known Cambridge to claim him. Lodge and Peele were at Oxford, so were Francis Beaumont and his brother Sir John. Philip Massinger, Shakerley Marmion, and John Marston are of Oxford, also Watson and Warner. Henry Vaughan the Silurist, Sir John Davies, George Sandys, Samuel Daniel, Dr. Donne, Lovelace, and Wither belong to the sister University, so did Dr. Brady—but Oxford must not claim all the merit of the metrical version of the Psalms, for Brady's colleague, Dr. Nahum Tate, was a Dublin man. Otway and Collins, Young, Johnson, Charles Wesley, Southey, Landor, Hartley Coleridge, Beddoes, Keble, Isaac Williams, Faber, and Clough are names of which their University may well be proud. But surely, when compared with the Cambridge list, a falling-off must be admitted.

A poet indeed once came into residence at University College, whose single name—for after all poets must be weighed and not counted—would have gone far to right the balance, but is Oxford bold enough to claim Shelley as her own? She sent him down, not for riotous living, for no purer soul than his ever haunted her courts, but for wanting to discuss with those whose business it was to teach him questions of high philosophy. Had Shelley only gone to Trinity in 1810 I feel sure wise and witty old Dr. Mansel would never have sent him down. Spenser, Milton, and Shelley! What a triad of immortal fames they would have made. As it is, we expect Oxford with her accustomed composure will insist upon adding Shelley to her score—but even when she has been allowed to do so, she must own herself beaten both in men and metal.

But this being so—why was it so? It is now my turn to own myself defeated. I cannot for the life of me tell how it happened.

NOTE, 1922.—I ought to have had the fairness and the courage to add to the score of Oxford the poets commemorated in the distich:

Alma novem genuit celebres Rhedecyna poetas—
Bubb, Stubb, Grubb, Crabb, Trapp, Young, Cary, Tickell, Evans.

" Bubb " was the well-known Dodington of the *Diary*, Stubb was " Bubb's " chaplain at the Madrid Embassy. Of Grubb and Crabb I know nothing, but the others are well-known Oxford poets, and one of them I had included—Young.

"PETER BELL"
1898

SIR;—Poetry has always been my passion. To know the best and to love it, my dream. I sometimes fear, but this is during my bad moments, in my dark hour, that I am not a little like Charles Lamb's friend, George Dyer, " to G. D. a poem is a poem, his own as good as anybody's, and (God bless him!) anybody's as good as his own, for I do not think he has the most distant guess of the possibility of one poem being better than another." I *think* I recognise the possibility, but I often find it difficult to establish the fact. But I work away all the same. My grandfather left me an edition of Johnson's *Poets* in fifty-three volumes, and an aunt gave me on my sixteenth birthday Campbell's *Specimens*, in seven volumes, and I have made as I went along a collection of my own. What terrifies me is the slowness of my progress. I am no longer young. I shall never see fifty again, and I am not yet within sight of the brotherhood and sisterhood of poets whose merits have been lately extolled by Mr. Archer with so evident a sincerity; indeed, I have yet to make the acquaintance of the poets belonging to that period.

At present I am stuck fast in *Peter Bell*, first published in 1819. The other poetical productions of that year I have mastered and made my own; but *Peter* still sticks in my gizzard—yet Wordsworth's

71

is a great name, and the poem was twenty-one
years maturing.   Wordsworth spared no pains
" to fit it for filling *permanently* " (the italics are
the poet's own) " a station however humble in the
literature of our country."   How dare I disregard
so solemn an assurance!   I have living with me a
nephew, not wholly illiterate, but hopelessly flippant, who, when I confessed to him that I had read
Peter Bell some scores of times without apprehend-
ing its true poetical significance, murmured to
himself, actually quoting from the very poem, and
thus, as it were, hurling at me the very stone of
my stumbling:

> Meanwhile the persevering Ass.

This was no help, and therefore, for the first time
in my life, I turn to my neglected contemporaries,
and beseech them to tell me what is thought of
Peter Bell in the best literary circles?

My aforesaid nephew also tells me that he has
long since left off reading Wordsworth, except in a
selection made by another poet, whose name is on
my list, and that in this selection *Peter Bell* is not
to be found.   But what does this *prove?*   In my
opinion, which is probably worthless, the poem
contains stanzas of glorious merit:

> He, two-and-thirty years or more,
> Had been a wild and woodland rover—
> Had heard the Atlantic surges roar
> On farthest Cornwall's rocky shore,
> And trod the cliffs of Dover.
>
> And he had seen Caernarvon's towers,
> And well he knew the spire of Sarum;
> And he had been where Lincoln bell
> Flings o'er the fen that ponderous knell—
> A far-renowned alarum!

At Doncaster, at York, and Leeds,
And merry Carlisle had he been;
And all along the lowlands fair,
All through the bonny shire of Ayr
And far as Aberdeen.

And he had trudged through Yorkshire dales,
Among the rocks and winding scars,
Where deep and low the hamlets lie
Beneath their little patch of sky
And little lot of stars;

And all along the indented coast,
Bespattered with the salt sea foam,
Where'er a knot of houses lay
On headland or in hollow bay;—
Sure never man like him did roam.

A magnificent itinerary! It has made me long to pitch my books into the fire and take to the road.

Though Nature could not touch his heart
By lovely forms and silent weather
And tender sounds—yet you might see
At once that Peter Bell and she
Had often been together.

A savage wildness round him hung,
As of a dweller out of doors.
In his whole figure and his mien,
A savage character was seen,
Of mountains and of dreary moors.

His face was keen as is the wind
That cuts along the hawthorn-fence.

There was a hardness in his cheek,
There was a hardness in his eye,
As if the man had fixed his face
In many a solitary place,
Against the wind and open sky!

He trudged along through copse and brake,
He trudged along o'er hill and dale,
Nor for the moon cared he a tittle,
And for the stars he cared as little,
And for the murmuring River Swale.

'Tis not a plover of the moors,
'Tis not a bittern of the fen;
Nor can it be a barking fox,
Nor night-bird chambered in the rocks,
Nor wild cat in a woody glen!

And now is Peter taught to feel
That man's heart is a holy thing;
And Nature through a world of death
Breathes into him a second breath
More searching than the breath of spring.

Am I wrong in thinking these unforgettable
verses? But what about the Ass? the poor Ass,
the little Ass, the miserable Ass, the pleased and
thankful Ass, the listening Ass, the strenuous Ass,
the grinning Ass, the unheeding Ass, the meek
Ass, the persevering Ass, the trusty Ass, the gentle
Ass. What in the name of all the Asses does it
mean? Whom or what does it portray? " In the
woods of Alfoxden," says the poet, " I used to
take great delight in noticing the habits, tricks and
physiognomy of asses, and I have no doubt that I
was thus put upon writing the poem out of liking
for the creature that is so often dreadfully abused."
Like his *Excursion*, in the opinion of the Scotch
Reviewer, " This will never do." *Peter Bell* is no
tract against cruelty to animals. Yet it all turns
upon that Ass.

Only the Ass, with motion dull,
Upon the pivot of his skull
Turns round his long left ear.

Who or what is he?
I have made a careful study of the Wordsworthian
epithets applied by him to the Ass and find that
they are all equally applicable to the READING
PUBLIC and to nothing else. Who else is poor and
n iserable and little, pleased and thankful? Who

else listens, is strenuous—grins? Who else is unheeding, meek, persevering, trusty, and gentle?
Who else is so often, so dreadfully abused? If the
Ass represents the Reading Public, Peter Bell himself, the vagrant tinker, who steals and sells, and
sells and steals pots and pans, is clearly the Living
Poet, the dealer in words and phrases, primroses
by the river's brim, who, finding the Ass—that is,
the Reading Public—half starved and mournful
by the tomb of his dead master—that is, the poetry
of the last age—mounts him, and tries to ride off
upon his back. I do not say that this interpreta-
tion makes all plain, but it certainly gives meaning
to a great deal that is otherwise obscure.

> He (Peter) lifts his head and sees the Ass
> Yet standing in the clear moonshine:
> " When shall I be as good as thou?
> Oh! would, poor beast, that I had now
> A heart but half as good as thine! "

How often must poets have felt their moral
inferiority to their readers; but how rarely have
they had the candour to avow it.

If only this proves the right solution I shall feel
myself free forthwith to tackle the poetry of 1820,
and who knows but that I may yet live to enter that
" nest of spicery," Mr. John Lane's shop in Vigo
Street, and become acquainted with the poets and
poetesses by whom the happy Mr. Archer lives
surrounded. But with *Peter Bell* in your gizzard,
progress is impossible.—Believe me, Sir, Yours
obediently,

GIDEON GOSLOWLY
(Faint yet Pursuing).

BOOK-BUYING

1887

THE most distinguished of living Englishmen, who, great as he is in many directions,
is perhaps inherently more a man of letters
than anything else, has been overheard mournfully
to declare that there were more booksellers' shops
in his native town sixty years ago when he was a
boy in it than are to-day to be found within its
boundaries. And yet the place, "all unabashed,"
now boasts its bookless self a city!

Mr. Gladstone was, of course, referring to
second-hand bookshops. Neither he nor any
other sensible man puts himself out about new
books. When a new book is published, read an
old one, was the advice of a sound though surly
critic. It is one of the boasts of letters to have
glorified the term "second-hand," which other
crafts have "soiled to all ignoble use." But why
it has been able to do this is obvious. All the best
books are necessarily second-hand. The writers
of to-day need not grumble. Let them "bide a
wee." If their books are worth anything they too
one day will be second-hand. If their books are
not worth anything there are ancient trades still
in full operation amongst us—the pastrycooks and
the trunkmakers—who must have paper.

But is there any substance in the plaint that

nobody now buys books, meaning thereby second-hand books? The late Mark Pattison, who had 16,000 volumes, and whose lightest word has therefore weight, once stated that he had been informed, and verily believed, that there were men of his own University of Oxford who, being in uncontrolled possession of annual incomes of not less than £500, thought they were doing the thing handsomely if they expended £50 a year upon their libraries. But we are not bound to believe this unless we like. There was a touch of morosity about the late Rector of Lincoln which led him to take gloomy views of men, particularly Oxford men.

No doubt arguments *à priori* may readily be found to support the contention that the habit of book-buying is on the decline. I confess to knowing one or two men, not Oxford men either, but Cambridge men (and the passion of Cambridge for literature is a by-word), who, on the plea of being pressed with business, or because they were going to a funeral, have passed a bookshop in a strange town without so much as stepping inside " just to see whether the fellow had anything." But painful as facts of this sort necessarily are, any damaging inference we might feel disposed to draw from them is dispelled by a comparison of price-lists. Compare a bookseller's catalogue of 1862 with one of the present year, and your pessimism is washed away by the tears which unrestrainedly flow as you see what *bonnes fortunes* you have lost. A young book-buyer might well turn out upon Primrose Hill and bemoan his youth, after comparing old catalogues with new.

Nothing but American competition, grumble some old stagers.

Well! why not? This new battle for the books is a free fight, not a private one, and Columbia has " joined in." Lower prices are not to be looked for. The book-buyer of 1900 will be glad to buy at to-day's prices. I take pleasure in thinking he will not be able to do so. Good finds grow scarcer and scarcer. True it is that but a few short weeks ago I picked up (such is the happy phrase, most apt to describe what was indeed a " street casualty") a copy of the original edition of *Endymion* (Keats's poem—O subscriber to Mudie's!—not Lord Beaconsfield's novel) for the easy equivalent of half-a-crown—but then that was one of my lucky days. The enormous increase of booksellers' catalogues and their wide circulation amongst the trade has already produced a hateful uniformity of prices. Go where you will it is all the same to the odd sixpence. Time was when you could map out the country for yourself with some hopefulness of plunder. There were districts where the Elizabethan dramatists were but slenderly protected. A raid into the " bonnie North Countrie " sent you home again cheered with chap-books and weighted with old pamphlets of curious interest; whilst the West of England seldom failed to yield a crop of novels. I remember getting a complete set of the Brontë books in the original issues at Torquay, I may say, for nothing. Those days are over. Your country bookseller is, in fact, more likely, such tales does he hear of London auctions, and such catalogues does he receive by every post, to exaggerate the value of his wares than to part with them pleasantly, and as a country bookseller should, "just to clear my shelves, you know, and give me a bit of room." The only compensation for this is the catalogues themselves. You get *them*, at least, for nothing, and it cannot be denied that they make mighty pretty reading.

These high prices tell their own tale, and force upon us the conviction that there never were so many private libraries in course of growth as there are to-day.

Libraries are not made; they grow. Your first two thousand volumes present no difficulty, and cost astonishingly little money. Given £400 and five years, and an ordinary man can in the ordinary course, without undue haste or putting any pressure upon his taste, surround himself with this number of books, all in his own language, and thenceforward have at least one place in the world in which it is possible to be happy. But pride is still out of the question. To be proud of having two thousand books would be absurd. You might as well be proud of having two top-coats. After your first two thousand difficulty begins, but until you have ten thousand volumes the less you say about your library the better. *Then* you may begin to speak.

It is no doubt a pleasant thing to have a library left you. The present writer will disclaim no such legacy, but hereby undertakes to accept it, however dusty. But, good as it is to inherit a library, it is better to collect one. Each volume then, however lightly a stranger's eye may roam from shelf to shelf, has its own individuality, a history of its own. You remember where you got it, and how much you gave for it; and your word may safely be taken for the first of these facts, but not for the second.

The man who has a library of his own collection is able to contemplate himself objectively, and is justified in believing in his own existence. No other man but he would have made precisely such a combination as his. Had he been in any single respect different from what he is, his library, as it exists, never would have existed. Therefore, surely he may exclaim, as in the gloaming he contemplates the backs of his loved ones, " They are mine, and I am theirs."

But the eternal note of sadness will find its way even through the keyhole of a library. You turn some familiar page, of Shakespeare it may be, and his " infinite variety," his " multitudinous mind," suggests some new thought, and as you are wondering over it, you think of Lycidas, your friend, and promise yourself the pleasure of having his opinion of your discovery the very next time when by the fire you two " help waste a sullen day." Or it is, perhaps, some quainter, tenderer fancy that engages your solitary attention, something in Sir Philip Sidney or Henry Vaughan, and then you turn to look for Phyllis, ever the best interpreter of love, human or divine. Alas! the printed page grows hazy beneath a filmy eye as you suddenly remember that Lycidas is dead—" dead ere his prime,"—and that the pale cheek of Phyllis will never again be relumined by the white light of her pure enthusiasm. And then you fall to thinking of the inevitable, and perhaps, in your present mood, not unwelcome hour, when the " ancient

peace " of your old friends will be disturbed, when
rude hands will dislodge them from their accustomed nooks and break up their goodly company.

> Death bursts amongst them like a shell,
> And strews them over half the town.

They will form new combinations, lighten other
men's toil, and soothe another's sorrow. Fool that
I was to call anything *mine*!

AUTHORS IN COURT

1892

THERE is always something a little ludicrous about the spectacle of an author in pursuit of his legal remedies. It is hard to say why, but like a sailor on horseback, or a Quaker at the play, it suggests that incongruity which is the soul of things humorous. The courts are of course as much open to authors as to the really deserving members of the community; and, to do the writing fraternity justice, they have seldom shown any indisposition to enter into them—though if they have done so joyfully, it must be attributed to their natural temperament, which (so we read) is easy, rather than to the mirthful character of legal process.

To write a history of the litigations in which great authors have been engaged would indeed be *renovare dolorem*, and is no intention of mine; though the subject is not destitute of human interest—indeed, quite the opposite.

Great books have naturally enough, being longer lived, come into court even more frequently than great authors. *Paradise Lost, The Whole Duty of Man, The Pilgrim's Progress*, Thomson's *Seasons, Rasselas*, all have a legal as well as a literary history. Nay, Holy Writ herself has raised some nice points. The king's exclusive prerogative to print the authorised version has been based by some lawyers on the commercial circumstance that King James paid for it out of his own pocket. Hence, argued they, cunningly enough, it became his, and is now his successor's. Others have contended more strikingly that the right of multiplying copies of the Scriptures necessarily belongs to the king as head of the Church. A few have been found to question the right altogether, and to call it a job. As her present gracious Majesty has been pleased to abandon the prerogative, and has left all her subjects free (though at their own charges) to publish the version of her learned predecessor, the Bible does not now come into court on its own account. But whilst the prerogative was enforced, the king's printers were frequently to be found seeking injunctions to restrain the vending of the Word of God by (to use Carlyle's language) "Mr. Thomas Teggs and other extraneous persons." Nor did the judges, on proper proof, hesitate to grant what was sought. It is perhaps interesting to observe that the king never claimed more than the text. It was always open to anybody to publish even King James's version, if he added notes of his own. But how shamefully was this royal indulgence abused! Knavish booksellers, anxious to turn a dishonest penny out of the very Bible, were known to publish Bibles with so-called notes, which upon examination turned out not to be *bonâ-fide* notes at all, but sometimes mere indications of assent with what was stated in the text, and sometimes simple ejaculations. And as people as a rule preferred to be without notes of this character they used to be thoughtfully printed at the very edge of the sheet, so that the scissors of the binder should cut them off and prevent them annoying the reader. But one can fancy the question, "What is a *bonâ-fide* note?" exercising the legal mind.

Our great lawyers on the bench have always treated literature in the abstract with the utmost respect. They have in many cases felt that they too, but for the grace of God, might have been authors. Like Charles Lamb's solemn Quaker, "they had been wits in their youth." Lord Mansfield never forgot that, according to Mr. Pope, he was a lost Ovid. Before ideas in their divine essence the judges have bowed down. "A literary composition," it has been said by them, "so long as it lies dormant in the author's mind, is absolutely in his own possession." Even Mr. Horatio Sparkins, of whose brilliant table-talk this observation reminds us, could not more willingly have recognised an obvious truth.

But they have gone much further than this. Not only is the repose of the dormant idea left undisturbed, but the manuscript to which it, on ceasing to be dormant, has been communicated, is hedged round with divinity. It would be most unfair to the delicacy of the legal mind to attribute this to the fact, no doubt notorious, that whilst it is easy (after, say, three years in a pleader's chambers) to draw an indictment against a man for stealing paper, it is not easy to do so if he has only stolen the ideas and used his own paper. There are some quibbling observations in the second book of Justinian's *Institutes*, and a few remarks of Lord Coke's which might lead the thoughtless to suppose that in their protection

of an author's manuscripts the courts were thinking
more of the paper than of the words put upon it;
but that this is not so clearly appears from our
law as it is administered in the Bankruptcy branch
of the High Court.

Suppose a popular novelist were to become a
bankrupt — a supposition which, owing to the
immense sums these gentlemen are now known
to make, is robbed of all painfulness by its im-
possibility—and his effects were found to consist
of the three following items: first, his wearing
apparel; second, a copy of *Whitaker's Almanack*
for the current year; and third, the manuscript
of a complete and hitherto unpublished novel,
worth in the Row, let us say, one thousand pounds.
These are the days of cash payments, so we must
not state the author's debts at more than fifteen
hundred pounds. It would have been difficult
for him to owe more without incurring the charge
of imprudence. Now, how will the law deal with
the effects of this bankrupt? Ever averse to
exposing anyone to criminal proceedings, it will
return to him his clothing, provided its cash value
does not exceed twenty pounds, which, as authors
have left off wearing bloom-coloured garments
even as they have left off writing *Vicars of Wakefield*, it is not likely to do. This humane rule dis-
poses of item number one. As to *Whitaker's
Almanack*, if would probably be found necessary
to take the opinion of the court; since, if it be
a tool of the author's trade, it will not vest in
the official receiver and be divisible amongst the
creditors, but, like the first item, will remain the
property of the bankrupt—but otherwise, if not

such a tool. On a point like this the court would probably wish to hear the evidence of an expert— of some man like Mr. George Augustus Sala, who knows the literary life to the backbone. This point disposed of, or standing over for argument, there remains the manuscript novel, which, as we have said, would, if sold in the Row, produce a sum not only sufficient to pay the costs of the argument about the *Almanack* and of all parties properly appearing in the bankruptcy, but also, if judiciously handled, a small dividend to the creditors. But here our law steps in with its chivalrous, almost religious respect for ideas, and declares that the manuscript shall not be taken from the bankrupt and published without his consent. In ordinary cases everything a bankrupt has, save the clothes for his back and the tools of his trade, is ruthlessly torn from him. Be it in possession, reversion, or remainder, it all goes. His incomes for life, his reversionary hopes, are knocked down to the speculator. In vulgar phrase, he is " cleaned out." But the manuscripts of the bankrupt author, albeit they may be worth thousands, are not recognised as property; they are not yet dedicate to the public. The precious papers, despite all their writer's misfortunes, remain his— his to croon and to dream over, his to alter and re-transcribe, his to withhold, ay, his to destroy, if he should deem them, either in calm judgment, or in a despairing hour, unhappy in their expression or unworthy of his name.

There is something positively tender in this view. The law may be an ass, but it is also a gentleman.

Of course, in my imaginary case, if the bankrupt were to withhold his consent to publication, his creditors, even though it were held that the *Almanack* was theirs, would get nothing. I can imagine them grumbling, and saying (what will not creditors say?):

We fed this gentleman whilst he was writing this precious manuscript. Our joints sustained him, our bread filled him, our wine made him merry. Without our goods he must have perished. By all legal analogies we ought to have a lien upon that manuscript. We are wholly indifferent to the writer's reputation. It may be blasted for all we care. It was not as an author but as a customer that we supplied his very regular wants. It is now our turn to have wants. We want to be paid.

These amusing, though familiar, cries of distress need not disturb our equanimity or interfere with our admiration for the sublime views as to the sanctity of unpublished ideas entertained by the Court of Bankruptcy.

We have thus found, so far as we have gone, the profoundest respect shown by the law both for the dormant ideas and the manuscripts of the author. Let us now push boldly on, and inquire what happens when the author withdraws his interdict, takes the world into his confidence, and publishes his book.

Our old Common Law was clear enough. Subject only to laws or customs about licensing and against profane books and the like, the right of publishing and selling any book belonged exclusively to the author and persons claiming through him. Books were as much the subjects of property-rights as lands in Kent or money in the bank. The term of enjoyment knew no period.

Fine fantastic ideas about genius endowing the world and transcending the narrow bounds of property were not countenanced by our Common Law. Bunyan's *Pilgrim's Progress*, in the year 1680, belonged to Mr. Ponder: *Paradise Lost*, in the year 1739, was the property of Mr. Jacob Tonson. Mr. Ponder and Mr. Tonson had acquired these works by purchase. Property-rights of this description seem strange to us, even absurd. But that is one of the provoking ways of property-rights. Views vary. Perhaps this time next century it will seem as absurd that Ben Mac Dhui should ever have been private property as it now does that in 1739 Mr. Tonson should have been the owner " of man's first disobedience and the fruit of that forbidden tree." This is not said with any covered meaning, but is thrown out gloomily with the intention of contributing to the general depreciation of property.

If it be asked how came it about that authors and booksellers allowed themselves to be deprived of valuable and well-assured rights—to be in fact disinherited, without so much as an expostulatory ode or a single epigram—it must be answered, strange as it may sound, it happened accidentally and through tampering with the Common Law.

Authors are indeed a luckless race. To be deprived of your property by Act of Parliament is a familiar process, calling for no remarks save of an objurgatory character; but to petition Parliament to take away your property—to get up an agitation against yourself, to promote the passage through both Houses of the Act of spolia-tion, is unusual; so unusual indeed that I make bold to say that none but authors would do such things. That they did these very things is certain. It is also certain that they did not mean to do them. They did not understand the effect of their own Act of Parliament. In exchange for a term of either fourteen or twenty-one years, they gave up not only for themselves, but for all before and after them, the whole of time. Oh! miserable men! No enemy did this; no hungry mob clamoured for cheap books; no owner of copyrights so much as weltered in his gore. The rights were unquestioned: no one found fault with them. The authors and booksellers accomplished their own ruin. Never, surely, since the well-nigh incredible folly of our first parents lost us Eden and put us to the necessity of earning our living, was so fine a property —perpetual copyright—bartered away for so paltry an equivalent.

This is how it happened. Before the Revolution of 1688 printing operations were looked after, first by the Court of Star Chamber, which was not always engaged, as the perusal of constitutional history might lead one to believe, in torturing the unlucky, and afterwards by the Stationers' Company. Both these jurisdictions revelled in what is called summary process, which lawyers sometimes describe as *brevi manu*, and suitors as " short shrift." They hailed before them the Mr. Thomas Teggs of the period, and fined them heavily and confiscated their stolen editions. Authors and their assignees liked this. But then came Dutch William and the glorious Revolution. The Press was left free; and authors and their assignees were reduced to the dull level of unlettered persons; that is to say, if their rights were interfered with, they were compelled to bring an action, of the kind called " trespass on the case," and to employ astute counsel to draw pleadings with a pitfall in each paragraph, and also to incur costs; and in most cases, even when they triumphed over their enemy, it was only to find him a pauper from whom it was impossible to recover a penny. Nor had the law power to fine the offender or to confiscate the pirated edition; or if it had this last power, it was not accustomed to exercise it, deeming it unfamiliar and savouring of the Inquisition. Grub Street grew excited. A noise went up, " most musical, most melancholy,

> As of cats that wail in chorus."

It was the Augustan age of literature. Authors were listened to. They petitioned Parliament, and their prayer was heard. In the eighth year of good Queen Anne the first copyright statute was passed, which, " for the encouragement of learned men to compose and write useful books," provided that the authors of books already printed who had not transferred their rights, and the booksellers or other persons who had purchased the copy of any books in order to print or reprint the same, should have the sole right of printing them for a term of twenty-one years from the tenth of April, 1710, and no longer; and that authors of books not then printed, should have the sole right of printing for fourteen years, and no longer. Then followed, what the authors really wanted the Act for, special penalties for infringement. And there was peace in Grub Street for the space of twenty-one years. But at the expiration of this period the fateful question was stirred—what had happened to the old Common Law right in perpetuity? Did it survive this peddling Act, or had it died, ingloriously smothered by a statute? That fine old book—once on every settle—*The Whole Duty of Man*, first raised the point. Its date of publication was 1657, so it had had its term of twenty-one years. That term having expired, what then? The proceedings throw no light upon the vexed question of the book's authorship. Sir Joseph Jekyll was content with the evidence before him that, in 1735 at all events, *The Whole Duty of Man* was, or would have been but for the statute, the property of one Mr. Eyre. He granted an injunction, thus in effect deciding that the old Common Law had survived the statute. Nor did the defendant appeal, but sat down under the affront, and left *The Whole Duty of Man* alone for the future.

Four years later there came into Lord Hardwicke's court " silver-tongued Murray," afterwards Lord Mansfield, then Solicitor-General, and on behalf of Mr. Jacob Tonson moved for an injunction to restrain the publication of an edition of *Paradise Lost*. Tonson's case was, that *Paradise Lost* belonged to him, just as the celebrated ewer by Benvenuto Cellini once belonged to the late Mr. Beresford Hope. He proved his title by divers mesne assignments and other acts in the law, from Mrs. Milton—the poet's third wife, who exhibited such skill in the art of widowhood, surviving her husband as she did for fifty-three years. Lord Hardwicke granted the injunction.

It looked well for the Common Law. Thomson's *Seasons* next took up the wondrous tale. This delightful author, now perhaps better remembered by his charming habit of eating peaches off the wall with both hands in his pockets, than by his great work, had sold the book to Andrew Millar, the bookseller whom Johnson respected because, said he, " he has raised the price of literature." If so, it must have been but low before, for he only gave Thomson a hundred guineas for " Summer," " Autumn," and " Winter," and some other pieces. The " Spring " he bought separately, along with the ill-fated tragedy, *Sophonisba*, for one hundred and thirty-seven pounds ten shillings. A knave called Robert Taylor pirated Millar's Thomson's *Seasons* ; and on the morrow of All Souls in Michaelmas, in the seventh year of King George the Third, Andrew Millar brought his plea of trespass on the case against Robert Taylor, and gave pledges of prosecution, to wit, John Doe and Richard Roe. The case was recognised to be of great importance, and was argued at becoming length in the King's Bench. Lord Mansfield and Justices Willes and Aston upheld the Common Law. It was, they declared, unaffected by the statute. Mr. Justice Yates dissented, and in the course of a judgment occupying nearly three hours, gave some of his reasons. It was the first time the court had ever finally differed since Mansfield presided over it. Men felt the matter could not rest there. Nor did it. Millar died, and went to his own place. His executors put up Thomson's *Poems* for sale by public auction, and one Beckett bought them for five hundred and five pounds.

When we remember that Millar only gave two hundred and forty-two pounds ten shillings for them in 1729, and had therefore enjoyed more than forty years' exclusive monopoly, we realise not only that Millar had made a good thing out of his brother Scot, but what great interests were at stake. Thomson's *Seasons*, erst Millar's, now became Beckett's; and when one Donaldson of Edinburgh brought out an edition of the poems, it became the duty of Beckett to take proceedings, which he did by filing a bill in the Court of Chancery.[1]

These proceedings found their way, as all decent proceedings do, to the House of Lords—farther than which you cannot go, though ever so minded. It was now high time to settle this question, and their lordships accordingly, as was their proud practice in great cases, summoned the judges of the land before their bar, and put to them five carefully-worded questions, all going to the points —what was the old Common-Law right, and has it survived the statute? Eleven judges attended, heard the questions, bowed and retired to consider their answers. On the fifteenth of February, 1774, they reappeared, and it being announced that they differed, instead of being locked up without meat, drink, or firing until they agreed, they were requested to deliver their opinions with their reasons, which they straightway proceeded to do. The result may be stated with tolerable accuracy thus:

[1] Donaldson was a well-known man in Edinburgh. He was Boswell's first publisher, and on one occasion gave that gentleman a dinner consisting mainly of pig. Johnson's view of his larcenous proceedings is stated in the *Life*. Thurlow was his counsel in this litigation. Donaldson's Hospital in Edinburgh represents the fortune made by this publisher.

by ten to one they were of opinion that the old
Common Law recognised perpetual copyright. By
six to five they were of opinion that the statute
of Queen Anne had destroyed this right. The House
of Lords adopted the opinion of the majority,
reversed the decree of the Court below, and thus
Thomson's *Seasons* became your *Seasons*, my
Seasons, anybody's *Seasons*. But by how slender
a majority! To make it even more exciting, it
was notorious that the most eminent judge on
the Bench (Lord Mansfield) agreed with the
minority; but owing to the combined circumstances of his having already, in a case practically
between the same parties and relating to the same
matter, expressed his opinion, and of his being
not merely a judge but a peer, he was prevented
(by etiquette) from taking any part, either as a
judge or as a peer, in the proceedings. Had he not
been prevented (by etiquette), who can say what
the result might have been?

Here ends the story of how authors and their
assignees were disinherited by mistake, and forced
to content themselves with such beggarly terms
of enjoyment as a hostile legislature doles out
to them.

As the law now stands, they may enjoy their
own during the period of the author's life, *plus*
seven years, or the period of forty-two years,
whichever may chance to prove the longer.

So strangely and so quickly does the law colour
men's notions of what is inherently decent, that
even authors have forgotten how fearfully they
have been abused and how cruelly robbed. Their
thoughts are turned in quite other directions. I

do not suppose they will care for these old-world memories. Their great minds are tossing on the ocean which pants dumbly-passionate with dreams of royalties. If they could only shame the English-reading population of the United States to pay for their literature, all would be well. Whether they ever will, depends upon themselves. If English authors will publish their books cheap, Brother Sam may, and probably will, pay them a penny a copy, or some such sum. If they will not, he will go on stealing. It is wrong, but he will do it. " He says," observes an American writer, " that he was born of poor but honest parents. *I* say, ' Bah!' " [1]

---

[1] I was wrong, for the very volume which first contained this Essay (*Res Judicatæ*, 1892) was protected in the States. I do not think this protection put much money into my pocket, while it robbed me of the wide circulation *Obiter Dicta* had obtained in a cheap unauthorised twelve-cent edition.

A FEW WORDS ABOUT COPYRIGHT IN BOOKS

1905

COPYRIGHT, which is the exclusive liberty reserved to an author and his assigns of printing or otherwise multiplying copies of his book during certain fixed periods of time, is a right of modern origin.

There is nothing about copyright in Justinian's compilations.

It is a mistake to suppose that books did not circulate freely in the era of manuscripts. St. Augustine was one of the most popular authors that ever lived. His *City of God* ran over Europe after a fashion impossible to-day. Thousands of busy hands were employed, year out and year in, making copies for sale of this famous treatise. Yet Augustine had never heard of copyright, and never received a royalty on sales in his life.

The word "copyright" is of purely English origin, and came into existence as follows:

The Stationers' Company was founded by royal charter in 1556, and from the beginning has kept register-books, wherein, first, by decrees of the Star Chamber, afterwards by orders of the Houses of Parliament, and finally by Act of Parliament, the titles of all publications and reprints have had to be entered prior to publication.

None but booksellers, as publishers were then content to be called, were members of the Stationers' Company, and by the usage of the Company on entries could be made in their register-books except in the names of members, and thereupon the book referred to in the entry became the "copy" of the member or members who had caused it to be registered.

By virtue of this registration the book became, in the opinion of the Stationers' Company, the property *in perpetuity* of the member or members who had effected the registration. This was the " right " of the stationer to his " copy."

Copyright at first is therefore not an author's, but a bookseller's copyright. The author had no part or lot in it unless he chanced to be both an author and a bookseller, an unusual combination in early days. The author took his manuscript to a member of the Stationers' Company, and made the best bargain he could for himself. The stationer, if terms were arrived at, carried off the manuscript to his Company and registered the title in the books, and thereupon became, in his opinion, and in that of his Company, the owner, at common law, in perpetuity of his " copy."

The stationers, having complete control over their register-books, made what entries they chose, and all kinds of books, even Homer and the Classics, became the " property " of its members. The booksellers, nearly all Londoners, respected each other's " copies," and jealously guarded access to their registers. From time to time there were sales by auction of a bookseller's " copies," but the public —that is, the country booksellers, for there were no other likely buyers—were excluded from the sale-room. A great monopoly was thus created and maintained by the trade. There was never any examination of title to a bookseller's copy.

Every book of repute was supposed to have a bookseller for its owner.   Bunyan's *Pilgrim's Progress* was Mr. Ponder's copy, Milton's *Paradise Lost* Mr. Tonson's copy, *The Whole Duty of Man* Mr. Eyre's copy, and so on.   The thing was a corrupt trade combination.

The expiration of the Licensing Act, and the consequent cessation of the penalties it inflicted upon unlicensed printing, exposed the proprietors of " copies " to an invasion of their rights, real or supposed, and in 1703, and again in 1706 and 1709, they applied to Parliament for a Bill to protect them against the " ruin " with which they alleged themselves to be threatened.[1]

In 1710 they got what they asked for in the shape of the famous Statute of Queen Anne, the first copyright law in the world.   A truly English measure, ill considered and ill drawn, which did the very last thing it was meant to do—viz., destroy the property it was intended to protect.

By this Act, in which the " author " first makes his appearance actually in front of the " proprietor," it was provided that, *in case of new books*, the author and his assigns should have the sole right of printing them for fourteen years, and if at the end of that time the author was still alive, a second term of fourteen years was conceded.   In the case of *existing books*, there was to be but one term—viz., twenty-one years, from August 10th, 1710.

Registration at the Stationers' Company was still required, but nothing was said as to who

---

[1] What the booksellers wanted was not to be left to their common law remedy—*i.e.*, an action of trespass on the case—but to be supplied with penalties for infringement, and especially with the right to seize and burn unauthorised editions.

might make the entries, or into whose names they were to be made.

Then followed the desired penalties for infringement. The booksellers thought the terms of years meant no more than that the penalties were to be limited by way of experiment to those periods.

Many years flew by before the Stationers' Company discovered the mischief wrought by the statute they had themselves promoted. To cut a long matter short, it was not until 1774 that the House of Lords decided that, whether there ever had been a perpetuity in literary property at common law or not, it was destroyed by the Act of Queen Anne, and that from and after the passing of that law neither author, assignee, nor proprietor of "copy" had any exclusive right of multiplication, save for and during the periods of time the statute created.

It was a splendid fight—a Thirty Years' War. Great lawyers were fee'd in it; luminous and lengthy judgments were delivered. Mansfield was a booksellers' man ; Thurlow ridiculed the pretensions of the Trade. It can be read about in Boswell's *Johnson* and in Campbell's *Lives of the Lord Chancellors*. The authors stood supinely by, not contributing a farthing towards the expenses. It was a booksellers' battle, and the booksellers were beaten, as they deserved to be.

All this is past history, in which the modern money-loving, motoring author takes scant pleasure. Things are on a different footing now. The Act of 1842 has extended the statutory periods of protection. The perpetuity craze is over. A right in perpetuity to reprint Frank Fustian's novel or Tom Tatter's poem would not add a penny to the present value of the copyright of either of those productions. In business short views must prevail. An author cannot expect to raise money on his hope of immortality. Milton's publisher, good Mr. Symonds, probably thought, if he thought about it at all, that he was buying *Paradise Lost* for ever when he registered it as his " copy " in the books of his Company; but into the calculations he made to discover how much he could afford to give the author posterity did not and could not enter. How was Symonds to know that Milton's fame was to outlive Cleveland's or Flatman's ?

How many of the books published in 1905 would have any copyright cash value in A.D. 2000 ? I do not pause for a reply.

The modern author need have no quarrel with the statutory periods fixed by the Act of 1842,[1] though common sense has long since suggested that a single term, the author's life and thirty or forty years after, should be substituted for the alternative periods named in the Act.

What the modern author alone desiderates is a big, immediate, and protected market.

The United States of America have been a great disappointment to many an honest British author. In the wicked old days when the States took British books without paying for them they used to take them in large numbers, but now that they have turned honest and passed a law allowing the

---

[1] Author's life *plus* seven years, or forty-two years from date of publication, whichever term is the longer. The great objection to the second term is that an author's books go out of copyright at different dates, and the earlier editions go out first.

British author copyright on certain terms, they have in great measure ceased to take ; for, by the strangest of coincidences, no sooner were British novels, histories, essays, and the like, protected in America, than there sprang up in the States themselves, novelists, historians, and essayists, not only numerous enough to supply their own home markets, but talented enough to cross the Atlantic in large numbers and challenge us in our own. Such a reward for honesty was not contemplated.

International copyright and the Convention of Berne are things to be proud of and rejoice over. As the first chapter in a Code of Public European Law, they may mark the beginning of a time of settled peace, order, and disarmament, but they have not yet enriched a single author, though here-after possibly an occasional novelist or playwright may prosper greatly under their provisions.

The copyright question is now at last really a settled question, save in a single aspect of it. What, if anything, should be done in the case of those authors, few in number, whose literary lives prove longer than the period of statutory protection? Should any distinction in law be struck between a Tennyson and a Tupper? between—— But why multiply examples? There is no need to be unnecessarily offensive.

The law and practice of to-day give the meat that remains on the bones of the dead author after the expiration of the statutory period of protection to the Trade. Any publisher who likes to bring out an edition can do so, though by doing so he does not gain any exclusive rights. A brother publisher may compete with him. As a result the public is usually well served with cheap editions of those non-copyright authors whose works are worth reprinting the moment the copyright expires.

Some lovers of justice, however, think that it is unnecessary all at once to endow the Trade with these windfalls, and that if an author's family, or his or their assignees, were prepared to publish cheap editions immediately after the expiration of the usual period of protection, they ought to be allowed to do so for a further period of, say, forty years. If they failed within a reasonable time either to do so themselves or to arrange for others to do so, this extended period should lapse.

Were this to be the law nobody could say that it was unfair; but it is never likely to be the law. It would take time for discussion, and now there is no time left in which to discuss anything in Parliament. A much-needed Copyright Bill[1] has been in draft for years, has been mentioned in Queen's and King's speeches, but it has never been read even a first time. If it ever is read a first time, its only chance of becoming law will be if it is taken in a lump, as it stands, without consideration or amendment. To such a pass has legislation been reduced in this country!

This draft Bill does not contain any provision for specially protecting the families of authors whose works long outlive their mortal lives.[2] It makes no invidious distinctions. It leaves all the authors to hang together, the quick and the dead. Perhaps this is the better way.

[1] This Copyright Bill has now become law (1 and 2 George V., Chap. 46), and extends the period of protection to fifty years after the author's death.

[2] Nor does the new Act beyond fifty years.

ALEXANDER KNOX AND THOMAS DE QUINCEY

1894

AMONGST the many bizarre things that attended the events which led up to the Act of Union between Great Britain and Ireland, was the circumstance that Lord Castlereagh's private secretary during the period should have been that Mr. Alexander Knox whose *Remains* in four rather doleful volumes were once cherished by a certain school of theologians.

Mr. Knox was a man of great piety, some learning, and of the utmost simplicity of life and manners. He was one of the first of our moderns to be enamoured of primitive Christian times, and to seek to avoid the claims of Rome upon the allegiance of all Catholic-minded souls by hooking himself on to a period prior to the full development of those claims.

It is no doubt true that, for a long time past, Nonconformists of different kinds have boldly asserted that they were primitive; but it must be owned that they have never taken the least pains to ascertain the actual facts of the case. Now, Mr. Knox took great pains to be primitive. Whether he succeeded it is not for me to say, but at all events he went so far on his way to success as to leave off being modern both in his ways of thought and in his judgments of men and books.

English Nonconformity has produced many hundreds of volumes of Biography and Remains, but there is never a primitive one amongst them. To anyone who may wish to know what it is to be primitive, there is but one answer: Read the *Remains* of Alexander Knox. Be careful to get the right Knox. There was one Vicesimus, who is much better known than Alexander, and at least as readable, but (and this is the whole point) not at all primitive.

And it was this primitive, apostolic Mr. Knox who is held by some to be the real parent of the Tractarian movement, whose correspondence is almost entirely religious, and whose whole character stands revealed in his *Remains* as that of a man without guile, and as obstinate as a mule, who was chosen at a most critical moment of political history to share the guilty secrets of Mr. Pitt and Lord Castlereagh. It seems preposterous.

The one and only thing in Knox's *Remains* of the least interest to people who are not primitive is a letter addressed to him by Lord Castlereagh, written after the completion of the Union, and suggesting to him the propriety of his undertaking the task of writing the history of that event—the reason being his thorough knowledge of all the circumstances of the case.

Such a letter bids us pause.

By this time we know well enough how the Act of Union was carried. By bribery and corruption. Nobody has ever denied it for the last fifty years. It has been in the school text-books for generations. But the point is, Did Mr. Knox know? If he did, it must seem to all who have read his *Remains*—

and it is worth while reading them only to enjoy
the sensation—a most marvellous thing. It would
not be more marvellous had we learnt from Canon
Liddon's long-looked-for volumes that Mr. Pusey
was Mr. Disraeli's adviser in all matters relating
to the disposition of the secret service money
and the Tory election funds. If Knox did not
know anything about it, how was he kept in
ignorance, how was he sheltered from the greedy
Irish peers and borough-mongers and all the
other impecunious rascals who had the vending
of a nation? And what are we to think of the
foresight of Castlereagh, who secured for himself
such a secretary in order that, after all was over,
Mr. Knox might sit down and in all innocence
become the historian of proceedings of which he
had been allowed to know nothing, but which
sorely needed the cloak of a holy life and conversation to cover up their sores?

It is an odd problem. For my part, I believe in
Knox's innocence. Trying very hard to be worthy
of the second century was not good training
for seeing his way through the fag-end of the
eighteenth. Apart from this, it is amazing what
some men will not see. I recall but will not quote
the brisk retort of Mrs. Saddletree at her husband's
expense, which relates to the incapacity of that
learned saddler to see what was going on under his
nose. The test was a severe one, but we have no
doubt whatever that Alexander Knox could have
stood it as well as Mr. Bartoline Saddletree.

Another strange incident connected with the
same event is that the final ratification of the Act
of Union in Dublin was witnessed by, and made,

as it could not fail to do, a great impression upon,
the most accomplished rhetorical writer of our
time. De Quincey, then a precocious boy of
fifteen, happened by a lucky chance to be in
Ireland at the time, and as the guest of Lord
Altamount, an Irish peer, he had every opportunity
both of seeing the sight and acquainting himself
with the feelings of some of the leading actors in
the play, call it tragedy, comedy, or farce, as
you please.

De Quincey's account of the scene, and his
two chapters on the Irish Rebellion, are to be
found in the first volume of his *Autobiographic
Sketches*.

De Quincey hints that both Lord Altamount
and his son, " who had an Irish heart," would have
been glad if at the very last moment the populace
had stepped in between Mr. Pitt and the Irish
peers and commoners and compelled the two
Houses to perpetuate themselves. Internally, says
De Quincey, they would have laughed. But it was
written otherwise in Heaven's chancery, and " the
Bill received the Royal assent without a muttering
or a whispering or the protesting echo of a sigh.
. . . One person only I remarked whose features
were suddenly illuminated by a smile—a sarcastic
smile, as I read it—which, however, might be all
fancy. It was Lord Castlereagh." Can it possibly
be that this was the very moment when it occurred
to his lordship's mind that Mr. Knox was the man
to be the historian of the event thus concluded?

The new edition of De Quincey's writings has
naturally provoked many critics to attempt to
do for him what he was fond enough of doing

for others, often to their dismay—to give some account, that is, of the author and the man. De Quincey does not lend himself to this familiar treatment. He eludes analysis and baffles description. His great fault as an author is best described, in the decayed language of the equity draughtsman, as multifariousness. His style lacks the charm of economy, and his workmanship the dignity of concentration.

A literary spendthrift is, however, a very endurable sinner in these stingy days. Mr. Mill speaks somewhere (I think in his *Political Economy*) almost sorrowfully of De Quincey's strange habit of scattering fine thoughts up and down his merely miscellaneous writings. The habit has ceased to afflict the reader. The fine maxim, " Waste not, want not," is now inscribed over the desks of our miscellaneous writers. Such extravagance as De Quincey's, as it is not likely to be repeated, need not be too severely reprobated.

De Quincey's magnificence, the apparent boundlessness of his information, the liberties he takes, relying upon his mastery of language, his sportiveness and freakish fancies, make him the idol of all hobbledehoys of a literary turn. By them his sixteen volumes are greedily devoured. Happy the country, one is tempted to exclaim, that has such reading to offer its young men and maidens!

The discovery that De Quincey wrote something else besides the *Opium Eater* marks a red-letter day in many a young life. The papers on *The Twelve Cæsars*; on the *Essenes and Secret Societies*; on *Judas Iscariot, Cicero,* and *Richard Bentley*; *The Spanish Nun, The Female Infidel, The Tartars,* seemed the very climax of literary well-doing, and to unite the learning of the schools with all the fancy of the poets and the wit of the world.

As one grows older, one grows sterner—with others.

> Prune thou thy words, the thoughts control
> That o'er thee swell and throng;
> They will condense within thy soul,
> And change to purpose strong.

The lines have a literary as well as a moral value.

But though paradox may cease to charm, and a tutored intellect seem to sober age a better guide than a lawless fancy, and a chastened style a more comfortable thing than impassioned prose and pages of *bravura*, still, after all, " the days of our youth are the days of our glory," and for a reader who is both young and eager the Selections Grave and Gay of Thomas de Quincey will always be above criticism, and belong to the realm of rapture.

NATIONALITY

1892

NOTHING can well be more offensive than the abrupt asking of questions, unless indeed it be the glib assurance which professes to be able to answer them without a moment's doubt or consideration. It is hard to forgive Sir Robert Peel for having once asked, " What is a pound ? " Cobden's celebrated question, " What next ? And next ? " was perhaps less objectionable, being vast and vague, and, to employ Sir Thomas Browne's well-known phrase, capable of a wide solution.

But in these disagreeable days we must be content to be disagreeable. We must even accept being so as our province. It seems now recognised that he is the best Parliamentary debater who is most disagreeable. It is not so easy as some people imagine to be disagreeable. The gift requires cultivation. It is easier, no doubt, for some than for others.

What is a nation—socially and politically, and as a unit to be dealt with by practical politicians ? It is not a great many things. It is not blood, it is not birth, it is not breeding. A man may have been born at Surat and educated at Lausanne, one of his four great-grandfathers may have been a Dutchman, one of his four great-grandmothers a French refugee, and yet he himself may remain, from his cradle in Surat to his grave at Singapore, a true-born Englishman, with all an Englishman's fine contempt for mixed races and struggling nationalities.

Where the English came from is still a matter of controversy, but where they have gone to is writ large over the earth's surface. Yet their nationality has suffered no eclipse. Caviare is not so good in London as in Moscow, but it is caviare all the same. No foreigner needs to ask the nationality of the man who treads on his corns, smiles at his religion, and does not want to know anything about his aspirations.

England has all the notes of a nation. She has a National Church, based upon a view of history peculiarly her own. She has a National Oath, which, without any undue pride, may be pronounced adequate for ordinary occasions. She has a Constitution, the admiration of the world, and of which a fresh account has to be written every twenty years. She has a History, glorious in individual feats, and splendid in accomplished facts; she has a Literature which makes the poorest of her children, if only he has been taught to read, rich beyond the dreams of avarice. As for the national character, it may be said of an Englishman, what has been truly said of the great English poet Wordsworth—take him at his best and he need own no superior. He cannot always be at his best; and when he is at his worst the world shudders.

But what about Scotland and Ireland? Are they nations? If they are not, it is not because their separate characteristics have been absorbed

by John Bullism. Scotland and Ireland are no
more England than Holland or Belgium. It may
be doubted whether, if the three countries had
never been politically united, their existing unlikeness would have been any greater than it is.
It is a most accentuated unlikeness. Scotland has
her own prevailing religion. Mr. Arnold recognised
this when he observed, in that manner of his which
did not always give pleasure, that Dr. Chalmers
reminded him of a Scotch thistle valorously trying
to look as much like the rose of Sharon as possible.
This distorted view of Mr. Arnold's at all events
recognises a fact. Then there is Scotch law. If
there is one legal proposition which John Bull—
poor attorney-ridden John Bull—has grasped for
himself, it is that a promise made without a
monetary or otherwise valuable consideration is
in its legal aspect a thing of nought, which may
be safely disregarded. Bull's views about the
necessity of writing and sixpenny stamps are
vague, but he is quite sound and certain about
promises going for nothing unless something
passed between the parties. Thus, if an Englishman, moved, let us say, by the death of his father,
says hastily to a maiden aunt who has made the
last days of his progenitor easy, " I will give you
fifty pounds a year," and then repents him of his
promise, he is under no legal obligation to make
it good. If he is a gentleman he will send her a
ten-pound note at Christmas and a fat goose at
Michaelmas, and the matter drops as being but
the babble of the sick-room. But in Scotland the
maiden aunt, provided she can prove her promise,
can secure her annuity and live merrily in Peebles

for the rest of a voluptuous life. Here is a difference indeed!

Then, Scotland has a history of her own. The late Dr. Hill Burton wrote it in nine comfortable volumes. She has a thousand traditions, foreign connections, feelings to which the English breast must always remain an absolute stranger. Scottish fields are different from English fields; her farms, roads, walls, buildings, flowers, are different; her schools, universities, churches, household ways, songs, foods, drinks, are all as different as may be. Boswell's Johnson, Lockhart's Scott! What a host of dissimilarities, what an Iliad of unlikenesses, do the two names of Johnson and Scott call up from the vasty deep of national differences!

One great note of a nation is possessed to the full by Scotland. I mean the power of blending into one state of national feeling all those who call what is contained within her geographical boundaries by the sacred name of "Home." The Lowlander from Dumfries is more at home at Inverness than in York. Why is this? Because Scotland is a nation. The great Smollett, who challenges Dickens for the foremost place amongst British comic writers, had no Celtic blood in his veins. He was neither a Papist nor a Jacobite, yet how did his Scottish blood boil whilst listening in London to the cowardly exultations of the cockneys over the brutalities that followed the English victory at Culloden! and how bitterly— almost savagely—did he contrast that cowardly exultation with the depression and alarm that had prevailed in London when but a little while before the Scotch had reached Derby!

What patriotic feeling breathes through Smollett's noble lines, *The Tears of Scotland*, and with what delightful enthusiasm, with what affectionate admiration, does Sir Walter Scott tell us how the last stanza came to be written!

He [Smollett] accordingly read them the first sketch of *The Tears of Scotland*, consisting only of six stanzas, and on their remarking that the termination of the poem, being too strongly expressed, might give offence to persons whose political opinions were different, he sat down without reply, and with an air of great indignation, subjoined the concluding stanza:

> " While the warm blood bedews my veins,
> And unimpaired remembrance reigns,
> Resentment of my country's fate
> Within my filial breast shall beat.
> Yes, spite of thine insulting foe,
> My sympathising verse shall flow:
> Mourn, hapless Caledonia, mourn,
> Thy banished peace, thy laurels torn."

In the same sense is the story told by Mr. R. L. Stevenson, how, when the famous Celtic regiment, the Black Watch, which then drew its recruits from the now unpeopled glens of Ross-shire and Sutherland, returned to Scotland after years of foreign service, veterans leaped out of the boats and kissed the shore of Galloway.

The notes of Irish nationality have been, by conquest and ill-usage, driven deeper in. Her laws were taken from her, and her religion brutally proscribed. In the great matter of higher education she has not been allowed her natural and proper development. Her children have been driven abroad to foreign seminaries to get the education Protestant England denied them at home. Her nationality has thus been checked and mutilated, but that it exists in spirit and in fact can hardly be questioned by any impartial traveller. Englishmen have many gifts, but one gift they have not—that of making Scotsmen and Irishmen forget their native land.

The attitude of some Englishmen towards Scotch and Irish national feelings requires correction. The Scotsman's feelings are laughed at. The Irishman's insulted. So far as the laughter is concerned, it must be admitted that it is good-humoured. Burns, Scott, and Carlyle, Scotch moors and Scotch whisky, the royal game of golf, all have mollified and beatified English feelings. In candour, too, it must be admitted that Scotsmen are not conciliatory. They do not meet people half-way. I do not think the laughter does much harm. Insults are different. . . .

Mr. Arnold, in a now scarce pamphlet published in 1859, on the Italian Question, with the motto prefixed, " Sed nondum est finis," makes the following interesting observations :

> Let an Englishman or a Frenchman, who respectively represent the two greatest nationalities of modern Europe, sincerely ask himself what it is that makes him take pride in his nationality, what it is which would make it intolerable to his feelings to pass, or to see any part of his country pass, under foreign dominion. He will find that it is the sense of self-esteem generated by knowing the figure which his nation makes in history; by considering the achievements of his nation in war, government, arts, literature, or industry. It is the sense that his people, which has done such great things, merits to exist in freedom and dignity, and to enjoy the luxury of self-respect.

This is admirable, but not, nor does it pretend to be, exhaustive. The love of country is something a little more than mere *amour-propre*. You may love your mother, and wish to make a home for her, even though she never dwelt in kings' palaces, and is clad in rags. The children of misery and misfortune are not all illegitimate. Sometimes you may discern amongst them high hope and pious endeavour. There may be, indeed, there is, a Niobe amongst the nations, but tears are not always of despair.

" The luxury of self-respect." It is a wise phrase. To make Ireland and Irishmen self-respectful is the task of statesmen.

NATIONALITY AND THE LEAGUE OF NATIONS

AN ADDRESS DELIVERED BY THE PRESIDENT OF
THE SOCIAL AND POLITICAL EDUCATION LEAGUE
ON JULY 9TH, 1919. THE DEAN OF ST. PAUL'S
IN THE CHAIR.

YOU choose your President annually, and each year his task becomes harder, and this year it excites, or should do so, compassion in every human breast. The problems, as the Press loves to call them, some of which your President may be expected, not indeed to solve but to glide over, ascending as they do into the highest heaven of men's fancies, sick and healthy, and descending into the grimmest depths of our social machinery, accumulate month by month, while the presidential wits—I refer exclusively to my own—decay with equal rapidity.

Yours is a League to promote our nation's social and political education. Society, Politics, Education—what great words are these! and yet they are in common use. Indeed, the contrast between our simply magnificent vocabulary, so easily invoked by us, whether we are upon our knees before God or only talking in the street, and the miserably restricted range and depth of our knowledge and piety are painfully marked. Could we but charge our words with meaning and our prayers with reality, I might this very afternoon take upon myself to dissolve your League, and hold my peace for the rest of the day. No such cheerful prospect is immediately before you.

In choosing a title for this address I own to drawing upon my past melancholy experience of parliamentary draftsmanship. Before introducing a Bill to the notice of Parliament, leave to do so has first to be obtained, and in order to get this leave the would-be law-maker is required, perhaps not unreasonably, to say in general terms what his Bill is about; in other words, he has to invent a title for it, and then, if, after the measure has been discussed and, probably, amended, an enemy finds it to contain something not so much as hinted at in the original title, why, then, trouble ensues, and the whole thing may have to be withdrawn, and the palaver begun over again. Consequently, the experienced draftsman, when concocting his title, casts the net of his verbiage very wide, so that whatever kind of fish he may chance to catch he may lawfully retain.

Nationality and the League of Nations is wide enough to satisfy the draftsman within me, for, after all, my only object in composing and submitting to your notice the following desultory observations was, and is, first to stir my own thoughts on these subjects, and then possibly some of yours, and thus to force ourselves to think about them as clearly as we can. This process of stirring is often a muddy one, but a muddy stream is clearer than a stagnant pool.

Nationality, though a word to-day in common employment, is not to be found in Johnson's two

folios of 1755, where you will only discover *Nation*
and *National*, the latter being defined as " bigoted
to one's own country "—a very good description
of the lexicographer himself. But if you consult
the New English Dictionary, 1905, you will find
that eleven columns are devoted to this root and
its various derivatives.

When engaged in turning over this new-fangled
word in our minds, we are somewhat disposed,
under the pressure of the moment, to think almost
exclusively of what are called *small* nationalities,
i.e., of oppressed national sentiments struggling
for freedom of expression, with not unnatural
enthusiasms for their own ancient languages and
native literatures, as well as for their once dis-
tinctive manners, customs, and dress. The big
political combinations, the Principal Allies, the
Masters of many legions and sea forces, the Proprietors of huge National Debts, with, I hope,
correspondingly solid credits, find it very difficult,
however hard they try (and to-day many of them
do try very hard) to avoid treading on the toes of
the small nations, by innocently ignoring their
aspirations, and naïvely exhibiting the most far-
reaching ignorance of their past histories, nay,
even of their previous existence. M. Masaryk,
who has lived all his life amid the small nations of
Europe involved in the present imbroglio, puts
them down at sixty-eight, and divides them into
twenty-eight States, of which seven alone are
homogeneous. In each of the other twenty-one
there is an Ulster. Allowing each of these sixty-
eight small nations the usual human allotment
of ten toes, how can we, knowing the extent of our

own ignorance, blame the big clumsy-footed Four
for occasionally treading on most of them?

We cannot expect our statesmen to be great
political geographers, our practice being first to
annex a country, and to find out about it afterwards.   One Prime Minister of the eighteenth
century is to-day best known to the ordinary
student because he discovered Cape Breton was
an island after he had taken it, and our present
Prime Minister honestly told the House of Commons, to the affected horror of *The Times*, that he
had just heard of the coalfields of Teschen.

The problem, vexed and troublesome as it is,
of rival nationalities is in Europe a modern trouble.
Lord Acton, in an illuminating, though, as indeed
his work is apt to be, toughish, discourse on
Nationality, contributed fifty-seven years ago to
the *Home and Foreign Review*, and now to be
studied in that volume of his essays called *The
History of Freedom and other Essays*, wrote as
follows:

In the old European system the rights of nationalities were
neither recognised by governments nor asserted by the people.
The interest of the reigning families, not those of the nations,
regulated the frontiers; and the administration was conducted generally without any reference to the popular desires.
Where all liberties were suppressed, the claims of national
independence were necessarily ignored, and a princess, in the
words of Fénelon, carried a monarchy in her wedding portion.
The eighteenth century acquiesced in this oblivion of cor-
porate rights on the Continent, for (*mark these words : much
turns on them*) the Absolutists cared only for the *State*, and
the Liberals only for the individual.   The Church, the nobles,
and the nation had no place in the popular theories of the
age, and they devised none in their own defence, for they were
not before the Revolution openly attacked.   The aristocracy
retained its privileges and the Church her property, and the
dynastic interest which overruled the natural inclination of
the nations and destroyed their independence, nevertheless

maintained their integrity. The national sentiment was not wounded in its most sensitive part. . . . In time of war, as there was no national cause at stake, there was no attempt to arouse national feeling. . . . The art of war became a slow and learned game. The monarchies were linked not only by a natural community of interests, but by family alliances. A marriage contract sometimes became the signal for an interminable war, whilst family connections often set a barrier to ambition. After the Wars of Religion came to an end at the peace of Westphalia in 1648, the only wars were those which were waged for an inheritance or dependency, or against countries whose systems of government exempted them from the common law of dynastic States. . . . Those countries were England and Holland.

Thus far Lord Acton.

There was, however, one country whose monarch was not admitted into this comity of Kings—this Alliance of dynasties regardless of nationalities. The name of this country is Poland. A monarch without the blood-royal, a crown bestowed by a nation as its own free gift, were things then hardly tolerable and were, in truth, almost " unthinkable," to use a word now commonly employed to describe the very things about which almost everybody is thinking his hardest, though it may be with apprehension or disgust. Hence came about the first partition of Poland in 1772, a shocking violation of the public law. It was a grim question asked by Burke—" The powers have breakfasted upon Poland; but when or where will they dine ? " I do not know what name to apply to the lengthy meal lately spread in the Hall of Mirrors in Versailles, but whatever its nature may have been, Poland had a " *plat* " all to herself.

This infamous partition aroused from its long slumber in Europe the spirit of nationality. Sentiment assumed the toga of politics. Thenceforward there was on the Continent of Europe at least one nation demanding State rights, a soul in search of a body, a wandering voice crying aloud that a people had been robbed of its birthright. Long before this cry had reached High Heaven—which, indeed, is disposed to be a little hard of hearing in such cases—the French Revolution appeared, and after a short while the old European system of dynasties, often represented by madmen, lay in ruins at the feet of the little Corporal from Corsica. To-day Poland reappears on the map in her original, somewhat histrionic part of a nation. Her reappearancere lights ancient and ardent hopes and antipathies, and well demands both the prayers of the pious and the early attention of the League of Nations.

After the Congress of Vienna—that stupendous failure, that blind and brutal blunder—Legitimism again raised its muddled head so high as to lead many good English patriots so far astray as to regret Napoleon. But Legitimism was but galvanised into a mischievous semblance of life, and ere long the cause of nationality passed into the glowing hands of Mazzini.

> Of God nor man was ever this thing said,
> That he could give
> Life back to her who gave it, whence his dead
> Mother might live.

To Mazzini the form of government for Italy was never an international question, but always a national—that is, an Italian question. In the *argot* of to-day the right of self-determination belonged to Italy alone. In Mazzini's view, wherever you can postulate a nation—not always an easy thing to do—it should, if it wishes, be enshrined and consecrated in an independent State, having as its chief *raison d'être* the preservation through the ages of that nationality.

Mr. J. S. Mill, in 1865, adopts, though with some cautionary limitations, the same view, and in the interesting chapter on Nationality in his *Considerations on Representative Government*, may be found declaring that he would hardly know what any division of the human race should be free to do, if not to determine with which of the various bodies of human beings they would choose to associate themselves, adding, in a fit of unusual martial ardour, that for one nationality by brute strength to reduce another to subjection would be a sheer mischief to the human race, "and one which civilised humanity with one accord should rise in arms to prevent." In 1865 Mr. Mill had Russia in his mind as a Power capable of such an atrocity.

It is, perhaps, going too far to say that we ought all to be left free to choose with which of the various collective bodies of human beings we should be associated. I am glad to know that for me, at all events, the choice, like most other things of real importance, was made for me, once for all, when nearly seventy years ago I was born, not within sight of the Parthenon in Athens, or of the Capitol of Rome, or even on the doorsteps of the Temple in Jerusalem, but in the vicinity of Liverpool.

This raises to the surface of our thoughts a distinction which has to be made between the natural, primitive emotion of patriotism and the claim of nationality for the pride and place of a State. You, Mr. Dean, in your Presidential address in 1915, chose patriotism as your stirring theme, and whilst striving to purge this instinct of our fallen nature from vulgar accessaries which dim its purity and lustre, were yet able to conclude as follows: "The deepest sympathy is potentially also the widest. He who loves not his home and country which he has seen, how shall he love humanity in general which he has not seen?"

So patriotism, like charity, begins at home.

> The old trees
> Which grew by our youth's home, the waving mass
> Of clustering plants, heavy with bloom and dew,
> The morning swallows with their songs like words—
> All these seem clear.

But, happily, it is possible to construct on the foundation of this ineradicable emotion an honest allegiance to a political law-giving State, although that State may not even include your "youth's home" within its boundaries, or, if it does do so, only by the slender tie of a federating union. Recent legal proceedings have revealed to us, in the case of a distinguished painter, how even that most delicate instrument known to us for the discovery of the truth about anything—cross-examination in open court—is too coarse, too clumsy, and too blunt a thing to disentangle contending emotions of the kind we are considering in an honest, truth-loving breast.

For if patriotism is to be of any use, it must be lifted out of the realm of clanship, which, though a romantic word in a "Waverley" novel, has a history full of sound and fury, signifying nothing! Patriotism must be expanded, taken out of itself, after some fashion or another, and in alliance with other patriotisms become part of a

State or a federation of States. Undoubtedly when
the word " State " comes upon the scene, the
natural, simple emotion of patriotism begins to
wear another hue. There is no need for moral
or political philosophers to prescribe for us our
duties towards our Homeland. We look into our
hearts and act in obedience to their dictates. But
what remarkable books have been written, what
loyal hearts broken, what martyrdoms endured,
what blood has been shed, on the subject of our
duty towards the State!

It was just hereabouts that Acton parted company with Mazzini, whose passionate patriotism
and historic pride forced him to make the somewhat vague boundaries of the Italian nation com-
mensurate with an Italian State. Lord Acton,
as all his readers know well, hugged to his honest
heart three ideals, or Faery Queens—first, the true
facts of history as revealed by archival research;
second, the supremacy of the moral law, and
particularly of the Commandment, *Thou shalt do
no murder*; and third, liberty, meaning by that
abused word, not licence to commit crime, but
the widest possible area for individual freedom of
action and thought. Now, it must be admitted
that patriots engaged in such a task as Mazzini's
would find themselves hampered by a too un-
swerving devotion to any one of Acton's three
Faery Queens. Impartial history is not likely to
be written by any patriot in hot pursuit of a State.
The Sixth Commandment has only too frequently
suffered patriotic amendment by striking out the
" not," whilst as for liberty, how many crimes
against freedom have been committed in that name!

The truth is, that any State, whether based on the right of kings to govern wrong, or on the rights of peoples to misgovern themselves, is absolute in theory and soon falls in love with her own absolutism, and brooks no rival near her throne. Every statesman of the true breed, whether he springs from the Court, the University, the Counting-house, the Mill, or the Mine, is at heart a Hobbist, and his demand, which grows with his power, is complete surrender. Authority, by whatever steps it climbed the throne, is *right*, and from the State mint alone is issued the current coin of the realm, and the fine words graven on the coins—obverse, reverse, or rim—make not a ha'porth of difference.

The pet aversion of the State, and its obedient servants, is the Conscientious Objector—who is sometimes a pacifist who won't kill Germans at the bidding of Parliament, sometimes an ex-Minister who declares he will call out his partially-armed forces if Ulster is required to modify the Act of Union, and sometimes a coal-owner who objects to be " nationalised "; but the Conscientious Objector, whoever he is or may become, is, in the eye of the Government, possibly a traitor, probably a fool, and always a nuisance.

Yet the State and due subordination to it are necessary, not only to make the liberty Acton so dearly loved possible, but also to secure what, after all, is at the bottom of everything—the right of *self-preservation*, to go on existing along the lines and on the paths history and our predecessors have marked out for us.

War used to be called the *ultima ratio* of kings,

and to-day self-preservation is the *ultima ratio* of States. Whenever the issue of self-preservation is raised, force of necessity follows. Can force be mobilised in the interests of peace? Where, amidst the clash of contending national egoisms and the pride of States, is there the hope of a peace that shall not merely be the temporary product of exhaustion, bloodshed, and suspended hatred, but of the growth of the principles of toleration and of a mutual respect, if not—for it does not do to ask too much — of affection, between independent States?

The three Faery Queens I have invoked turn away with angry frowns from the spectacle of a chimerical Something, believing itself to be a nation, developing, with the aid of an army and, if feasible, a navy, into an absolute State, bullying such other nationalities or undigested units of population that have the misfortune to live within the State boundaries. Where, in these circumstances, can these fine and gracious ladies hold their courts, and patronise impartial historians pursuing their archival researches, encourage stern and unbending moralists, and with feminine blandishments soothe the always wounded hearts of the true lovers of liberty? Where, indeed? I turn for the last time to Lord Acton:

If we take the establishment of liberty for the realisation of moral duties to be the end and object of civil society [and Acton did so take it], we must conclude that those States are substantially the most perfect which, like the British and the Austrian Empires, include various distinct nationalities without oppressing them. Those States in which *no* mixture of races has occurred are *imperfect*. A State which is incompetent to *satisfy* different races *condemns* itself. A State which labours to *neutralise*, to *absorb*, or *excel* them *destroys* its own vitality. A State which does not include them is destitute of the chief basis of self-government. The theory of nationality, pure and simple, is a retrograde step in history.

These concluding words clearly point to federation as a solution, but as that subject is obviously outside my title I pass it by regretfully, and will bring my remarks to an end by saying something about the Covenant of the League of Nations — a theme which, though beyond my powers, is within my scope. The Covenant of the League of Nations I have in mind is that Covenant and League proclaimed by and set out in the first twenty-six articles of the Treaty of Peace between Germany and the Allies, signed on the 28th of June at Versailles, and now awaiting ratification.

Part I.—The Covenant of the League of Nations.

> THE HIGH CONTRACTING PARTIES,
> In order to promote international co-operation and to achieve international peace and security
> by the acceptance of obligations not to resort to war,
> by the prescription of open, just, and honourable relations between nations,
> by the firm establishment of the understandings of international law as the actual rule of conduct among Governments, and
> by the maintenance of justice and a scrupulous respect for all treaty obligations in the dealings of organised peoples with one another,
> Agree to this Covenant of the League of Nations.

All this is signed, and probably will be ratified. None the less, we must feel that to covenant to build a house, even according to signed plans and specifications, is one thing, and actually to construct it is another, whilst for a large and ill-assorted family to live happily in it for ever afterwards is a different proposition altogether. All must depend on good faith to start with, and a fixed and honest determination to adhere to the Covenant in times of strain, whilst throughout there must be a continuous, genuine, heart-felt horror of war.

How does this great project of the League of Nations—for it is great and is still a project— stand to-day in the minds of men and women? Are we warm or cold, eager or indifferent—have we faith or are we sceptical? First of all, who are *we*? A League of Nations can hardly help being of a little use, but to be of great use in the hour of danger, the nation must be behind it, and where are we to look for the nation, and where are its lively oracles? It is foolish to ask questions unless you have provided yourself with answers; but I can only say with piety and some measure of hope, "Thank God! we are a nation yet," and whenever the nation does get a word in edgeways it obtains a hearing.

It seems to me that the weather is favourable for the first flight of this messenger of peace and goodwill. In the first place, all the literary hum- bug about the "pride, pomp and circumstance of glorious war" has perished in the trenches. Militarism is not dead—we know that only too well—but its gilt spurs and epaulettes are sorely tarnished in the sight of men and women. A demobilised citizen soldier, were he ever again to encounter a recruiting sergeant, will this time know what to ask him. The two novels of M. Henri Barbusse, both in their native French and in English being live literature, have a power of filtration through the strata of society beyond the control of field-marshals, plenipo's, and politicians.

There is another favourable consideration which I will hardly mention, and certainly shall not dwell upon, for I do not much believe in frightening people into decent behaviour, still it is a powerful consideration, and much in men's minds—I mean the almost unimaginable horrors of war as wars will in the future be waged. A great change is here noticeable. When I was young I had to read treatises on International Law and the conduct of war between civilised States. I found myself submerged under a torrent of talk about mitigating the horrors of war, chiefly in the interests of trade and commerce. Privateering was abolished, free ships carried free goods, except contraband of war. There were those who advocated the complete immunity of private property at sea. The rights of neutrals were to be extended and most jealously maintained, on the assumption that Great Britain would usually be a neutral and carrying on her business as before. All this philandering with the devil has gone by the board. We know now that the next great war will, when it comes, know no bounds on land, sea, or air. Torpedoes, huge and well-directed bombs, food blockades, poisoned gases, and all the pleasing possibilities of chemistry! Our children are already counting them up on their fingers. And as for the causes of War:

> With a frown,
> *Revenge* impatient rose.
> He threw his blood-stained sword in thunder down,
> And with a withering look,
> The war-denouncing trumpet took,
> And blew a blast so loud and dread,
> Were ne'er prophetic sounds so full of woe.

It is not cowardice but horror that makes the world shudder at such a prospect.

What obstacles can be placed in the path of war—of such war? The cause of the Covenant and League of Nations has been injured in the public estimate in two ways. First, by our magnificent vocabulary, always far, far ahead of either the facts of the case or the sincerity of our intentions. No sooner had the war with Germany begun than our leading Vocabularists, ever in search of a phrase, proclaimed to all the world that *this was a war to end war*, and for a while the welkin rang with the appreciatory yells of the folk who stayed at home. But no sooner was the war over than the zeal of our Vocabularists for that particular phrase began to cool, and their great gifts were devoted to coin other phrases, to accomplish other ends. Fine phrases are good starters, but seldom pass the winning post.

There is no need to decorate the Covenant and League with fine phrases. It is a *business* proposal having for its object to make wars difficult of commencement and to forge bonds of peace in the hope that they may, if not always, at least occasionally, prove unbreakable. When you have said this much, you have said enough to make our grief-stricken multitudes clutch to their bosoms the desire, and revive the unconquerable hope, that their heavy sorrow may hereafter in the breasts of men be turned into peace, comfort, and joy. Fine phrases are quite out of place.

> Prune thou thy words, the thoughts control,
> That o'er thee swell and throng,
> They will condense within thy soul
> And change to purpose strong.

> But he who lets his feelings run
>   In soft, luxurious flow,
> Shrinks when hard service must be done,
>   And faints at every woe.

There is much hard service to be done, both here and in the United States of America, ere we shall see a League of Nations duly enthroned.

There is another lion in the path of noble and enduring enterprises such as this one as well as our innate passion for fine language. I mean the juristic pedantry of some writers who seek to frighten us with the word (and words as easily frighten as inflame us) *sovereignty*. The State, say these Hobbists, must be *supreme*, always and everywhere, else it becomes a vassal to another's will and ceases to be an independent State. Can we allow, so we are asked to shout in a passion, the sovereignty of our national State to be mutilated and flouted by an adverse vote cast in Geneva? May we not be free to go or not to go to war, as and when we choose, in pursuit of British interests, and whenever the lion within us, poked up by the Press morning and evening, roars for its prey? It would probably be useless to point out to irritated men that under the proposed code no such decision can be arrived at without unanimity. " Unanimity! " they will cry with a sneer. " We know how that may be brought about—by secret bargaining ' behind the chair,' by the ' hidden hand,' and unacknowledged influences." It is best, therefore, boldly to take this bull by the horns and to ask this dread abstraction, Sovereignty, what it is, and where it resides, " Sir, your name and college? " Who to-day is the sovereign power in these realms or in the United States? No one can tell you. And yet we all know there is such a thing, and that it is always a question of fact, though jurists may quarrel where to look for it. And what is more, it is a fact that cannot be nullified by any vote in any city.

There is nothing more foolish in human affairs than to test them by extreme instances. I have heard of an old lady—though in justice to her sex I declare I have never met her—who is said to pray nightly that the Pope may be brought to see his way to become President of the United Protestant Alliance, and so by one single act of faith or folly destroy Sacramentarianism throughout the world. These things do not happen, and if a League of Nations ever flouted the clear, convinced, expressed will and purpose of a great nation, why, then, so much the worse for the League of Nations; and if in the meantime the small nations are kept from cutting each other's throats, so much the better for the small nations.

But as great wars are oftener than not the results of misunderstandings and weakness of purpose, of foreign policies never thought out and only half-pursued, why, then, to submit to careful consideration the direst of all questions, war— before and not after the button is pressed that repeals the decalogue—is and must be the plainest and most pressing of all duties, and therefore cannot harm any State—for there is no such thing on God's earth, Hobbes notwithstanding, as unlimited authority.

Once it was thought a wicked thing to assign limits to a king's authority, and yet was it not well said long ago by a wise foreigner that if the King of England is content to be the first of his own subjects, his is a position far prouder than that of any autocrat, whose autocracy is always tempered by assassination and periodically destroyed by revolution? We need not tremble at the thought of the tyranny of a League of Nations forbidding us from going to war. If it ever does grow into such a tyranny we can deal with it on Johnsonian principles.

Apart from this Covenant and League of Nations, the prospect before our children is doleful in the extreme. This planet may some day cease to be inhabited by our branch of the human family, but for the residue of our time upon it we shall do well to labour to obtain some measure of security against the recurrence of war, as war will in future be waged. If we fail to secure this measure of security, then when the curtain does eventually fall upon the last scene of the last act of the drama of the life of man upon earth, the best epilogue to be chosen from a large repertoire will be Edgar Allan Poe's:

> Lo! 'tis a gala night,
>   Within the lonesome latter years!
> An angel throng, bewinged, bedight
>   In veils, and drowned in tears,
> Sits in a theatre, to see
>   A play of hopes and fears,
> While the orchestra breathes fitfully
>   The music of the spheres.
>
> That motley drama—oh, be sure
>   It shall not be forgot!—
> With its Phantom chased for evermore
>   By a crowd that seize it not,
> Through a circle that ever returneth in
>   To the self-same spot,
> And much of Madness, and more of Sin
>   And Horror the soul of the plot.

But see, amid the mimic rout,
　A crawling shape intrude!
A blood-red thing that writhes from out
　The scenic solitude!
It writhes! it writhes! with mortal pangs
　The mimes become its food,
And the seraphs sob at vermin fangs
　In human blood imbrued.

Out—out are the lights—out all!
　And over each quivering form
The curtain—a funeral pall—
　Comes down with the rush of a storm.
And the angels, all pallid and wan,
　Uprising, unveiling, affirm
That the play is the tragedy, " Man,"
　And its hero, the Conqueror Worm!

BOOKS OLD AND NEW

1894

NOW that our century has entered upon its last decade, and draws near the hour which will despatch it to join its too frequently and most unjustly despised predecessor, it is pleasing to note how well it has learnt to play the old man's part. One has only to compare the *Edinburgh Review* of, say, October, 1807, with its last number, to appreciate the change that has come over us. Cocksureness, once the badge of the tribe of critics, is banished to the schoolroom. The hearty hatreds of our early days would ill befit a death-bed. A keen critic has observed what a noisy place England used to be. Everybody cried out loud in the market-place, in the Senate-house, in the Law Courts, in the Reviews and Magazines. In the year 1845 the *Times* newspaper incurred the heavy and doubtless the just censure of the Oxford Union for its unprincipled tone as shown in its " violent attempts to foment agitation as well by inflammatory articles as by the artifices of correspondents." How different it now is! We all move about as it were in list slippers. Our watchword is " Hush! " Dickens tells us how, at Hone's funeral, Cruikshank, being annoyed at some of the observations of the officiating minister, whispered in Dickens's ear as they both moved to kneel at prayer, " If this wasn't a funeral I would punch his head." It was a commendable restraint. We are now, all of us, exercising it.

A gloomy view is being generally taken of our literary future in the next century. Poetry, it is pretty generally agreed, has died with Lord Tennyson. Who, it is said, can take any pride or pleasure in the nineties, whose memory can carry him back to the sixties? What days those were that gave us brand-new from the press *Philip* and *The Four Georges*, *The Mill on the Floss* and *Silas Marner*, *Evan Harrington* and *Rhoda Fleming*, *Maud*, the *Idylls of the King*, and *Dramatis Personæ*, Mr. Arnold's *New Poems*, the *Apologia pro Vitâ Suâ*, and *Verses on Various Occasions*, four volumes of *Frederick the Great*, and *The Origin of Species*! One wonders in the retrospect how human stupidity was proof against such an onslaught of wit, such a shower of golden fancies. Why did not Folly's fortress fall? We know it did not, for it is standing yet. Nor has any particular halo gathered round the sixties—which, indeed, were no better than the fifties or the forties.

From what source, so ask " the frosty pows," are you who call yourselves " jolly candidates " for 1900, going to get your supplies? Where are your markets? Who will crowd the theatre on your opening nights? What well-graced actors will then cross your stage? Your boys and girls will be well provided for, one can see that. Storybooks and handbooks will jostle for supremacy; but your men and women, all a-hungered, how are you going to feed them and keep their tempers sweet? It is not a question of side dishes, but of joints. Sermons and sonnets, and even " clergy-poets," may be counted upon, but they will only affront the appetites they can never satisfy. What will be wanted are Sam Wellers, Captain Costigans, and Jane Eyres—poetry that lives, controversy that bites, speeches that stir the imagination.

Thus far the aged century. To argue with it would be absurd; to silence it cruel, and perhaps impossible. Greedy Time will soon do that.

But suppose it should turn out to be the fact that we are about to enter upon a period of well-cultivated mediocrity. What then? Centuries cannot be expected to go on repeating the symptoms of their predecessors. We have had no Burns. We cannot, therefore, expect to end with the beginnings of a Wordsworth and a Coleridge; there may likely be a lull. The lull may also be a relief. Of all odd crazes, the craze to be for ever reading new books is one of the oddest.

Hazlitt may be found grappling with this subject, and, as usual, " punishing " it severely in his own inimitable style. " I hate," says he, in the second volume of *The Plain Speaker*—in the essay entitled " On Reading Old Books "—" to read new books "; and he continues, a page further on, " Contemporary writers may generally be divided into two classes—one's friends or one's foes. Of the first we are compelled to think too well, and of the last we are disposed to think too ill, to receive much genuine pleasure from the perusal, or to judge fairly of the merit of either. One candidate for literary fame who happens to be of our acquaintance writes finely and like a man of genius, but unfortunately has a foolish face, which spoils a delicate passage; another inspires us with the highest respect for his personal talents and character, but does not come up to our expectations in print. All these contradictions and petty details interrupt the calm current of our reflections."

Hazlitt was no doubt a good hater. We are now of milder mood. It ought not to be difficult for any of us, if we but struggle a little, to keep a man's nose out of his novel. But, for all that, it is certain that true literary sway is borne but by the dead. Living authors may stir and stimulate us, provoke our energies, and excite our sympathy, but it is the dead who rule us from their urns.

Authority has no place in matters concerning books and reading, else it would be well were some proportion fixed between the claims of living and dead authors.

There is no sillier affectation than that of old-worldism. To rave about Sir Thomas Browne and know nothing of William Cobbett is foolish. To turn your back upon your own time is simply to provoke living wags, with rudimentary but effective humour, to chalk opprobrious epithets upon your person. But, on the other hand, to depend upon your contemporaries for literary sustenance, to be reduced to scan the lists of " Forthcoming Works " with a hungry eye, to complain of a dearth of new poems, and new novels, and new sermons, is worse than affectation—it is stupidity.

There was a time when old books were hard to procure and difficult to house. With the exception of a few of the greatest, it required as much courage to explore the domains of our old authors as it did

to visit Wast Water or Loch Maree before the era
of roads and railways. The first step was to turn
the folios into octavos, and to publish complete
editions; the second was to cheapen the price of
issue. The first cheap booksellers were, it is sometimes alleged, men of questionable character in
their trade. Yet their names should be cherished.
They made many young lives happy, and fostered
better taste than either or both the Universities.
Hogg, Cooke, Millar, Donaldson, Bell, even Tegg,
the "extraneous Tegg" of Carlyle's famous Parliamentary petition, did good work in their day.
Somehow or another the family libraries of the
more respectable booksellers hung fire. They did
not find their way about. Perhaps their authors
were selected with too much care.

He wales a portion with judicious care.

The pious Cottar did well, but the world is larger
than the family; besides which it is not always
"Saturday Night." Cooke had no scruples. He
published *Tom Jones* in fortnightly, and (I think)
sixpenny parts, embellished with cuts, and after
the same appetising fashion proceeded right through
the "British Novelists." He did the same with the
"British Poets." It was a noble enterprise. You
never see on a stall one of Cooke's books but it is
soiled by honest usage; it odour speaks of the
thousand thumbs that have turned over its pages
with delight. Cooke made an immense fortune,
and deserved to do so. He believed both in genius
and his country. He gave the people cheap books,
and they bought them gladly. He died at an
advanced age in 1810. Perhaps when he came to

do so he was glad he had published a series of
" Sacred Classics," as well as *Tom Jones.*

We are now living in an age of handsome reprints. It is possible to publish a good-sized book
on good paper and sell it at a profit for fourpence
halfpenny. But of course to do this, as the profit
is too small to bear division, you must get the
Authors out of the way. Our admirable copyright
laws and their own sedentary habits do this on
the whole satisfactorily and in due course. Consequently dead authors are amazingly cheap. Not
merely Shakespeare and Milton, Bunyan and Burns,
but Scott and Macaulay, Thackeray and Dickens.
Living authors are deadly dear. You may buy
twenty books by dead men at the price of one
work by a living man. The odds are fearful. For
my part, I hope a *modus vivendi* may be established
between the publishers of the dead and those of the
living; but when you examine the contents of the
" Camelot Classics," the " Carisbrooke Library,"
the " Chandos Classics," the " Canterbury Poets,"
the " Mermaid Series of the Old Dramatists," and
remember, or try to remember, the publishing lists
of Messrs. Routledge, Mr. Black, Messrs. Warne,
and Messrs. Cassell, it is easy for the reader to snap
his fingers at Fate. It cannot touch him—he can
dine for many a day. Even were our " lyrical cry "
to be stifled for half a century, what with Mr.
Bullen's *Elizabethan Lyrics,* and *More Elizabethan
Lyrics,* and *Lyrics from the Dramatists,* and *Lyrics
from the Romances,* and Mr. Palgrave's *Golden
Treasury,* " a man," as Mr. Markham observes in
David Copperfield, " might get on very well here,"
even though that man were, as Markham asserted

himself to be, " hungry all day long." A British
poet does not cease to be a poet because he is
dead, nor is he, for that matter, any the better a
poet for being alive.

As for a scarcity of living poets proving national
decadence, it would be hard to make out that case.
Who sang Chatham's victories by sea and land?

BOOK-BINDING

1894

THERE is a familiar anecdote of the ingenious author of *The Seasons*, *Rule*, *Britannia*, and other excellent pieces, that when he sent a well-bound copy of his poems to his father, who had always regarded him, not altogether unjustly, as a " feckless loon," that canny Scot handled the volume with unfeigned delight, and believing that his son had bound it, cried out admiringly, " Who would have thought our Jamie could have done the like of this? " This particular copy has not been preserved, and it is therefore impossible for us to determine how far its bibliopegic merits justified the rapture of the elder Thomson, whose standard is not likely to have been a high one. Indeed, despite his rusticity, he was probably a better judge of poetry than of binding.

This noble craft has revived in our midst. Twenty years ago, in ordinary circles, the bookbinder was a miscreant who, by the aid of a sharp knife, a hideous assortment of calf-skins and of marbled papers, bound your books for you by slaughtering their margins, stripping their sides, and returning them upon your hands cropped and in prison garb, and so lettered as to tell no man what they were. And the worst of it was we received them with complacency, gave them harbourage upon our shelves, and only grumbled that the price was so high as four shillings a volume. Those days are over. Yet it is well to be occasionally reminded of the rock from whence we were hewn, and the pit out of which we were digged. I have now lying before me a first edition of *The Essays of Elia* which, being in boards, I allowed to be treated by a provincial called Shimmin, in the sixties. I remember its coming home, and how I thought it was all right. Infancy was no excuse for such ignorance.

The second-hand booksellers, a race of men for whom I have the greatest respect, are to blame in this matter. They did not play the part they might have been expected to do. They gave no prominence in their catalogues, which are the true textbooks of literature, to specimens of book-binding, nor did they instil into the minds of their young customers the rudiments of taste. Worse than this, some of the second-hand booksellers in the country were themselves binders, and, for the most part, infamous ones.

One did, indeed, sometimes hear of Roger Payne and of the Harleian style, but dimly, and as a thing of no moment, nor were our eyes ever regaled in booksellers' catalogues with facsimiles of the exquisite bindings of the French and English masters. Nor was it until we went further afield, and became acquainted with the booksellers of Paris, that this new world swam into our ken. It was a great day when a stray copy of a *Bulletin Mensuel* of Damascene Morgand, the famous bookseller in the Passage des Panoramas, fell into the hands of a mere country book-buyer. Then he knew how brutally he had been deceived—then he looked with loathing on his truncated tomes and their abominable devices. The first really bound book I ever saw was a copy of the works of Pierre de Ronsard bearing the devices of Marguerite de Valois. The price was so far beyond my resources that I left the shop without a touch of envy, but the scales had fallen from my eyes, and I walked down the Passage des Panoramas as one who had awakened from a dream.

Nowadays it is quite different. The Arts and Crafts Exhibition did much, and the second-hand booksellers, in quite ordinary places, are beginning to give in their catalogues reproductions of noble specimens. Nothing else is required. To see is enough. There was recently, as most people know, a wonderful exhibition of bindings to be seen at the Burlington Fine Art Club, but what is not so generally known is that the Club has published a magnificent catalogue of the contents of that Exhibition, with no less than 114 plates reproducing with the greatest possible skill and delicacy some of the finest specimens. Mr. Gordon Duff, who is credited with a profounder knowledge of pigskins than any living man, has contributed a short preface to the volume, whilst Miss Prideaux, herself a binder of great merit, has written a general introduction, in which she traces the history of the craft, and duly records the names of the most famous binders of Europe. A more fascinating picture-book cannot be imagined, for to the charm of colour and design is added all the feeling which only a book can impart. Such a book as this marks an epoch, and ought to be the beginning of a time when even sale-catalogues shall take pains to be splendid.

When the library of the Baron de Lacarelle came to be dispersed at his death a few years ago, the auctioneer's catalogue, as issued by Charles Porquet, of the Quai Voltaire, made a volume which, wherever it goes, imparts dignity to human endeavour, and consecrates a virtuoso's whim. It was but a small library—only 540 books—and to call it well selected would be to abuse a term one has learnt to connect with Major Ponto's library in *The Book of Snobs*. " My library's small," says Ponto, with the most amazing impudence, " but well selected, my boy, well selected. I have been reading the History of England all the morning." He could not have done this in the Baron's library.

As you turn the pages of this glorified catalogue, his treasures seem to lie before you—you can almost stroke them. A devoted friend, *de la Société des Bibliophiles français*, contributes an ecstatic sketch of the Baron's character, and tells us of him how he employed in his hunt after a book infinite artifice, and called to his aid all the resources of learned strategy—" poussant ses approches et manœuvrant, autour de la place, avec la prudence et le génie d'un tacticien consommé, si bien que le malheureux libraire, enlacé, fasciné, hypnotisé par ce grand charmeur, finissait presque toujours par capituler et se rendre." This great man only believed in one modern binder: Trautz. The others did not exist for him. " Cherchez-vous à le convertir ? Il restait incorruptible et répétait invariablement, avec cet esprit charmant, mais un peu railleur, dont il avait le privilège, que s'il était jamais damné, son enfer serait de remuer une reliure de Capé ou de Lortic! "

It is all very splendid and costly and grand, yet still from time to time,

From the soul's subterranean depth upborne,

there comes the thought of Charles Lamb amidst " the ragged veterans " he loved so well, and then in an instant a reaction sets in, and we almost hate this sumptuous Baron. " Thomson's *Seasons*, again, looks best (I maintain it) a little torn and dog's-eared. How beautiful to a genuine lover of reading are the sullied leaves and worn-out appearance, nay, the very odour (beyond Russia), if we would not forget kind feelings in fastidiousness, of an old ' circulating library ' *Tom Jones* or the *Vicar of Wakefield*! " Thus far, Elia.

Let us admit that the highest and noblest joys are those which are in widest commonalty spread, and that accordingly the clay pipe of the artisan is more truly emotional than the most marvellous meerschaum to be seen in the shop-windows of Vienna—still, the collector has his joys and his uses, his triumphant moments, his hours of depression, and, if only he publishes a catalogue, may be pronounced in small type a benefactor of the human race.

POETS LAUREATE

1894

ABOUT forty years ago two ingenious gentlemen, Mr. Austin, of Exeter College, and Mr. Ralph, a member of the Bar, published a book containing short sketches of the lives of Poets Laureate of this realm, beginning with Ben Jonson and ending with Wordsworth, and also an essay on the Title and Office. It has sometimes been rudely said that Laureates came into fashion when fools and jesters went out, but the perusal of Messrs. Austin and Ralph's introductory essay, to say nothing of the most cursory examination of the table of contents of their volume, is enough to disprove the truth of this saying.

A Laureate was originally a purely University title, bestowed upon those Masters of Arts who had exhibited skill in the manufacture of Latin verses, and had nothing to do with the civil authority or royal favour. Thus, the famous Skelton (1460–1529) was laureated at Oxford, and afterwards obtained permission to wear his laurel at Cambridge; but though tutor to King Henry VIII., and, according to Miss Strickland, the original corrupter of that monarch, he was never a Poet Laureate in the modern sense of the word; that is, he was never appointed to hold the place and quality of Poet Laureate to his Majesty. I regret this, for he was a man of original genius.

Campbell, writing in 1819, admits his " vehemence
and vivacity," but pronounces his humour " vulgar
and flippant," and his style a texture of slang
phrases; but Mr. Churton Collins, in 1880, declares
that Skelton reminds him more of Rabelais than
any author in our language, and pronounces him
one of the most versatile and essentially original
of all our poets. We hold with Mr. Collins.

Skelton was popularly known as a Poet Laureate,
and in the earliest edition of his poems, which bears
no date, but is about 1520, he is described on the
title-page as " Mayster Skelton, Poet Laureate,"
as he also is in the first collected edition of 1568,
" Pithy pleasaunt and profitable works of Maister
Skelton, Poete Laureate." This title was the
University title and not a royal one.

Spenser is sometimes reckoned amongst the Poets
Laureate; but, as a matter of fact, he had no right
to the title at all, nor did he or his publishers ever
assume it. He is, of course, one of the poetical
glories of Cambridge, but he was never laureated
there, nor did Queen Elizabeth ever appoint him
her poet, though she granted him £50 a year.

The first Laureate, in the modern sense of the
word, is undoubtedly Ben Jonson, to whom Charles
I. made out a patent conferring upon this famous
man £100 a year and " a terse of Canary Spanish
wine," which latter benefit the miserable Pye com-
muted for £27. From Jonson to Tennyson there
is no breach of continuity, for Sir William Davenant, who was appointed in 1638, survived till the
Restoration, dying in 1668. The list is a curious
one, and is just worth printing: Jonson, Davenant,
Dryden, Shadwell, Nahum Tate, Rowe, the Rev.

Laurence Eusden, Colley Cibber, William White-
head, the Rev. Thomas Warton, Henry James
Pye, Robert Southey, William Wordsworth, Lord
Tennyson.

One must be charitable in these matters. Here
are fourteen names and four great ones—Jonson,
Dryden, Wordsworth and Tennyson; two distinguished ones—Nicholas Rowe and Robert Southey;
two clever names—Shadwell and Colley Cibber;
two respectable names—Tate and Warton; one
interesting name—Davenant; and three unutter-
able names—Eusden, Whitehead and Pye. After
all, it is not so very bad. The office was offered
to Gray, and he refused it. Pope, as a Roman Catholic, was out of the question. It would have
suited Thomson well enough, and have tickled
Goldsmith's fancy mightily. Collins died too young.

But Eusden, Whitehead and Pye, how did they
manage it? and what in the name of wonder did
they write? Eusden was of Irish extraction, but
was born the son of an English clergyman, and
was like most poets a Cambridge man. He owed
his appointment in 1718 to the Duke of Newcastle
of the period, whose favour he had won by a poem
addressed to him on the occasion of his marriage
with the Lady Henrietta Godolphin. But he had
also qualified for the office by verses sacred to the
memory of George I., and in praise of George II.

> Hail, mighty monarch! whom desert alone
> Would, without birthright, raise up to the throne.
> Thy virtues shine peculiarly nice,
> Ungloomed with a confinity to vice.

To do Grub Street justice, it was very angry
with this appointment, and " Hesiod " Cooke wrote

a poem called *The Battle of the Poets*, in which the new Laureate was severely but truthfully handled in verse not conspicuously better than his own:

> Eusden, a laurelled bard by fortune rais'd,
> By very few been read—by fewer prais'd.

Eusden is the author of *Verses Spoken at the Public Commencement in Cambridge*, published in quarto, which are said to be indecent. Our authors refer to them as follows:

" Those prurient lines which we dare not quote, but which the curious may see in the library of the British Museum, were specially composed and repeated for the edification and amusement of some of the noblest and fairest of our great-great-grandmothers." Eusden took to drinking and translating Tasso, and died at his living, for he was a parson, of Coningsby in Lincolnshire.

Of William Whitehead you may read in Campbell's *Specimens of the British Poets*. He was the son of a baker, was school-tutor to Lord Lymington, and having been treated at Oxford in the shabby way that seat of learning has ever treated poets—from Shirley to Calverley—proceeded to Cambridge, that true nest of singing-birds, where he obtained a Fellowship and the post of domestic tutor to the eldest son of the Earl of Jersey. He was always fond of the theatre, and his first effort was a little farce which was never published, but which tempted him to compose heavy tragedies which were. Of these tragedies it would be absurd to speak; they never enjoyed any popularity, either on the stage or in the closet. He owed his appointment—which he did not obtain till Gray had refused it—entirely to his noble friends.

Campbell had the courage to reprint a longish poem of Whitehead's called *Variety: a Tale for Married People*. It really is not very, very bad, but it will never be reprinted again; and so I refer "the curious" to Mr. Campbell's seventh volume.

As for Pye, he was a scholar and a gentleman, a barrister, a member of Parliament, and a police magistrate. On his father's death he inherited a large estate, which he actually sold to pay his parent's debts, though he was under no obligation to do so, as in those days a man's real estate was not liable to pay the debts he might chance to leave undischarged at his death. To pay a dead man's debts out of his land was to rob his heir. Pye was not famous as a Parliamentary orator, but he was not altogether silent, like Gibbon; for we read that in 1788 he told the House that his constituents had suffered from a scanty hay-harvest. He was appointed Laureate in 1790, and he died in 1813. He was always made fun of as a poet, and, unfortunately for him, there was another poet in the House at the same time, called Charles Small Pybus; hence the jest, " Pye et Parvus Pybus," which was in everyone's mouth. He was a voluminous author and diligent translator, but I do not recollect ever seeing a single book of his in a shop, or on a stall, or in a catalogue. As a Poet Great Pye is dead—as dead as Parvus Pybus, M.P., but let us all try hard to remember that he paid his father's debts out of his own pocket.

> Only the actions of the just,
> Smell *sweet* and blossom in *their* dust.

PARLIAMENTARY CANDIDATES

1894

THE best time to study at leisure the habits and manners of the candidate for Parliament is shortly before an anticipated dissolution. Even as once in a series of years the astronomer furbishes up his telescope and observes the transit of a planet across the surface of the sun, so, as a General Election approaches, and when, consequently, candidates are numerous, the curious observer of human nature in all its wayward manifestations hastens to some place where experience has taught him candidates will be found gathered together.

No spot is so favourable for an investigation of this kind as the scene of a contested by-election which takes place when a General Election is at no great distance. The investigation cannot with safety be postponed until a General Election. Then all is hurry and confusion. There is a fight in every constituency. No man can help his neighbour. Everybody is on his own war-path. There is, therefore, no concentration of candidates. They are scattered up and down the land, and so flurried that it is almost impossible to observe their humours. To appreciate a candidate properly takes time—a great deal of time. But at a by-election shortly before a General Election candidates are to be found in shoals—genuine candidates who have all gone through the proud process of selection, who enjoy a status peculiarly their own, who have a part to play, and play it with spirit. They hurry to the contest from afar. With what readiness do they proffer their services! Like sea-birds, they come screaming and flapping their wings, and settle down at the same hotel, which for days resounds with their cheerful cries. This is quite the best place to observe them. In the smoking-room at night, after their oratorical labours are over, they are very great, very proud, very happy. Their talk is of their constituencies, as they are pleased to designate the districts which have chosen them. They retail the anecdotes with which they are wont to convulse their audiences. The stories are familiar, but not as they tell them.

What a contrast do these bright, hopeful creatures present to their taciturn, cynical companions!—sombre figures, who sit sucking at their pipes, the actual members of Parliament, who, far from flying joyfully to the field of battle, as the candidate has just done, have been driven there, grunting and grumbling, by the angry crack of the party Whips.

As you listen to the frank, exuberant speech of the candidate, recounting the points he has made during the day, the conviction he has brought home to the waverer, the dilemmas he has thrust upon his opponents, the poor show made by somebody who thought to embarrass him by an interruption, and compare it with the gloomy asides of the member, who, however brave a figure he may have made upon the platform an hour or two before, seems now painfully alive to the inherent weakness of his cause, doubtful of victory any-where, certain of defeat where he is, it is almost impossible to believe that once upon a time the member was himself a candidate.

Confidence is the badge of the tribe of candidates. How it is born, where it is bred, on what it feeds save vanity, we cannot tell. Figures cannot shake it. It is too majestical to be affected by ridicule. From scorn and brutal jest it turns contemp-tuously away. When a collision occurs between the boundless confidence of the candidate and the bottomless world-wearied scepticism of the member, it is interesting to note how wholly ineffectual is the latter to disturb, even for a moment, the beautifully poised equilibrium of the former.

" I always forget the name of the place you are trying for," I lately overheard a member, during an election contest, observe at breakfast-time to a candidate.

" The Slowcombe Division of Mudfordshire," replied the candidate.

" Oh! " said the member, with a groan, as he savagely chipped at his egg; " I thought they had given you something better than that."

" I wish for nothing better," said the candidate; " I'm safe enough."

And so saying, he rose from the table, and, taking his hat, went off on to the Parade, where he was soon joined by another candidate, and the pair whiled away a couple of hours in delightful converse.

The politics of candidates are fierce things. In this respect the British commodity differs materially from the American. Mr. Lowell introduces the American candidate as saying:

> Ez to my princerples, I glory
> In hevin' nothin' o' the sort.
> I ain't a Whig, I ain't a Tory—
> I'm just a Canderdate, in short.

Our candidates—good, excellent fellows that they are—are not a bit like Mr. Lowell's. They have as many principles as a fish has bones; their vision is clear. The following expressions are constantly on their lips:

> I can see no difficulty about it—I have explained it all to my people over and over again, and no more can they. I and my constituency are entirely at one in the matter. I must say our leaders are very disappointing. My people are getting a little dissatisfied, though, of course, I tell them they must not expect everything at once, and I think they see that—

and so on for an hour or two.

There is nothing a candidate hates more than a practical difficulty; he feels discomfited by it. It destroys the harmony of his periods, the sweep of his generalisations. All such things he dismisses as detail, " which need not now detain us, gentlemen."

Herein, perhaps, consists the true happiness of the candidate. He is the embodied Hope of his party. He will grapple with facts—when he becomes one. In the meantime he floats about, cheered wherever he goes. It is an intoxicating life.

Sometimes when candidates and members meet together—not to aid their common cause at a by-election, but for the purpose of discussing the prospects of their party—the situation gets a little accentuated. Candidates have a habit of glaring around them, which is distinctly unpleasant; whilst some members sniff the air, as if that were a recognised method of indicating the presence of candidates. Altogether, the less candidates and members see of one another, the better. They are antipathetic; they harm one another.

The self-satisfaction and hopefulness of the candidate, his noisy torrent of talk ere he is dashed below, his untiring enunciation of platitudes and fallacies, his abuse of opponents, the weight of whose arm he has never felt—all these things, harmless as they are, far from displeasing in themselves, deepen the gloom of the sitting member, into whose soul the iron of St. Stephen's has entered, relax the tension of his mind, unnerve his vigour, corrode his faith; whilst, on the other hand, his demeanour and utterances, his brutal recognition of failure on his own side, and of merit in his opponent's, are puzzling to the candidate.

The leaders of parties will do well if they keep members and candidates apart. The latter should always herd together.

To do candidates justice, they are far more amusing, and much better worth studying, than members.

THE *BONÂ-FIDE* TRAVELLER

1894

THIS thirsty gentleman is threatened with extinction. His Sabbatical pint is in danger. He has been reported against by a Royal Commission. Threatened men, I know, live long, and it is not for me to raise false alarms, but though the end of the *bonâ-fide* traveller may be not yet, his glory has departed. His more than Sabbath-day journeys in search of the liquor that he loves, extended though they are by statute over three dreary, dusty miles of turnpike, have been ridiculed, and, worse than that, his *bonâ-fide* character—hitherto his proud passport to intoxication—has been roughly condemned as pleonastic. A pretty pleonasm, truly, which has broached many a barrel. The Commissioners say, " We think it would be advisable to eliminate the words *bonâ-fide*. No sensible person could suppose that the Legislature in using the word ' traveller ' meant to include persons who make a pretence only of being such, and are not travellers really and in fact." At present there are two classes of Sunday travellers: there is the real traveller and there is the *bonâ-fide* traveller. It is the latter whose existence is menaced. The sooner he dies the better, for, in plain English, he is a drunken dog.

The Report of the Royal Commission as to the operation of the Welsh Sunday Closing Act of 1881 has been published, and, as the phrase runs, will repay perusal. It is full of humanity and details about our neighbours, their habits and customs. However true it may have been, or still may be, that one half of the world does not know how the other half lives, it is a libel upon the curiosity of mankind to attribute this ignorance to indifference. No facts are more popular than those which relate to people's lives. Could it be discovered how many people prefer tea without sugar, the return would be printed in every newspaper of Great Britain, and be made the text of tens of thousands of leading articles. We are all alike in this respect, though some of us are ashamed to own it. We are by no means sure that the man answered badly who, when asked which of George Eliot's characters was lodged most firmly in human memories, replied boldly, Mrs. Linnet. Everybody remembers Mrs. Linnet, and grins broadly at the very mention of her name. " On taking up the biography of a celebrated preacher, she immediately turned to the end to see what disease he died of; and if his legs swelled as her own occasionally did, she felt a stronger interest in ascertaining any earlier facts in the history of the dropsical divine; whether he had ever fallen off a stage-coach, whether he had married more than one wife, and, in general, any adventures or repartees recorded of him prior to the epoch of his conversion. Then she glanced over the letters and diary, and wherever there was a predominance of Zion, the River of Life, and notes of exclamation, she turned over to the next page; but any passage in which she saw such promising nouns as ' small-pox,' ' pony,' or ' boots and shoes,' at once arrested her." How inimitable it is! And

yet Mr. Oscar Browning prefers *Daniel Deronda.*
It is a comforting reflection that whether you write
well or whether you write ill, you have always
an audience.

But Mrs. Linnet's deep-rooted popularity proves
how fond we all are of escaping from abstractions
and predictions, and seizing hold of the things
about which we really feel ourselves entitled to
an opinion. Mrs. Linnet would have read a great
part of the Report to which I have referred with
much interest. It is full of most promising nouns.
Mrs. Linnet's opinion as to a *bonâ-fide* traveller would
be quite as valuable as Lord Balfour of Burleigh's.

But who is a *bonâ-fide* traveller? He is a person
who seeks drink on Sunday during hours when by
law public-houses are closed. He has therefore to
make out a special case for being supplied with
drink. The fact that he is thirsty counts for
nothing. Everybody is thirsty on Sunday. His
special case is that he is not a resident, but a
traveller, and wants refreshment to enable him to
go on travelling. But here the law steps in, " big-
wigged, voluminous-jawed," and adds this quali-
fication—that nobody shall be considered a *bonâ-
fide* traveller who is not three miles away from his
last bed. An attorney's clerk of three months'
standing could have foretold what has happened,
namely, that everybody who is three miles from
home becomes at once and *ipso facto* a *bonâ-fide*
traveller. You rap with your knuckles at the door
of the shut inn; it is partially opened, and the
cautious publican or his spouse inquires of you
where you come from; you name a city of the plain
four miles off, and the next moment finds you

comfortably seated in the bar-parlour. Falsely to represent yourself as a *bonâ-fide* traveller is a misdemeanour, but assuming you are three miles away from home, how can such a representation be made falsely? We are all pilgrims in this world. If my sole motive for walking three miles on Sunday is to get a pint of beer at the Griffin, doubtless I am not a *bonâ-fide* traveller, but if my motive be to get both the walk and the beer, who dare asperse my good faith? Should I have taken the walk but for the beer, or should I have taken the beer but for the walk? are questions far too nice to be made the subject of summary process.

The Commissioners cannot be accused of shirking this difficult question. They brace up their minds to it, and deliver themselves as follows. There is, say they, in language of almost Scriptural simplicity, first the traveller who makes a journey either by railway or otherwise, on business or for some other necessary cause. His case, in the opinion of the Commissioners, is a simple one. He is entitled to drink by the way. But next, proceed the Commissioners in language of less merit, " there is the individual who leaves his place of residence in the morning, or it may be later in the day, intending to be absent for some hours, inclusive perhaps, but not necessarily, of his mid-day meal, his object being primarily change of air and scene, exercise, relaxation of some kind, a visit to friends, or some reasonable cause other than merely to qualify for entrance into a licensed house." This is the mixed-motive case already hinted at. Then, thirdly, there is the bold bad man " who goes from his home to a point not less than three miles distant, either on foot or by wheeled vehicle by road or rail, primarily if not solely to procure the drink which the Act denies him within three miles of where he lodged the previous night." This gentleman is the genuine *bonâ-fide* traveller known to all policemen and magistrates, and it is he who is threatened with extinction. But how is he to be differentiated from the individual who leaves his place of residence in the morning and goes to a place, not in search of drink, but where, for all that, drink is? For example, it appears from this Report that near Swansea is a place of resort called the Mumbles. A great many people go there every Sunday, and a considerable number return home drunk at night; but, say the Commissioners, and we entirely believe them, " it is impossible for us to say what proportion of them go for change and exercise and what proportion for the sake of drink." But if it be impossible, how is the distinction between the individual who leaves his place of residence in the morning, and the bold bad man, to be maintained?

There are those who would abolish the exemption in favour of travellers altogether. Let him who travels on Sunday take his liquor with him in a flask. There are others who would allow his glass to the traveller who is not on pleasure bent, but would refuse it to everybody else. A third party hold that a man who takes exercise for his health is as much entitled to refreshment as the traveller who goes on business. No one has been found bold enough to say a word for the man who travels in order that he may drink.

The Commissioners, after the wont of such men,

steer a middle course. They agree with the Rev. Dr. Parry, Moderator of the General Assembly of the Calvinistic Methodists of Wales, who declared that he would not exclude from reasonable refreshment " a man who goes from his place of residence on Sunday to see the country "! I confess I should like to have both Dr. Parry's and a Welsh collier's opinion as to what is reasonable refreshment. Then, again, " to see the country " is a vague phrase.

The Commissioners suggest a new clause, to run as follows:

No person shall be deemed to be within the exception relating to travellers unless he proves that he was actually engaged in travelling for some purpose other than that of obtaining intoxicating liquor, and that he has not remained on the licensed premises longer than was reasonably required for the transaction of his necessary business or for the purpose of necessary rest, refreshment, or shelter from the weather.

This is nothing but a repeal of the three-mile limit. How is a wayfaring man to prove that he is travelling for some purpose other than that of obtaining intoxicating liquor? He can only assert the fact, and unless he is a notorious drunkard, both the publican and the magistrate are bound to believe him. Were the suggestion of the Commissioners to be carried out, it probably would be found that our old friend the *bonâ-fide* traveller could get his liquor and curtail his walk.

I should like Mrs. Linnet's opinion; but failing hers, can only express my own, which is that Sunday drinking is so bad a thing that if it can be stopped it ought to be so, even though it were to follow as a consequence that no traveller could get drink from Saturday night till Monday morning except at the place where he spent the night.

"HOURS IN A LIBRARY"

1894

IN spite of the proverb about the pavement of the road to hell, I am prepared to maintain that good intentions are better than bad, and that evil is the wretch who is not full of good intentions and holy plans at the beginning of each New Year. Time, like a fruitful plain, then lies stretched before you; the eye rests on tuneful groves, cool meadow-lands, and sedgy streams, whither you propose to wander, and where you promise yourself many happy, well-spent hours. I speak in metaphors, of course—pale-faced Londoner that I am—my meadows and streams are not marked upon the map: they are (coming at once to the point, for this is a generation which is only teased by allegory) the old books I mean to read over again during the good year of grace 1894. Yonder stately grove is Gibbon; that thicket, Hobbes; where the light glitters on the green surface (it is black mud below) is Sterne; healthful but penetrating winds stir Bishop Butler's pages and make your naked soul shiver, as you become more and more convinced, the longer you read, that "someone has blundered," though whether it is you or your Maker remains, like everything else, unsolved. Each one of us must make out his own list. It were cruelty to prolong mine, though it is but begun.

As a grace before meat, or, if the simile be preferred, as the *Zakuska* or *Vorschmack* before dinner, let me urge upon all to read the three volumes, lately reissued and very considerably enlarged, called *Hours in a Library*, by Mr. Leslie Stephen.

Mr. Stephen is a bracing writer. His criticisms are no sickly fruit of fond compliance with his authors. By no means are they this, but hence their charm. There is much pestilent trash now being talked about "Ministry of Books," and the "Sublimity of Art," and I know not what other fine phrases. It almost amounts to a religious service conducted before an altar of first editions. Mr. Stephen takes no part in such silly rites. He remains outside with a pail of cold water.

It sometimes strikes readers of books that literature is, on the whole, a snare and a delusion. Writers, of course, do not generally share that impression; and on the contrary have said a great many fine things about the charm of conversing with the choice minds of all ages, with the innuendo, to use the legal phrase, that they themselves modestly demand some place amongst the aforesaid choice minds. But at times we are disposed to retort upon our teachers. "Are you not," we observe, "exceedingly given to humbug?"

Mr. Stephen has indeed, by way of preface to his own three volumes, collected a goodly number of these very fine things, but then he has, with grim humour, dubbed them "Opinions of Authors," thus reducing them to the familiar level of "Nothing like leather!"

But of course, though Mr. Leslie Stephen, like the wise man he is, occasionally hits his idol over the costard with a club just to preserve his own independence, he is and frankly owns himself to be a bookish man from the crown of his head to the sole of his foot. He even confesses he loves the

country best in books; but then it must be in real
country-books and not in descriptive poetry, which,
says he with Johnsonian calmness, is for the most
part " intolerably dull."

There is no better living representative of the
great clan of sensible men and women who delight
in reading for the pleasure it gives them than Mr.
Stephen. If he is only pleased, it is quite shocking
what he will put up with, and even loudly commend.

We are indeed told dogmatically that a novelist should
never indulge in little asides to a reader. Why not? . . . I
like to read about Tom Jones or Colonel Newcome; but I
am also very glad when Fielding or Thackeray puts his puppets
aside for the moment and talks to me in his own person. A
child, it is true, dislikes to have the illusion broken, and is
angry if you try to persuade him that Giant Despair was not
a real personage like his favourite Blunderbore. But the
attempt to produce such illusions is really unworthy of work
intended for full-grown readers.

Puppets indeed! It is evil and wicked treason
against our Sovereign Lady, the Art we serve, to
talk of puppets. The characters of our living
Novelists live and move and have an independent
being all their very own. They are clothed in
flesh and blood. They talk and jostle one another.
Where, we breathlessly inquire, do they do all or
any of these fine things? Is it in the printed page?
Alas! no. It is only in the minds of their Authors,
whither we cannot follow them even if we would.

Mr. Stephen has great enthusiasm, which ought
to reconcile us to his discriminating judgment
and occasional easterly blast. Nobody loves a
good book better than he. Whether his subject
be Nathaniel Hawthorne or Daniel Defoe, it is
handled cunningly, as by a man who knows. But
his highest praise is his unbought verdict. He is

his own man. He is dominated by no prevailing taste or fashion. Even his affection does not bias him. He yields to none in his admiration for the " good Sir Walter," yet he writes:

It is a question perhaps whether the firmer parts of Scott's reputation will be sufficiently coherent to resist after the removal of the rubbish.

" Rubbish." It is a harsh word, and might well make Dean Stanley and a bygone generation of worshippers and believers in the plenary inspiration of Scott stir uneasily in their graves. It grates upon my own ear. But if it is a true word, what then? Why even then it does not matter very much, for when Time, that old ravager, has done his very worst, there will be enough left of Sir Walter to carry down his name and fame to the remotest age. He cannot be ejected from his native land. Loch Katrine and Loch Leven are not exposed to criticism, and they will pull Sir Walter through.

Mr. Stephen has another recommendation. Every now and again he goes hopelessly wrong. This is most endearing. Must I give instances? If I must I will, but without further note or comment. He is wrong in his depreciation of *Wuthering Heights*, and wrong, amazingly wrong, in his unaccountable partiality for *Henrietta Temple*.

The author of *Hours in a Library* belongs, it is hardly necessary to say, to the class of writers who use their steam for the purpose of going straight ahead. He is always greatly concerned with his subject. If he is out fox-hunting, he comes home with the brush, and not with a spray of blackberries; but if, on the other hand, he goes out

blackberrying, he will return deeply dyed the true
tint, and not dragging behind him a languishing
coil of seaweed. Metaphors will, I know, ultimately
be my ruin, but in the meantime I hope I make
myself reasonably plain. In this honest characteristic Mr. Leslie Stephen resembles his distinguished brother, Sir James Stephen, who, in his
admirable *Horæ Sabbaticæ* (Macmillan, 3 vols.),
may be discovered at any time tearing authors
into little bits and stripping them of their fringe,
and then presenting to you in a few masterly
pages the marrow of their arguments and the pith
of their position.

Much genuine merriment is, however, almost
always to be extracted from writers of this kind.
Mr. Leslie Stephen's humour, none the worse for
belonging to the sardonic species, is seldom absent
from a page. It would be both pleasant and easy
to collect a number of his epigrams, witty sayings,
and humorous terms—but it is better to leave
them where they are. The judicious will find them
for themselves for many a long day to come. The
sensible and truthful writers are the longest livers.

AMERICANISMS AND BRITICISMS

1894

MESSRS. HARPER BROS., of New York, have lately printed and published, and Mr. Brander Matthews has written, the prettiest possible little book, called *Americanisms and Briticisms, with other Essays on other Isms.* To slip it into your pocket when first you see it is an almost irresistible impulse, and yet—would you believe it?—this pretty little book is in reality a bomb, intended to go off and damage British authors by preventing them from being so much as quoted in the States. Mr. Brander Matthews, however, is so obviously a good-natured man, and his little fit of the spleen is so evidently of a passing character, that it is really not otherwise than agreeable to handle his bombshell gently and to inquire how it could possibly come about that the children of one family should ever be invited to fall out and strive and fight over their little books and papers.

It is easy to accede something to Mr. Matthews. Englishmen are often provoking, and not infrequently insolent. The airs they give themselves are ridiculous, but nobody really minds them in these moods; and, *per contra*, Americans are not easily laughed out of a good conceit of themselves, and have been known to be as disagreeable as they could.

To try to make " an international affair " over

the " u " in honour and the second " l " in traveller
is surely a task beneath the dignity of anyone who
does not live by penning paragraphs for the evening
papers, yet this is very much what Mr. Matthews
attempts to do in this pleasingly-bound little
volume. It is rank McKinleyism from one end
to the other. " Every nation," says he, " ought to
be able to supply its own second-rate books, and
to borrow from abroad only the best the foreigner
has to offer it." What invidious distinctions! Who
is to prepare the classification? I don't understand
this Tariff at all. If anything of the kind were true,
which it is not, I should have said it was just the
other way, and that a nation, if it really were one,
would best foster its traditions and maintain its
vitality by consuming its own first-rate books—
its Shakespeares and Bacons, its Taylors and
Miltons, its Drydens and Gibbons, its Wordsworths
and Tennysons—whilst it might very well be glad
to vary the scene a little by borrowing from abroad
less vitalising but none the less agreeable wares.

But the whole notion is preposterous. In Fish
and Potatoes a ring is possible, but hardly in
Ideas. What is the good of being educated and
laboriously acquiring foreign tongues and lingoes
—getting to know, for instance, what a " freight "
train is and what a bobolink—if I am to be prevented by a diseased patriotism from reading
whatever I choose in any language I can? Mr.
Matthews' wrath, or his seeming wrath—for it is
impossible to suppose that he is really angry—
grows redder as he proceeds. " It cannot," he
exclaims, " be said too often or too emphatically
that the British are foreigners, and their ideals in

life, in literature, in politics, in taste, in art " (why
not add " in victuals and drink " ?) " are not
our ideals."

What rant this is! Mr. Matthews, however
frequently and loudly he repeats himself, cannot
unchain the canons of taste and compel them to
be domiciled exclusively in America; nor can he
hope to persuade the more intelligent of his coun-
trymen to sail to the devil in an ark of their own
sole construction. Artists all the world over are
subject to the same laws. Nations, however big,
are not the arbiters of good taste, though they may
be excellent exemplars of bad. As for Mr. Matthews'
determination to call Britons foreigners, that is his
matter, but feelings of this kind, to do any harm,
must be both reciprocal and general. The majority
of reasonable Englishmen and Americans will,
except when angry, feel it as hard to call one
another foreigners, as John Bright once declared
he would find it hard to shout " bastard " after
the issue of a marriage between a man and his
deceased wife's sister.

There is a portrait of Mr. Matthews at the beginning of this book or bomb of his, and he does not
look in the least like a foreigner. I am sorry to
disappoint him, but truth will out. The fact is
that Mr. Matthews has no mind for reciprocity;
he advises Cousin Sam to have nothing to do with
John Bull's second-rate performances, but he feels
a very pardonable pride in the fact that John Bull
more and more reads his cousin's short stories and
other things of the kind.

He gives a countrywoman of his, Miss Agnes
Repplier, quite a scolding for quoting in a little

book of hers no less than fifteen British authors of very varying degrees of merit. Why, in the name of common-sense, should she not if they serve her turn? Was a more ludicrous passage than the following ever penned? It follows immediately after the enumeration of the fifteen authors just referred to:

But there is nothing from Lowell, than whom a more quotable writer never lived. In like manner, we find Miss Repplier discussing the novels and characters of Miss Austen and of Scott, of Dickens, of Thackeray, and of George Eliot, but never once referring to the novels or characters of Hawthorne. Just how it was possible for any clever American woman to write nine essays in criticism, rich in references and quotations, without once happening on Lowell or on Hawthorne, is to me inexplicable.

O Patriotism! what follies are committed in thy name!

The fact is, it is a weak point in certain American writers of "the patriotic school" to be for ever dragging in and puffing the native article, just because it is native and for no other reason whatever; as if it mattered an atom whether an author whom, whilst you are discussing literature, you find it convenient to quote was born in Boston, Lincoln, or Boston, Massachusetts. One wearies of it indescribably. It is always Professor This or Colonel That. If you want to quote, quote and let your reader judge your samples; but do not worry him into rudeness by clawing and scraping.

Here we all are, Heaven knows how many million of us, speaking, writing and spelling the English language more or less ungrammatically in a world as full as it can hold of sorrows and cares, and fustian and folly. Literature is a solace and a charm. I will not stop for a moment in my headlong

course to compare it with tobacco; though if it
ever came to the vote, mine would be cast for
letters. Men and women have been born in America,
as in Great Britain and Ireland, who have written
books, poems, and songs which have lightened
sorrow, eased pain, made childhood fascinating,
middle-age endurable, and old age comfortable.
They will go on being born and doing this in both
places. What reader cares a snap of his finger
where the man was cradled who makes him for
awhile forget himself? Nationality indeed! It is
not a question of Puffendorf or Grotius or Wheaton,
even in the American edition with Mr. Dana's
notes, but of enjoyment, of happiness, out of
which we do not intend to be fleeced. Let us
throw all our books into hotch-pot. Who cares
about spelling? Milton spelt " dog " with two g's.
The American Milton, when he comes, may spell
it with three, while all the world wonders, if he is
so minded.

But we are already in hotch-pot. Cooper and
Irving, Longfellow, Bryant and Poe, Hawthorne,
Lowell, and Whitman, and living writers by the
score from the other side of the sea, are indistin-
guishably mixed with our own books and authors.
The boundaries are hopelessly confused, and it is
far too late for Mr. Brander Matthews to come
upon the scene with chalk and tape, and try to
mark us off into rival camps.

There is some girding and gibing, of course.
Authors and critics cannot help nagging at one
another. Some affect the grand air, " assume the
god," and attempt to distinguish, as Mr. Matthews
himself does in this little book of his, " between the

authors who are not to be taken seriously, between the man of letters who is somebody and the scribbler who is merely, in the French phrase, *quelconque*, nobody in particular." Others, again, though leading quiet, decent lives, pass themselves off in literature as swaggering Bohemians, cut-and-thrust men. When these meet there must be blows —pen-and-ink blows, as bloodless as a French duel. All the time the stream of events flows gigantically along. But to the end of all things Man will require to be interested, to be taken out of himself, to be amused; and that interest, that zest, that amuse-ment, he will find where he can—at home or abroad, with alien friends or alien enemies: what cares he?

AUTHORS AND CRITICS

1894

A T the gracious Christmas season of the year we are reminded by nearly every post of our duty towards our neighbours, meaning thereby not merely those who live within what Wordsworth, with greater familiarity than precision, has defined as " an easy walk," but, with few exceptions, mainly of a party character, all mankind. The once wide boundaries of an Englishman's sphere of hatred are sorely circumscribed. We are now expected not only to love all peoples, which in theory is easy enough, particularly if we are no great travellers, but to read their publications in translations unverified by affidavit, which in practice is very hard. Yet if we do not do it, we are Chauvinists, which has a horrid sound.

Much is now expected of a man. Even in his leisure hours, when his feet are on the hob, he must be zealous in some cause, say Realism; serious, as he reflects upon the interests of literature and the position of authors; and, above all and hardest of all, he must be sympathetic. Irony he should eschew, and levity, but disquisitions on duty are never out of place.

This disposition of mind, however praiseworthy, makes the aspect of things heavy, and yet this is the very moment selected by certain novelists, playwrights, and irresponsible persons of that kind, to whom we have been long accustomed to look for relaxation, to begin prating, not of their duty to please us, but of our duty to appreciate them. It appears that we owe a duty to our contemporaries who write, which is not merely passive, that is, to abstain from slandering them, but active, namely, to read and admire them.

The authors who grumble and explain the merits of their own things are not the denizens of Grub Street, or those poor neglected souls to one of whom Mr. Alfred Austin lately addressed these consolatory words:

> Friend, be not fretful if the voice of fame,
> Along the narrow way of hurrying men,
> Where unto echo echo shouts again,
> Be all day long not noisy with your name.

No; it is the shouted authors who are most discontented; the men who have best availed themselves of all the resources of civilisation, who belong to syndicates, employ agents, have a price-current, and know what it is to be paid half a dozen times over for the same thing. Even the prospect of American copyright and taxing all the intelligence of a reading Republic—even this does not satisfy them. They want to be classics in their own lifetime, and to be spoken and written of as if they were already embalmed in the memory of a grateful nation. To speak or write lightly of departed genius is offensive, but people who have the luck to be alive must not expect to be taken quite so seriously. But they do. Everything is taken seriously in these grim days, even short stories. There is said to be a demand for short stories, begotten, amongst many other things, by that reckless parent, the

Spirit of the Age. There is no such demand. The one and only demand poor wearied humanity has ever made, or will ever make, of the story-teller, be he as long-winded as Richardson or as breathless as Kipling, is to be made self-forgetful for a season. Interest me somehow, anyhow; make me mindless of the room I am sitting in, of the people about me; soothe me, excite me, tickle me, make me better, make me worse; do what you like with me, only make it possible for me to keep reading on, and a joy to do so. This is our demand. There is nothing unreasonable in it. It is matter of experience. Authors have done all this for us, and are doing it to-day. It is their trade, and a glorious one.

But the only thing that concerns the reader is the book he holds in his hand. He cannot derive inspiration from any other quarter. To the author the characters may be living, he may have lived amongst them for months; they may be inexpressibly dear to him, and his fine eyes may fill with tears as he thinks of Jane or Sarah, but this avails naught to the reader. Our authors are too apt to forget this, and to tell us what they think of their own figments, and how they came to write their books. The imitation of Carlyle cannot be generally recommended, but in one respect, at all events, his example should be followed. Though he made fuss enough whilst he was writing a book, as soon as he had done with it he never mentioned it again.

This sudden display of nervousness on the part of authors is perhaps partly due to their unreasonable confusion of the Reviewers with the Readers.

The great mass of criticism is delivered *vivâ voce*, and never appears in print at all. This spoken criticism is of far greater importance than printed criticism. It is repeated again and again, in all sorts of places, on hundreds of occasions, and cannot fail to make dints in people's minds, whereas the current printed criticism of the week runs lightly off the surface. " Press notices," as they are called, have no longer " boodle " in them, if I may use a word the genius of Mr. Stevenson has already consecrated for all delightful use. The pen may, in peaceful times, be mightier than the sword, but in this matter of criticism of our contemporaries the tongue is mightier than the pen. Authors should remember this.

The volume of unprinted criticism is immense, and its force amazing. Lunching last year at a chop-house, I was startled to hear a really important oath emerge from the lips of a clerkly-looking man who sat opposite me, and before whom the hurried waiter had placed a chump-chop. " Take the thing away," cried the man with the oath aforesaid, " and bring me a loin-chop." Then, observing the surprise I could not conceal that an occurrence so trifling should have evoked an expression so forcible, the man muttered half to himself and half to me: " There is nothing I hate so much in the wide world as a chump-chop, unless indeed it be " (speaking slowly and thoughtfully) " the poetry of Mr. ——," and here the fellow, unabashed, named right out the name of a living poet who, in the horrid phrase of the second-hand booksellers, is " much esteemed " by himself and some others. After this explosion of feeling the conversation between us became frankly literary, but I contrived to learn in the course of it that this chump-chop-hater was a clerk in an insurance office, and had never printed a line in his life. He was, as sufficiently appears, a whimsical fellow, full of strange oaths and stranger prejudice, but for criticism of contemporary authors—keen, searching, detached, genuine—it would be impossible to find his equal in the Press. The man is living yet—he was lately seen in Cheapside, elbowing his way through the crowd with a masterful air; and so long as he lives he criticises, and what is more, permeates his circle—for he must live somewhere—with his opinions. These are your gods, O Authors! It is these voices which swell the real chorus of praise or blame. These judges are untainted by hatreds, strangers to jealousy; your vanity, your egotism, your necktie, your anecdotes, do not prevent *them* from enjoying your books or revelling in your humour, be it new or old, for they do not know you by sight; but neither will the praise of the *Athenæum*, or any newspaper, or the conventional respect of other authors save your productions, your poem, your novel, your drama, your collected trifles, from the shafts of their ridicule or the dust of their indifference.

But do we owe any duty to contemporary authors? Clearly we are at liberty to talk about them and their " work " as much as ever we choose—at dinner-tables, in libraries and smoking-rooms, in railway carriages (if we like shouting and do not mind being inaudible), in boats, at balls, in Courts of Justice, and other places *ejusdem generis*, at Congresses (before, during, and after the speeches), and, indeed, everywhere and at all times, if we are so disposed and can find anybody to listen, or even to seem to listen, to us. Of this liberty we can never be deprived even by a veto of authors *ad hoc*, and, as already stated, the free exercise of it is a far more important constituent in the manufacture of literary opinion than printed notices of books.

But though we are just as much entitled to express in conversation our delight in, or abhorrence of, a contemporary author as we are to bless or curse the weather, it cannot be said to be our duty to do so. No adult stands in a fiduciary relationship to another adult in the matter of his reading. If we like a book very much, it is only natural to say so; but if we do not like it, we may say so or hold our tongues as we choose.

Suppose one dreamt (gentle reader, remember this is nothing but a dream) that there was one woebegone creature alive at this moment in this Britain of ours who cordially disliked, and shrank from, the poetry of Sir Edwin Arnold, Mr. Lewis Morris, and Mr. Alfred Austin, who could not away with *Robert Elsmere*, *The Wages of Sin*, or *Donovan*, who abhorred the writings of Mrs. Lynn Linton, Archdeacon Farrar, and Mr. Shorthouse, who hated *Amiel's Journal*, Marie Bashkirtseff, and *Little Lord Fauntleroy*, who found it easy, and even helpful, to live for six months at a time without reading a new novel by Mr. Hall Caine or Mr. Black, who failed to respond to the careful and often-repeated raptures of those wise critics who assured him that the author of *Amos Barton* and

Middlemarch cowers and crouches by the side of Mr. Hardy and Mr. Meredith; who, when he wants to laugh very heartily indeed, does not take down the works of—— But my list is long enough for a dream—could you honestly advise that man to run amuck in print against all these powerful and delightful writers? What good could come of it? The good people who like a writer will not like him or her any the less because you don't. Reading is a democratic pursuit, else why are children taught it—very badly, no doubt—out of the rates? Sensible men and foolish men alike resent being dictated to about their contemporaries. They are willing to learn about the dead, but they crave leave to lay their own hands upon the living.

"Who set you up as a judge over us?" they cry testily, when they are told by a perfect stranger that they ought not to like what they do like, and ought to like what they go to sleep over.

Schopenhauer, a man who hated much, in his *Parerga*, fervently desires a literary journal which "should be a dam against the unconscionable scribbling of the age, the everlasting deluge of bad and useless books."

He proceeds (I am quoting from Mr. Saunders' translation):

If there were such a paper as I mean, every bad writer, every brainless compiler, every plagiarist from others' books, every hollow and incapable place-hunter, every sham philosopher, every vain and languishing poetaster, would shudder at the prospect of the pillory in which his bad work would inevitably have to stand soon after publication.

It is an animated passage, and reeks of the shambles. How awkward for poor So-and-so! one murmurs whilst reading. But even were the

thing possible, I demur to the ferocity. There is
no need to be so angry. A dishonest and lazy
plumber does more harm in a week than all the
poetasters of the Christian era. But the thing is
not possible, as the robust sense of Schopenhauer
made plain to him. He goes on:

> The ideal journal could, to be sure, be written only by
> people who joined incorruptible honesty with rare know-
> ledge and still rarer power of judgment, so that, perhaps,
> there could, at the very most, be one, *and even hardly one*,
> in the whole country; but there it would stand, like a just
> Areopagus, every member of which would have to be elected
> by all the others.

Who, I wonder, would elect the first member of
this just Ruin? He would, I suppose, be nominated
by the subscribers of the necessary capital, and
would then proceed to gather round him, were his
terms better than his quarters, the gang we all
know so well, incorruptible as Robespierre, not
quite so learned as Selden, and with powers of
judgment which can only be described as varying.

It is of course obvious that no journal, be its
contributors who they may, can exercise criminal
jurisdiction over bad or stupid authors. The hue
and cry has before now been raised at the heels
of a popular author, but always to the great en-
richment of the rascal. The reading community
owes no allegiance, and pays no obedience, to the
critical journals, who, if they really want to injure
an author, and deprive him of his little meed of
contemporary praise and profit, should leave him
severely alone. To refer to him is to advertise him.

The principles of taste, the art of criticism, are
not acquired amidst the hurly-burly of living
authors and the hasty judgments thereupon of

hasty critics, but by the study, careful and reverential, of the immortal dead.   In this study
the critics are of immense use to us.   Dryden,
Addison, Gray, Coleridge, Lamb, Hazlitt, Bagehot,
Swinburne, reveal to us their highest critical powers
not whilst vivisecting a contemporary, but when
expounding the anatomy of departed greatness.

Teach me rightly to admire Milton and Keats,
and I will find my own criticism of living poets.
Help me to enjoy, however feebly, Homer and
Dante, and I will promise not to lose my head
over Pollok's *Course of Time*, or Mr. Bailey's
Festus.   Fire my enthusiasm for Henry Vaughan
and George Herbert, and I shall be able to distinguish between the muse of Miss Frances Ridley
Havergal and of Miss Christina Rossetti.   Train
me to become a citizen of the true Republic of
Letters, and I shall not be found on my knees
before false gods, or trooping with the vulgar to
crown with laurel brazen brows.

In conclusion, one may say that though authors
cannot be expected to love their critics, they might
do well to remember that it is not the critics who
print, but the reading community whose judgments
determine an author's place amongst contemporary
writers.   It may be annoying to be sneered at by
an anonymous critic in the *Saturday Review*, but
it is quite as bad to be sneered at by a stranger in
a railway carriage.   The printed sneer may be read
by more people than overheard the spoken sneer;
but printed sneers are not easily transferred from
writer to reader in their original malice.   One may
enjoy a sneer without sneering.

Authors may also advantageously remember that

we live in hurried times, and enjoy scanty leisure for reading, and that of necessity the greater fraction of that leisure belongs to the dead. Merely a nodding acquaintance with Shakespeare is not maintained without a considerable expenditure of time. The volumes with which every man of ordinary literary taste would wish to be familiar can only be numbered by thousands. We must therefore be allowed time, and there is always plenty. Every good poem, novel, play, at once joins and becomes part and parcel of the permanent stock of English literature, and some time or another will be read and criticised. It is quite safe. Every author of spirit repudiates with lofty scorn the notion that he writes in obedience to any mandate from the public. It is the wretched, degraded politician whose talk is of mandates; authors know nothing of mandates, they have missions. But if so, they must be content to bide their time. If a town does turn out to meet a missionary, it is usually not with loud applause, but with large stones.

As for the critics, the majority of them no doubt only do what they are told. It is a thousand pities the habit of reviewing so many new books in the literary papers has become general. It is a trade thing. Were a literary paper to have no advertising columns, do you suppose it would review half the new books it does? Certainly not. It gets the books, and it gets the advertisements, and then it does the best it can for itself and its readers by distributing the former amongst its contributors with the request that they will make as lively " copy " as they can out of the materials thus provided them. The reviews are written and printed; then begins the wail of the author: My reviewer, says he, has not done me justice; his object appears to have been, not to show me off, but himself. There is no sober exposition of *my* plan, *my* purpose, *my* book, but only a parade of the reviewer's own reading and a crackling of his thorns under my pot. The author's complaint is usually just, but he should remember that in nine cases out of ten his book calls for no review, and certainly would receive none on its merits. The review is not written for those who have read or intend to read the book, but for a crowd of people who do not mean to read it, but who want to be amused or interested by a so-called review of it, which must therefore be an independent, substantive literary production.

What a mercy it would be if the critical journals felt themselves free to choose their own subjects, new and old, and recognised that it was their duty to help to form the taste of their readers, and not merely to pick their provender for them or to promote the prosperity of publishers, which, as a matter of fact, they can no longer do.

The critics who criticise in print, were they left to themselves, would be found praising enthusiastically all they found praiseworthy in contemporary effort. Even now, when their tempers must be sorely tried by the dreary wilderness in which they are compelled to sojourn, it is marvellous how quick they are to snuff the fresh, blowing airs of genuine talent. It is slander to say that present-day critics are grudging of praise. They are far too free with it. Had they less hack-work, they

might by chance become a little more fastidious;
but even if this were so, it would only increase
their joy, delight, and satisfaction in making the
discovery that somebody or another—some Stevenson, some Barrie, some Kipling—had actually
written something which was not only in form
but in fact a new book.

Fiery souls there would no doubt always be who
would insist, on occasions, in rushing out to strike
the shield of some many-editioned living author,
and defy him to mortal combat. An occasional
fray of the kind is always an agreeable incident,
but a wise editor would do his best to control
the noble rage of his contributors, bidding them
remember the words of John Keats: " The sure
way, Bailey, is first to know a man's faults, and
then be passive."

The time and space liberated by giving up the
so-called criticism of bad and insignificant books
could be devoted to the real criticism of the few
living and the many dead classics; and, for one
does occasionally get a little weary of the grand
style, with arguments and discussions about smaller
folk. If basting there must be, let it be the basting
of the brainless compilers, the plagiarists, the sham
philosophers, and the languishing poetasters of the
past. Dead donkeys are far more amusing than
living ones, and make much better texts for fierce
critics than men with wives and families dependent
upon them. The vagaries of great authors have
often done harm in their generation; the follies of
small ones, including the supreme and most visible
of all their follies, that of thinking themselves great,
have never harmed a human creature.

"IN THE NAME OF THE BODLEIAN"

1905

WITH what feelings, I wonder, ought one to approach in a famous University an already venerable foundation, devoted by the last will and indented deed of a pious bene-factor to the collection and housing of books and the promotion of learning? The Bodleian at this moment harbours within its walls well-nigh half a million of printed volumes, some scores of precious manuscripts in all the tongues, and has become a name famous throughout the whole civilised world. What sort of a poor scholar would he be whose heart did not beat within him when, for the first time, he found himself, to quote the words of "Elia," "in the heart of learning, under the shadow of the mighty Bodley"?

Grave questions these!

The following episode occurred during one of Calverley's (then Blayds) appearances at "Collections," the Master (Dr. Jenkyns) officiating. *Question :* "And with what feelings, Mr. Blayds, ought we to regard the decalogue?" Calverley who had no very clear idea of what was meant by the decalogue, but who had a due sense of the importance both of the occasion and of the question, made the following reply: "Master, with feelings of devotion, mingled with awe!" "Quite right, young man; a very proper answer," exclaimed the Master.[1]

"Devotion mingled with awe" might be a very proper answer for me to make to my own questions,

[1] *Literary Remains of C. S. Calverley*, p. 31.

186

but possessing that acquaintance with the history of the most picturesque of all libraries which anybody can have who loves books enough to devote a dozen quiet hours of rumination to the pages of Mr. Macray's *Annals of the Bodleian Library,* second edition, Oxford, " at the Clarendon Press, 1890," I cannot honestly profess to entertain in my breast, with regard to it, the precise emotions which C. S. C. declared took possession of him when he regarded the decalogue. A great library easily begets affection, which may deepen into love: but devotion and awe are plants hard to rear in our harsh climate: besides, can it be well denied that there is something in a huge collection of the ancient learning, of mediæval folios, of controversial pamphlets, and in the thick black dust these things so woefully collect, provocative of listlessness and enervation and of a certain Solomonic dissatisfaction? The two writers of modern times, both pre-eminently sympathetic towards the past, who have best described this somewhat melancholy and disillusioned frame of mind are both Americans: Washington Irving, in two essays in *The Sketch-Book*, " The Art of Bookmaking," and "The Mutability of Literature "; and Nathaniel Hawthorne, in many places, but notably in the famous chapter on " The Emptiness of Picture Galleries," in *The Marble Faun.*

It is perhaps best not to make too great demands upon our slender stock of deep emotions, not to rhapsodise too much, or vainly to pretend, as some travellers have done, that to them the collections of the Bodleian, its laden shelves and precious cases, are more attractive than wealth, fame, or family, and that it was stern Fate that alone compelled them to leave Oxford by train after a visit rarely exceeding twenty-four hours in duration.

Sir Thomas Bodley's Library at Oxford is, all will admit, a great and glorious institution, one of England's sacred places: and springing, as it did, out of the mind, heart, and head of one strong, efficient, and resolute man, it is matter for rejoicing with every honest gentleman to be able to observe how quickly the idea took root, how well it has thriven, by how great a tradition it has become consecrated, and how studiously the wishes of the founder in all their essentials are still observed and carried out.

Saith the prophet Isaiah, " The liberal deviseth liberal things; and by liberal things he shall stand." The name of Thomas Bodley still stands all the world over by the liberal thing he devised.

A few pages about this " second Ptolemy " will be grudged me by none but unlettered churls.

He was a west-countryman, an excellent thing to be in England if you want backing through thick and thin, and was born in Exeter on March 2nd, 1544—a most troublesome date. It seems our fate in the old home never to be for long quit of the religious difficulty—which is very hard upon us, for nobody, I suppose, would call the English a " religious " people. Little Thomas Bodley opened his eyes in a land distracted with the religious difficulty. Listen to his own words: they are full of the times:

My father, in the time of Queen Mary, being noted and known to be an enemy to Popery, was so cruelly threatened and so narrowly observed by those that maliced his religion, that for the safeguard of himself and my mother, who was

wholly affected as my father, he knew no way so secure as to
fly into Germany, where after a while he found means to call
over my mother with all his children and family, whom he
settled for a time in Wesel in Cleveland.   (For there there
were many English which had left their country for their
conscience and with quietness enjoyed their meetings and
preachings.)   From thence he removed to the town of Frank-
fort, where there was in like sort another English congregation.
Howbeit we made no longer tarriance in either of these two
towns, for that my father had resolved to fix his abode in the
city of Geneva.

Here the Bodleys remained " until such time
as our Nation was advertised of the death of
Queen Mary and the succession of Elizabeth, with
the change of religion which caused my father
to hasten unto England."

In Geneva young Bodley and his brothers
enjoyed what now would be called great educational
advantages. Small creature though he was, he yet
attended, so he says, the public lectures of Cheva-
lerius in Hebrew, Bersaldus in Greek, and of Calvin
and Beza in Divinity. He had also " domestical
teachers," and was taught Homer by Robert
Constantinus, who was the author of a Greek
lexicon, a luxury in those days.

On returning to England, Bodley proceeded, not
to Exeter College, as by rights he should have done,
but to Magdalen, where he became a " reading
man," and graduated Bachelor of Arts in 1563.
The next year he shifted his quarters to Merton,
where he gave public lectures on Greek. In 1566
he became a Master of Arts, took to the study of
natural philosophy, and three years later was
Junior Proctor. He remained in residence until
1576, thus spending seventeen years in the University. In the last-mentioned year he obtained
leave of absence to travel on the Continent, and

for four years he pursued his studies abroad, mastering the French, Spanish, and Italian languages. Some short time after his return home he obtained an introduction to Court circles and became an Esquire to Queen Elizabeth, who seems to have entertained varying opinions about him, at one time greatly commending him and at another time wishing he were hanged—an awkward wish on Tudor lips. In 1588 Bodley married a wealthy widow, a Mrs. Ball, the daughter of a Bristol man named Carew. As Bodley survived his wife and had no children, a good bit of her money remains in the Bodleian to this day. Blessed be her memory! Nor should the names of Carew and Ball be wholly forgotten in this connection. From 1588 to 1596 Bodley was in the diplomatic service, chiefly at The Hague, where he did good work in troublesome times. On being finally recalled from The Hague, Bodley had to make up his mind whether to pursue a public life. He suffered from having too many friends, for not only did Burleigh patronise him, but Essex must needs do the same. No man can serve two masters, and though to be the victim of the rival ambitions of greater men than yourself is no uncommon fate, it is a currish one. Bodley determined to escape it, and to make for himself after a very different fashion a name *ære perennius.*

I resolved thereupon to possess my soul in peace all the residue of my days, to take my full farewell of State employments, to satisfy my mind with the mediocrity of worldly living that I had of mine own, and so to retire me from the Court.

But what was he to do?

Whereupon, examining exactly for the rest of my life what

course I might take, and having sought all the ways to the wood to select the most proper, I concluded at the last to set up my staff at the Library door in Oxford, being thoroughly persuaded that in my solitude and surcease from the Commonwealth affairs I could not busy myself to better purpose than by reducing that place (which then in every part lay ruined waste) to the publick use of students.

It is pleasant to be admitted into the birth-chamber of a great idea destined to be translated into action. Bodley proceeds to state the four qualifications he felt himself to possess to do this great bit of work : first, the necessary knowledge of ancient and modern tongues and of "sundry other sorts of scholastical literature"; second, purse ability ; third, a great store of honourable friends; and fourth, leisure.

Bodley's description of the state of the old library as lying in every part ruined and in waste was but too true.

Richard of Bury, the book-loving Bishop of Durham, seems to have been the first donor of manuscripts on anything like a large scale to Oxford, but the library he founded was at Durham College, which stood where Trinity College now stands, and was in no sense a University library. The good Bishop, known to all book-hunters as the author of the *Philobiblon*, died in 1345, but his collection remained intact, subject to rules he had himself laid down, until the dissolution of the monasteries, when Durham College, which was attached to a religious house, was put up for sale, and its library, like so much else of good learning at this sad period, was dispersed and for the most part destroyed.

Bodley's real predecessor, the first begetter of a University library, was Thomas Cobham, Bishop of Worcester, who in 1320 prepared a chamber above a vaulted room in the north-east corner of St. Mary's Church for the reception of the books he intended to bestow upon his University. When the Bishop of Worcester (as a matter of fact, he had once been elected Archbishop of Canterbury; but that is another story, as Laurence Sterne has said) died in 1327, it was discovered that he had by his will bequeathed his library to Oxford, but he was insolvent! No rich relict of a defunct Ball was available for a Bishop in those days. The executors found themselves without sufficient estate to pay for their testator's funeral expenses, even then the first charge upon assets. They are not to be blamed for pawning the library. A good friend redeemed the pledge, and despatched the books — all, of course, manuscripts — to Oxford. For some reason or another Oriel took them in, and, having become their bailee, refused to part with them, possibly and plausibly alleging that the University was not in a position to give a valid receipt. At Oriel they remained for ten years, when all of a sudden the scholars of the University, animated by their notorious affection for sound learning and a good " row," took Oriel by storm, and carried off the books in triumph to Bishop Cobham's room, where they remained in chests unread for thirty years. In 1367 the University by statute ratified and confirmed its title to the books, and published regulations for their use, but the quarrel with Oriel continued till 1409, when the Cobham Library was for the first time properly furnished and opened as a place for study and reference.

The librarian of the old Cobham Library had an advantage over Mr. Nicholson, the Bodley librarian of to-day. Being a clerk in Holy orders before the time when, in Bodley's own phrase, already quoted, we " changed " our religion, he was authorised by the University to say masses for the souls of all dead donors of books, whether by gifts *inter vivos* or by bequest.

The first great benefactor of Cobham's Library was Duke Humphrey of Gloucester, the youngest son of Henry IV., and perhaps the most " pushful " youngest son in our royal annals. Though a dissipated and unprincipled fellow, he lives in history as " the good Duke Humphrey," because he had the sense to patronise learning, collect manuscripts, and enrich Universities. He began his gifts to Oxford as early, so say some authorities, as 1411, and continued his donations of manuscripts with such vivacity that the little room in St. Mary's could no longer contain its riches. Hence the resolution of the University in 1444 to build a new library over the Divinity School. This new room, which was completed in 1480, forms now the central portion of that great reading-room so affectionately remembered by thousands of still living students.

Duke Humphrey's Library, as the new room was popularly called, continued to flourish and receive valuable accessions of manuscripts and printed books belonging to divinity, medicine, natural science, and literature until the ill-omened year 1550. Oxford has never loved Commissioners revising her statutes and reforming her schools, but the Commissioners of 1550 were worse than prigs, worse even than Erastians; they were barbarians and wreckers. They were deputed by King Edward VI., " in the spirit of the Reformation," to make an end of the Popish superstition. Under their hands the library totally disappeared, and for a long while the tailors and shoemakers and bookbinders of Oxford were well supplied with vellum, which they found useful in their respective callings. It was a hard fate for so splendid a collection. True it is that for the most part the contents of the library had been rescued from miserable ill-usage in the monasteries and chapter-houses where they had their first habitations, but at last they had found shelter over the Divinity School of a great University. There at least they might hope to slumber. But our Reformers thought otherwise. The books and manuscripts being thus dispersed or destroyed, a prudent if unromantic Convocation exposed for sale the wooden shelves, desks, and seats of the old library, and so made a complete end of the whole concern, thus making room for Thomas Bodley.

On February 23rd, 1597/8, Thomas Bodley sat himself down in his London house and addressed to the Vice-Chancellor of his University a certain famous letter:

SIR,

Altho' you know me not as I suppose, yet for the farthering of an offer of evident utilitie to your whole University I will not be too scrupulous in craving your assistance. I have been alwaies of a mind that if God of his goodness should make me able to do anything for the benefit of posteritie, I would shew some token of affection that I have ever more borne to the studies of good learning. I know my portion is too slender to perform for the present any answerable act to my willing disposition, but yet to notify some part of my desire in that behalf I have resolved thus to deal. Where there hath been heretofore a public library in Oxford which you know is apparent by the room itself remaining and by your statute records, I will take the charge and cost upon me to reduce it again to its former use and to make it fit and handsome with seats and shelves and desks and all that may be needful to stir up other mens benevolence to help to furnish it with books. And this I purpose to begin as soon as timber can be gotten to the intent that you may be of some speedy profit of my project. And where before as I conceive it was to be reputed but a store of books of divers benefactors because it never had any lasting allowance for augmentation of the number or supply of books decayed, whereby it came to pass that when those that were in being were either wasted or embezzled, the whole foundation came to ruin. To meet with that inconvenience, I will so provide hereafter (if God do not hinder my present design) as you shall be still assured of a standing annual rent to be disbursed every year in buying of books, or officers stipends and other pertinent occasions, with which provision and some order for the preservation of the place and the furniture of it from accustomed abuses, it may perhaps in time to come prove a notable treasure for the multitude of volumes, an excellent benefit for the use and ease of students, and a singular ornament of the University.

The letter does not stop here, but my quotation has already probably wearied most of my readers, though for my own part I am not ashamed to confess that I seldom tire of retracing with my own hand the *ipsissima verba* whereby great and truly notable gifts have been bestowed upon nations or Universities or even municipalities for the advancement of learning and the spread of science. Bodley's language is somewhat involved, but through it glows the plain intention of an honest man.

Convocation, we are told, embraced the offer with wonderful alacrity, and lost no time in accepting it in good Latin.

From February 1598 to January 1613 (when he died), Bodley was happy with as glorious a hobby-horse as ever man rode astride upon. Though Bodley, in one of his letters, modestly

calls himself a mere " smatterer," he was, as indeed
he had the sense to recognise, excellently well
fitted to be a collector of books, being both a good
linguist and personally well acquainted with the
chief cities of the Continent and with their booksellers. He was thus able to employ well-selected
agents in different parts of Europe to buy books
on his account, which it was his pleasure to receive,
his rapture to unpack, his pride to despatch in
what he calls " dry-fats "—that is, weather-tight
chests—to Dr. James, the first Bodleian librarian.
Despite growing and painful infirmities (stone,
ague, dropsy), Bodley never even for a day dis-
mounted his hobby, but rode it manfully to the
last. Nor had he any mean taint of nature that
might have grudged other men a hand in the great
work. The more benefactors there were, the better
pleased was Bodley. He could not, indeed—for
had he not been educated at Geneva and attended
the Divinity Lectures of Calvin and Beza?—
direct Dr. James to say masses for the souls of
such donors of money or books as should die, but
he did all a poor Protestant can do to tempt
generosity; he opened and kept in a very public
place in the library a great register-book, containing the names and titles of all benefactors. Bodley
was always on the look-out for gifts and bequests
from his store of honourable friends; and in the
case of Sir Henry Savile he even relaxed the rule
against lending books from the library, because,
as he frankly admits to Dr. James, he had hopes
(which proved well founded) that Sir Henry would
not forget his obligations to the Bodleian.

The library was formally opened on November

8th, 1602, and then contained some 2000 volumes. Two years later its founder was knighted by King James, who on the following June directed letters patent to be issued styling the library by the founder's name and licensing the University to hold land in mortmain for its maintenance. The most learned and by no means the most foolish of our kings, this same James I., visited the Bodleian in May 1605. Sir Thomas was not present. There it was that the royal pun was made that the founder's name should have been Godly and not Bodley. King James handled certain old manuscripts with the familiarity of a scholar, and is reported to have said, I doubt not with perfect sincerity, that were he not King James he would be a University man, and that were it his fate at any time to be a captive, he would wish to be shut up in the Bodleian and to be bound with its chains, consuming his days amongst its books as his fellows in captivity. Indeed, he was so carried away by the atmosphere of the place as to offer to present to the Bodleian whatever books Sir Thomas Bodley might think fit to lay hands upon in any of the royal libraries, and he kept this royal word so far as to confirm the gift under the Privy Seal. But there it seems to have stopped, for the Bodleian does not contain any volumes traceable to this source. The King's librarians probably obstructed any such transfer of books.

Authors seem at once to have recognised the importance of the library, and to have made presentation copies of their works, and in 1605 we find Bacon sending a copy of his *Advancement of*

Learning to Bodley, with a letter in which he said: "You, having built an ark to save learning from deluge, deserve propriety [ownership] in any new instrument or engine whereby learning should be improved or advanced." The most remarkable letter Bodley ever wrote, now extant, is one to Bacon; but it has no reference to the library, only to the Baconian philosophy. We do not get many glimpses of Bodley's habits of life or ways of thinking, but there is no difficulty in discerning a strenuous, determined, masterful figure, bent during his later years, perhaps tyrannously bent, on effecting his object. He was not, we learn from a correspondent, "hasty to write but when the posts do urge him, saying there need be no answer to your letters till more leisure breed him opportunity." "Words are women, deeds are men," is another saying of his which I reprint without comment.

By an indenture dated April 20th, 1609, Bodley, after reciting how he had, out of his zealous affection to the advancement of learning, lately erected upon the ruins of the old decayed library of Oxford University "a most ample, commodious, and necessary building, as well for receipt and conveyance of books as for the use and ease of students, and had already furnished the same with excellent writers on all sorts of sciences, arts, and tongues, not only selected out of his own study and store, but also of others that were freely conferred by many other men's gifts," proceeded to grant to trustees lands and hereditaments in Berkshire and in the city of London for the purpose of forming a permanent endowment of his library: and so they, or the proceeds of sale thereof, have remained unto this day.

Sir Thomas Bodley died on January 20th, 1613, his last days being soothed by a letter he received from the Vice-Chancellor of Oxford University condoling his sickness and signifying how much the Heads of Houses, etc., prayed for his recovery. A cynical friend—not much of a friend, as we shall see—called John Chamberlain, was surprised to observe what pleasure this assurance gave to the dying man. " Whereby," writes Chamberlain to Sir Ralph Winwood, " I perceive how much fair words work, as well upon wise men as upon others, for indeed it did affect him very much."

Bodley was rather put out in his last illness by the refusal of a Cambridge doctor, Batter, to come to see him, the doctor saying: " Words cannot cure him, and I can do nothing else for him." There is an occasional curtness about Cambridge men that is hard but not impossible to reconcile with good feeling.

Bodley's will gave great dissatisfaction to some of his friends, including this aforesaid John Chamberlain, and yet, on reading it through, it is not easy to see any cause for just complaint. Bodley's brother did not grumble, there were no children, Lady Bodley had died in 1611, and everybody who knew the testator must have known that the library would be (as it was) the great object of his bounty. What annoyed Chamberlain seems to be that, whilst he had (so he says, though I take leave to doubt it) put down Bodley for some trifle in his will, Bodley forgot to mention Chamberlain in his. There is always a good deal of human nature exhibited on these occasions. I will transcribe a bit of one of this gentleman's grumbling letters, written, one may be sure, with no view to publication, the day after Bodley's death:

Mr. Gent came to me this morning as it were to bemoan himself of the little regard hath been had of him and others, and indeed for ought I hear there is scant anybody pleased, but for the rest it were no great matter if he had had more consideration or commiseration where there was most need. But he was so carried away with the vanity and vain-glory of his library, that he forgot all other respects and duties, almost of Conscience, Friendship, or Good-nature, and all he had was too little for that work. To say the truth I never did rely upon his conscience, but I thought he had been more real and ingenuous I cannot learn that he hath given anything, no, not a good word nor so much as named any old friend he had, but Mr. Gent and Thos. Allen, who like a couple of Almesmen must have his best and second gown, and his best and second cloak, but to cast a colour or shadow of something upon Mr. Gent, he says he forgives him all he owed him, which Mr. Gent protests is never a penny. I must intreat you to pardon me if I seem somewhat impatient on his [*i.e.*, Gent's] behalf, who hath been so servile to him, and indeed such a perpetual servant, that he deserved a better reward. Neither can I deny that I have a little indignation for myself that having been acquainted with him for almost forty years, and observed and respected him so much, I should not be remembered with the value of a spoon, or a mourning garment, whereas if I had gone before him (as poor a man as I am), he should not have found himself forgotten.[1]

Bodley did no more by his will, which is dated January 2nd, 1613, and is all in his own handwriting, than he had bound himself to do in his lifetime, and I feel as certain as I can feel about anything that happened nearly three hundred years ago, that Mr. Gent, of Gloucester Hall, did owe Bodley money, though, as many another member of the University of Oxford has done with his debts, he forgot all about it.

[1] *Winwood's Memorials*, vol. iii., p. 429.

The founder of the Bodleian was buried with proper pomp and circumstance in the chapel of Merton College on March 29th, 1613. Two Latin orations were delivered over his remains, one, that of John Hales (the ever-memorable), a Fellow of Merton, being of no inconsiderable length. After all was over, those who had mourning weeds or " blacks " retired, with the Heads of Houses, to the refectory of Merton and had a funeral dinner bestowed upon them, " amounting to the sum of £100," as directed by the founder's will.

The great foundation of Sir Thomas Bodley has, happily for all of us, had better fortune than befell the generous gifts of the Bishops of Durham and Worcester. The Protestant layman has had the luck, not the large-minded prelates of the old religion. Even during the Civil War Bodley's books remained uninjured, at all events by the Parliament men.

When Oxford was surrendered [June 24th, 1646], the first thing General Fairfax did was to set a good guard of soldiers to preserve the Bodleian Library. 'Tis said there was more hurt done by the Cavaliers [during their garrison] by way of embezzling and cutting of chains of books than there was since. He was a lover of learning, and had he not taken this special care that noble library had been utterly destroyed, for there were ignorant senators enough who would have been contented to have it so. (*See* Macray, p. 101.)

Oliver Cromwell, while Lord Protector, presented to the library twenty-two Greek manuscripts he had purchased, and, what is more, when Bodley's librarian refused the Lord Protector's request to allow the Portugal Ambassador to borrow a manuscript, sending instead of the manuscript a copy of the statutes forbidding loans, Oliver commended the prudence of the founder, and subsequently made the donation just mentioned.

A great wave of generosity towards this foundation was early noticeable. The Bodleian got hold of men's imaginations. In those days there were learned men in all walks of life, and many more who, if not learned, were endlessly curious. The great merchants of the city of London instructed their agents in far lands to be on the look-out for rare things, and transmit them home to find a resting-place in Bodley's buildings. All sorts of curiosities found their way there — crocodiles, whales, mummies, and black negro boys in spirits. The Ashmolean now holds most of them; the negro boy has been conveniently lost.

In 1649 the total of 2000 printed books had risen to more than 12,000—viz., folios, 5889; quartos, 2067; octavos, 4918; whilst of manuscripts there were 3001. One of the first gifts in money came from Sir Walter Raleigh, who in 1605 gave £50, whilst among the early benefactors of books and manuscripts it were a sin not to name the Earl of Pembroke, Archbishop Laud (one of the library's best friends), Robert Burton (of the *Anatomy of Melancholy*), Sir Kenelm Digby, John Selden, Lord Fairfax, Colonel Vernon, and Barlow, Bishop of Lincoln. No nobler library exists in the world than the Bodleian, unless it be in the Vatican at Rome. The foundation of Sir Thomas Bodley, though of no antiquity, shines with unrivalled splendour in the galaxy of Oxford

Amidst the stars that own another birth.

I must not say, being myself a Cambridge man,

that the Bodleian dominates Oxford, yet to many an English, American, and foreign traveller to that city, which, despite railway-stations and motor-cars and the never-ending villas and perambulators of the Banbury Road, still breathes the charm of an earlier age, the Bodleian is the pulsing heart of the University. Colleges, like ancient homesteads, unless they are yours, never quite welcome you, though ready enough to receive with civility your tendered meed of admiration. You wander through their gardens, and pace their quadrangles with no sense of co-ownership; not for you are their clustered memories. In the Bodleian every lettered heart feels itself at home.

Bodley drafted with his own hand the first statutes or rules to be observed in his library. Speaking generally, they are wise rules. One mistake, indeed, he made—a great mistake, but a natural one. Let him give his own reasons:

> I can see no good reason to alter my rule for excluding such books as Almanacks, Plays, and an infinite number that are daily printed of very unworthy matters—handling such books as one thinks both the Keeper and Under-Keeper should disdain to seek out, to deliver to any man. Haply some plays may be worthy the keeping—but hardly one in forty. . . . This is my opinion, where in if I err I shall err with infinite others; and the more I think upon it, the more it doth distaste me that such kinds of books should be vouchsafed room in so noble a library.[1]

" Baggage-books " was the contemptuous expression elsewhere employed to describe this " light infantry " of literature—*Belles Lettres*, as it is now more politely designated.

One play in forty is liberal measure, but who is to say out of the forty plays which is the one worthy

---

[1] See correspondence in *Reliquiæ Bodleianæ*, London, 1703.

to be housed in a noble library? The taste of Vice-Chancellors and Heads of Houses, of keepers and under-keepers of libraries—can anybody trust it? The Bodleian is entitled by imperial statutes to receive copies of all books published within the realm, yet it appears, on the face of a Parliamentary return made in 1818, that this "noble library" refused to find room for Ossian, the favourite poet of Goethe and Napoleon, and labelled Miss Edgeworth's *Parent's Assistant* and Miss Hannah More's *Sacred Dramas* " Rubbish." The sister University, home though she be of nearly every English poet worth reading, rejected *The Siege of Corinth*, though the work of a Trinity man; would not take in the *Thanksgiving Ode* of Mr. Wordsworth, of St. John's College; declined Leigh Hunt's *Story of Rimini* ; vetoed the *Headlong Hall* of the inimitable Peacock, and, most wonderful of all, would have nothing to say to Scott's *Antiquary*, being probably disgusted to find that a book with so promising a title was only a novel.

Now this is altered, and everything is collected in the Bodleian, including, so I am told, Christmas-cards and bills of fare.

Bodley's rule has proved an expensive one, for the library has been forced to buy at latter-day prices " baggage-books " it could have got for nothing.

Another ill-advised regulation got rid of duplicates. Thus, when the third Shakespeare Folio appeared in 1664, the Bodleian disposed of its copy of the first Folio. However, this wrong was righted in 1821, when, under the terms of Edmund Malone's bequest, the library once again became the possessor of the edition of 1623. Quite lately the original displaced Folio has been recovered.

Against lending books Bodley was adamant, and here his rule prevails. It is pre-eminently a wise one. The stealing of books, as well as the losing of books, from public libraries is a melancholy and ancient chapter in the histories of such institutions; indeed, there is too much reason to believe that not a few books in the Bodleian itself were stolen to start with. But the long possession by such a foundation has doubtless purged the original offence. In the National Library in Paris is at least one precious manuscript which was stolen from the Escurial. There are volumes in the British Museum on which the Bodleian looks with suspicion, and *vice versâ*. But let sleeping dogs lie. Bodley would not give the divines who were engaged upon a bigger bit of work even than his library—the translation of the Bible into that matchless English which makes King James's version our greatest literary possession—permission to borrow " the one or two books " they wished to see.

Bodley's Library has sheltered through three centuries many queer things besides books and strangely-written manuscripts in old tongues; queerer things even than crocodiles, whales, and mummies—I mean the librarians and sub-librarians, janitors and servants. Oddities many of them have been. Honest old Jacobites, non-jurors, primitive thinkers, as well as scandalously lazy drunkards and illiterate dogs. An old foundation can afford to have a varied experience in these matters.

One of the most original of these originals was the famous Thomas Hearne, an " honest gentleman "

—that is, a Jacobite—and one whose collections and diaries have given pleasure to thousands. He was appointed janitor in 1701, and sub-librarian in 1712, but in 1716, when an Act of Parliament came into operation which imposed a fine of £500 upon anyone who held any public office without taking the oath of allegiance to the Hanoverians, Hearne's office was taken away from him; but he shared with his King over the water the satisfaction of accounting himself still *de jure*, and though he lived till 1735, he never failed each half-year to enter his salary and fees as sub-librarian as being still unpaid. He was perhaps a little spiteful and vindictive, but none the less a fine old fellow. I will write down as specimens of his humour a prayer of his and an apology, and then leave him alone. His prayer ran as follows:

O most gracious and merciful Lord God, wonderful in Thy Providence, I return all possible thanks to Thee for the care Thou hast always taken of me. I continually meet with most signal instances of this Thy Providence, and one act yesterday, *when I unexpectedly met with three old manuscripts*, for which in a particular manner I return my thanks, beseeching Thee to continue the same protection to me, a poor helpless sinner, and that for Jesus Christ his sake. (*Aubrey's Letters*, i. 118.)

His apology, which I do not think was actually published, though kept in draft, was after this fashion:

I, Thomas Hearne, A.M. of the University of Oxford, having ever since my matriculation followed my studies with as much application as I have been capable of, and having published several books for the honour and credit of learning, and particularly for the reputation of the foresaid University, am very sorry that by my declining to say anything but what I knew to be true in any of my writings, and especially in the last book I published entitled, etc., I should incur the displeasure of any of the Heads of Houses, and as a token of my sorrow for their being offended at truth, I subscribe my name to this paper and permit them to make what use of it they please.

Leaping 140 years, an odd tale is thus lovingly recorded of another sub-librarian, the Rev. A. Hackman, who died in 1874:

> During all the time of his service in the library (thirty-six years) he had used as a cushion in his plain wooden arm-chair a certain vellum-bound folio, which by its indented side, worn down by continual pressure, bore testimony to the use to which it had been put. No one had ever the curiosity to examine what the book might be, but when, after Hackman's departure from the library, it was removed from its resting-place of years, some amusement was caused by finding that the chief compiler of the last printed catalogue had omitted from his catalogue the volume on which he sat, of which, too, though of no special value, there was no other copy in the library. (Macray, p. 388a.)

The spectacle in the mind's eye of this devoted sub-librarian and sound divine sitting on the vellum-bound folio for six-and-thirty years, so absorbed in his work as to be oblivious of the fact that he had failed to include in what was his *magnum opus*, the Great Catalogue, the very book he was sitting upon, tickles the midriff.

Here I must bring these prolonged but wholly insufficient observations to a very necessary conclusion. Not a word has been said of the great collection of bibles, or of the unique copies of the Koran and the Talmud and the *Arabian Nights*, or of the Dante manuscripts, or of Bishop Tanner's books (many bought on the dispersion of Archbishop Sancroft's great library), which in course of removal by water from Norwich to Oxford fell into the river and remained submerged for twenty hours, nor of many other splendid benefactions of a later date.

One thing only remains, not to be said, but to

be sent round—I mean the hat. Ignominious to relate, this glorious foundation stands in need of money. Shade of Sir Thomas Bodley, I invoke thy aid to loosen the purse-strings of the wealthy! The age of learned and curious merchants, of high-spirited and learning-loving nobles, of book-collecting bishops, of antiquaries, is over. The Bodleian cannot condescend to beg. It is too majestical. But I, an unauthorised stranger, have no need to be ashamed.

Especially rich is this great library in *Americana*, and America suggests multi-millionaires. The rich men of the United States have been patriotically alive to the first claims of their own richly endowed universities, and long may they so continue: but if by any happy chance any one of them should accidentally stumble across an odd million or even half a million of dollars hidden away in some casual investment he had forgotten, what better thing could he do with it than send it to this, the most famous foundation of his Old Home? It would be acknowledged by return of post in English and in Latin, and the donor's name would be inscribed, not indeed (and this is a regrettable lapse) in that famous old register which Bodley provided should always be in a prominent place in his library, but in the Annual Statement of Accounts now regularly issued. To be associated with the Bodleian is to share its fame and partake of the blessing it has inherited. " The liberal deviseth liberal things; and by liberal things he shall stand."

BOOKWORMS

1905

GREAT is bookishness and the charm of books.
No doubt there are times and seasons in
the lives of most reading men when they
rebel against the dust of libraries and kick against
the pricks of these monstrously accumulated heaps
of words. We all know " the dark hour " when the
vanity of learning and the childishness of merely
literary things are brought home to us in such a
way as almost to avail to put the pale student
out of conceit with his books, and to make him
turn from his best-loved authors as from a friend
who has outstayed his welcome, whose carriage
we wish were at the door. In these unhappy
moments we are apt to call to mind the shrewd
men we have known, who have been our blithe
companions on breezy fells, heathery moor, and
by the stream side, who could neither read nor
write, or who, at all events, but rarely practised
those Cadmean arts. Yet they could tell the time
of day by the sun, and steer through the silent
night by the stars; and each of them had—as
Emerson, a very bookish person, has said—a dial
in his mind for the whole bright calendar of the
year. How racy was their talk; how wise their
judgments on men and things; how well they did
all that at the moment seemed worth doing; how
universally useful was their garnered experience—

their acquired learning! How wily were these illiterates in the pursuit of game—how ready in an emergency! What a charm there is about out-of-door company! Who would not sooner have spent a summer's day with Sir Walter's humble friend, Tom Purday, than with Mr. William Wordsworth of Rydal Mount! It is, we can only suppose, reflections such as these that make country gentlemen and farmers the sworn foes they are of education and the enemies of School Boards.

I only indicate this line of thought to condemn it. Such temptations come from below. Great, we repeat, is bookishness and the charm of books. Even the writings, the ponderous writings, of that portentous parson, the Rev. T. F. Dibdin, with all their lumbering gaiety and dust-choked rapture over first editions, are not hastily to be sent packing to the auction-room. Much red gold did they cost us, these portly tomes, in bygone days, and on our shelves they shall remain till the end of our time, unless our creditors intervene—were it only to remind us of years when our enthusiasms were pure though our tastes may have been crude.

Some years ago Mr. Blades, the famous printer and Caxtonist, published in vellum covers a small volume which he christened *The Enemies of Books*. It made many friends, and now a revised and enlarged version in comely form, adorned with pictures, and with a few prefatory words by Dr. Garnett, has made its appearance. Mr. Blades himself has left this world for a better one, where —so piety bids us believe—neither fire nor water nor worm can despoil or destroy the pages of heavenly wisdom. But the book-collector must

not be caught nursing mere sublunary hopes.
There is every reason to believe that in the realms
of the blessed the library, like that of Major Ponto,
will be small though well selected. Mr. Blades
had, as his friend Dr. Garnett observes, a debonair
spirit—there was nothing fiery or controversial
about him. His attitude towards the human race
and its treatment of rare books was rather mournful
than angry. For example, under the head of
" Fire," he has occasion to refer to that great
destruction of books of magic which took place
at Ephesus, to which St. Luke has called attention
in his Acts of the Apostles. Mr. Blades describes
this holocaust as righteous, and only permits himself to say in a kind of undertone that he feels a
certain mental disquietude and uneasiness at the
thought of the loss of more than £18,000 worth of
books, which could not but have thrown much
light (had they been preserved) on many curious
questions of folk-lore. Personally, I am dead
against the burning of books. A far worse, because a corrupt, proceeding, was the scandalously
horrid fate that befell the monastic libraries at
our disgustingly conducted, even if generally bene-
ficent, Reformation. The greedy nobles and landed
gentry, who grabbed the ancient foundations of
the old religion, cared nothing for the books they
found cumbering the walls, and either devoted
them to vile domestic uses or sold them in ship-
loads across the seas. It may well be that the
monks—fine, lusty fellows!—cared more for the
contents of their fish-ponds than of their libraries;
but, at all events, they left the books alone to
take their chance—they did not rub their boots

with them or sell them at the price of old paper. A man need have a very debonair spirit who does not lose his temper over our blessed Reformation. Mr. Blades, on the whole, managed to keep his.

Passing from fire, Mr. Blades has a good deal to say about water, and the harm it has been allowed to do in our collegiate and cathedral libraries. With really creditable composure he writes: " Few old libraries in England are now so thoroughly neglected as they were thirty years ago. The state of many of our collegiate and cathedral libraries was at that time simply appalling. I could mention many instances—one especially— where, a window having been left broken for a long time, the ivy had pushed through and crept over a row of books, each of which was worth hundreds of pounds. In rainy weather the water was conducted as by a pipe along the tops of the books, and soaked through the whole." Ours is indeed a learned Church. Fancy the mingled amazement and dismay of the Dean and Chapter when they were informed that all this mouldering literary trash had " boodle " in it. " In another and a smaller collection the rain came through on to a bookcase through a skylight, saturating continually the top shelf, containing Caxtons and other English books, one of which, although rotten, was sold soon after by permission of the Charity Commissioners for £200." Oh, those scoundrelly Charity Commissioners! How impertinent has been their interference with the loving care and guardianship of the Lord's property by His lawfully consecrated ministers! By the side of these anthropoid apes, the genuine bookworm, the paper-eating insect, ravenous as he once was, has done comparatively little mischief. Very little seems known of the creature, though the purchaser of Mr. Blades's book becomes the owner of a life-size portrait of the miscreant in one, at all events, of his many shapes. Mr. Birdsall, of Northampton, sent Mr. Blades, in 1879, by post, a fat little worm he had found in an old volume. Mr. Blades did all, and more than all, that could be expected of a humane man to keep the creature alive, actually feeding him with fragments of Caxtons and seventeenth-century literature; but it availed not, for in three weeks the thing died, and as the result of a post-mortem was declared to be *Œcophera pseudopretella*. Some years later Dr. Garnett, who has spent a long life obliging men of letters, sent Mr. Blades two Athenian worms which had travelled to this country in a Hebrew Commentary; but, lovely and pleasant in their lives, in their deaths they were not far divided. Mr. Blades, at least, mourned their loss. The energy of bookworms, like that of men, greatly varies. Some go much farther than others. However fair they may start on the same folio, they end very differently. Once upon a time 212 worms began to eat their way through a stout folio printed in the year 1477, by Peter Schoeffer, of Mentz. It was an ungodly race they ran, but let me trace their progress. By the time the sixty-first page was reached all but four had given in, either slinking back the way they came, or perishing *en route*. By the time the eighty-sixth page had been reached but one was left, and he evidently on his last legs, for he failed to pierce his way through page 87. At the other end of the same book another lot of worms began to bore, hoping, I presume, to meet in the middle, like the makers of submarine tunnels, but the last survivor of this gang only reached the sixty-ninth page from the end. Mr. Blades was of opinion that all these worms belonged to the *Anobium pertinax*. Worms have fallen upon evil days, for, whether modern books are readable or not, they have long since ceased to be edible. The worm's instinct forbids him to " eat the china clay, the bleaches, the plaster of Paris, the sulphate of barytes, the scores of adulterants now used to mix with the fibre." Alas, poor worm! Alas, poor author! Neglected by the *Anobium pertinax*, what chance is there of anyone, man or beast, a hundred years hence reaching his eighty-seventh page!

Time fails me to refer to bookbinders, frontispiece collectors, servants and children, and other enemies of books; but the volume I refer to is to be had of the booksellers, and is a pleasant volume, worthy of all commendation. Its last words set me thinking; they are:

Even a millionaire will ease his toils, lengthen his life, and add 100 per cent. to his daily pleasures, if he becomes a biliophile; while to the man of business with a taste for books, who through the day has struggled in the battle of life, with all its irritating rebuffs and anxieties, what a blessed season of pleasurable repose opens upon him as he enters his sanctum, where every article wafts him a welcome and every book is a personal friend!

As for the millionaire, I frankly say I have no desire his life should be lengthened, and care nothing about adding 100 per cent. to his daily pleasures. He is a nuisance, for he has raised prices nearly 100 per cent. We curse the day when he was told it was the thing to buy old books; and, if he must buy old books, why is he not content with the works of Gibbon, Hume, and Robertson, and Flavius Josephus, that learned Jew? But it is not the millionaire who set me thinking; it is the harassed man of business; and what I am wondering is, whether, in sober truth and earnestness, it is possible for him, as he shuts his library door and finds himself inside, to forget his rebuffs and anxieties—his maturing bills and overdue argosies—and to lose himself over a favourite volume. The " article " that wafts him welcome I take to be his pipe. That he will put the " article " into his mouth and smoke it I have no manner of doubt; my dread is lest, in ten minutes' time, the book should have dropt into his lap and the man's eyes be staring into the fire. But for a' that, and a' that—great is bookishness and the charm of books.

CONFIRMED READERS

1906

D R. JOHNSON is perhaps our best example of a confirmed reader. Malone once found him sitting in his room roasting apples and reading a history of Birmingham. This staggered even Malone, who was himself a somewhat far-gone reader.

"Don't you find it rather dull?" he ventured to inquire.

"Yes," replied the Sage, "it is dull."

Malone's eyes then rested on the apples, and he remarked he supposed they were for medicine.

"Why, no," said Johnson; "I believe they are only there because I wanted something to do. I have been confined to the house for a week, and so you find me roasting apples and reading the history of Birmingham."

This anecdote pleasingly illustrates the habits of the confirmed reader. Nor let the worldling sneer. Happy is the man who, in the hours of solitude and depression, can read a history of Birmingham. How terrible is the story Welbore Ellis told of Robert Walpole in his magnificent library, trying book after book, and at last, with tears in his eyes, exclaiming: "It is all in vain: I cannot read!"

Edmund Malone, the Shakespearian commentator and first editor of *Boswell's Johnson*, was as confirmed a reader as it is possible for a book-collector to be. His own life, by Sir James Prior, is full of good things, and is not so well known as it should be. It smacks of books and bookishness.

Malone, who was an Irishman, was once, so he would have us believe, deeply engaged in politics; but he then fell in love, and the affair, for some unknown reason, ending unhappily, his interest ceased in everything, and he was driven as a last resource to books and writings. Thus are commentators made. They learn in suffering what they observe in the margin. Malone may have been driven to his pursuits, but he took to them kindly, and become a vigorous and skilful book-buyer, operating in the market both on his own behalf and on that of his Irish friends with great success.

His good fortune was enormous, and this although he had a severely restricted notion as to price. He was no reckless bidder, like Mr. Harris, late of Covent Garden, who, just because David Garrick had a fine library of old plays, was determined to have one himself at whatever cost. In Malone's opinion half a guinea was a big price for a book. As he grew older he became less careful, and in 1805, which was seven years before his death, he gave Ford, a Manchester bookseller, £25 for the Editio Princeps of *Venus and Adonis*. He already had the edition of 1596—a friend had given it him—bound up with Constable's and Daniel's *Sonnets* and other rarities, but he very naturally yearned after the edition of 1593. He fondly imagined Ford's copy to be unique: there he was wrong, but as he died in that belief, and only gave £25 for his treasure, who dare pity him? His copy now reposes in the Bodleian. He secured Shakespeare's *Sonnets* (1609) and the first edition of the

Rape of Lucrece for two guineas, and accounted half a crown a fair average price for quarto copies of Elizabethan plays.

Malone was a truly amiable man, of private fortune and endearing habits. He lived on terms of intimacy with his brother book-collectors, and when they died attended the sale of their libraries and bid for his favourite lots, grumbling greatly if they were not knocked down to him. At Topham Beauclerk's sale in 1781, which lasted nine days, Malone bought for Lord Charlemont " the pleas-auntest workes of George Gascoigne, Esquire, with the princely pleasures at Kenilworth Castle, 1587." He got it cheap (£1 7s.), as it wanted a few leaves, which Malone thought he had; but to his horror, when it came to be examined, it was found to want eleven more leaves than he had supposed. " Poor Mr. Beauclerk," he writes, " seems never to have had his books examined or collated, otherwise he would have found out the imperfections." Malone was far too good a book-collector to suggest a third method of discovering a book's imperfections —namely, reading it. Beauclerk's library only realised £5,011, and as the Duke of Marlborough had a mortgage upon it of £5,000, there must have been after payment of the auctioneer's charges a considerable deficit.

But Malone was more than a book-buyer, more even than a commentator: he was a member of the Literary Club, and the friend of Johnson, Reynolds, and Burke. On July 28, 1789, he went to Burke's place, the Gregories, near Beaconsfield, with Sir Joshua, Wyndham, and Mr. Courtenay, and spent three very agreeable days. The following extract from the recently published Charlemont papers has interest:

> As I walked out before breakfast with Mr. Burke, I proposed to him to revise and enlarge his admirable book on the *Sublime and Beautiful*, which the experience, reading, and observation of thirty years could not but enable him to improve considerably. But he said the train of his thoughts had gone another way, and the whole bent of his mind turned from such subjects, and that he was much fitter for such speculations at the time he published that book than now.

Between the Burke of 1758 and the Burke of 1789 there was a difference indeed, but the forcible expressions, " the train of my thoughts " and " the whole bent of my mind," serve to create a new impression of the tremendous energy and fertile vigour of this amazing man. The next day the party went over to Amersham and admired Mr. Drake's trees, and listened to Sir Joshua's criticisms of Mr. Drake's pictures. This was a fortnight after the taking of the Bastille. Burke's hopes were still high. The Revolution had not yet spoilt his temper.

Amongst the Charlemont papers is an amusing tale I do not remember having ever seen before of young Philip Stanhope, the recipient of Lord Chesterfield's famous letters:

> When at Berne, where he passed some of his boyhood in company with Harte and the excellent Mr., now Lord, Eliott (Heathfield of Gibraltar), he was one evening invited to a party where, together with some ladies, there happened to be a considerable number of Bernese senators, a dignified set of elderly gentlemen, aristocratically proud, and perfect strangers to fun. These most potent, grave, and reverend signors were set down to whist, and were so studiously attentive to the game, that the unlucky brat found little difficulty in fastening to the bags of their chairs the flowing tails of their ample periwigs and in cutting, unobserved by them, the tyes of their breeches. This done, he left the room, and presently re-entered crying out, "Fire! Fire!" The affrighted burgomasters

suddenly bounced up, and exhibited to the amazed spectators their senatorial heads and backs totally deprived of ornament or covering.

Young Stanhope was no ordinary child. There is a completeness about this jest which proclaims it a masterpiece. One or other of its points might have occurred to anyone, but to accomplish both at once was to show real distinction.

Sir William Stanhope, Lord Chesterfield's brother, felt no surprise at his nephew's failure to acquire the graces. "What," said he, " could Chesterfield expect? His mother was Dutch, he was educated at Leipsic, and his tutor was a pedant from Oxford."

Papers which contain anecdotes of this kind carry with them their own recommendation. We hear on all sides complaints—and I hold them to be just complaints—of the abominable high prices of English books. Thirty shillings, thirty-six shillings, are common prices. The thing is too barefaced. His Majesty's Stationery Office set an excellent example. They sell an octavo volume of 460 closely but well-printed pages, provided with an excellent index, for one shilling and elevenpence. There is not much editing, but the quality of it is good.

If anyone is confined to his room, even as Johnson was when Malone found him roasting apples and reading a history of Birmingham, he cannot do better than surround himself with the publications of the Historical Manuscripts Commission; they will cost him next to nothing, tell him something new on every page, revive a host of old memories and scores of half-forgotten names, and perhaps tempt him to become a confirmed reader.

FIRST EDITIONS

1906

THIS is an age of great publicity. Not only
are our streets well lighted, but also our
lives. The cosy nooks and corners, crannies,
and dark places where, in old-fashioned days, men
hugged their private vices without shamefacedness
have been swept away as ruthlessly as Seven Dials.
All the questionable pursuits, fancies, foibles of
silly, childish men are discussed grimly and at
length in the newspapers and magazines. Our
poor hobby-horses are dragged out of the stable,
and made to show their shambling paces before
the mob of gentlemen who read with ease. There
has been much prate lately of as innocent a foible
as ever served to make men self-forgetful for a few
seconds of time—the collecting of first editions.
Somebody hard up for " copy " denounced this
pastime, and made merry over a *virtuoso's* whim.
Somebody else—Mr. Slater, I think it was—thought
fit to put in a defence, and thereupon a dispute
arose as to why men bought first editions dear
when they could buy last editions cheap. Brutal,
domineering fellows bellowed their complete indifference to Shakespeare's Quartos till timid *dilettanti*
turned pale and fled.

The fact, of course, is that in such a dispute as
this there is but one thing to do—namely, to persuade the Attorney-General of the day to enter up

a *nolle prosequi*, and for him who collects first
editions to go on collecting. There is nothing to
be serious about in the matter. It is not literature.
Some of the greatest lovers of letters who have
ever lived—Dr. Johnson, for example, and Thomas
de Quincey and Carlyle—have cared no more for
first editions than I do for Brussels sprouts. You
may love Molière with a love surpassing your love
of woman without any desire to beggar yourself in
Paris by purchasing early copies of the plays. You
may be perfectly content to read Walton's *Lives*
in an edition of 1905, if there is one; and as for
Robinson Crusoe and *Gulliver* and *The Vicar of
Wakefield*—are they not eternal favourites, and
just as tickling to the fancy in their nineteenth-
century dress as in their eighteenth? The whole
thing is but a hobby—but a paragraph in one
chapter of the vast, but most agreeable, history
of human folly. If John Doe is blankly indifferent to Richard Roe's Elizabethan dramatists,
it is only fair to remember how sublime is Richard's
contempt for John's collection of old musical instruments. If these gentlemen are wise they will
discuss, when they meet, the weather, or the Death
Duties, or some other extraneous subject, and leave
their respective hobbies in the stable. Never mind
what your hobby is—books, prints, drawings, china,
scarabæi, lepidoptera—keep it to yourself and for
those like-minded with you. Sweet indeed is the
community of interest, delightful the intercourse
which a common foible begets; but correspondingly
bitter and distressful is the forced union of nervous
zeal and pitiless indifference. Spare us the so-called
friends who come and gape and stare and go! What

is more painful than the chatter of the connoisseur as it falls upon the long ears of the ignoramus! Collecting is a secret sin—the great pushing public must be kept out. It is sheer madness to puff and praise your hobby, and to invite Dick, Tom, and Harry to inspect your stable: such conduct is to invite rebuff, to expose yourself to just animadversion. Keep the beast in its box. This is my first advice to the hobby-hunter.

My second piece of advice is equally important, particularly at the present time, when the world is too much with us, and it is this—never convert a taste into a trade. The moment you become a tradesman you cease to be a hobbyist. When the love of money comes in at the window the love of books runs out at the door. There has been of late years a good deal of sham book-collecting. The morals of the Stock Exchange have corrupted even the library. Sordid souls have been induced by wily second-hand booksellers to buy books for no other reason than because the price demanded was a high one. This is the very worst possible reason for buying a book. Whether it is ever wise to buy a book, as Aulus Gellius used to do, simply because it is cheap, and regardless of its condition, is a debatable point, but to buy one dear at the mere bidding of a bookseller is to debase yourself. The result of this ungodly traffic has been to enlarge for the moment the circle of book-buyers by including in it men with commercial instincts, sham hobbyists. But these impostors have been lately punished in the only way they could be punished—namely, in their pockets—by a heavy fall of prices. The stuff they were induced to buy has not, and could not, maintain its price, and the shops are now full of the volumes which, seven or ten years ago, fetched fancy sums.

If a young book-collector does but bear in mind the two bits of advice I have proffered him, he may safely be bidden godspeed and congratulated on his choice of a hobby, for it is, without a shadow of a doubt, the cheapest he could have chosen. Even without means to acquire the treasures of a Quaritch or a Pickering, he may yet derive infinite delight from the perusal of the many hundreds of catalogues that now weekly issue from the second-hand booksellers in town and country. He may write an imaginary letter, ordering the books he has previously selected from the catalogue, and then he has only to forget to post it to avoid all disagreeable consequences.

The constant turnover of old books is amazing. There seems no rest in this world even for folios and quartos. The first edition of Burton's *Anatomy*, printed at Oxford in a small quarto in 1621, rises to the surface as a rule no less than four times a year; so, too, does Coryat's *Crudities*, hastily gobbled up in five months' travels in France, Savoy, Italy, Germany, etc., 1611. What a seething, restless place this world is, to be sure! The constant recurrence of copies of the same books is almost startling. Hardly a year passes but every book of first-rate importance and interest is knocked down to the highest bidder. No doubt there are still old libraries where, buried in dust and cobwebs, the folios and quartos lie undisturbed; but to turn the pages or examine the index of *Book Prices Current* is to have a vision before your eyes of whole regiments of books passing and repassing across the stage amidst the loud cries of auctioneers and the bidding of booksellers.

In the auction-mart taste is pretty steady. The old favourites hold their own. Every now and again an immortal joins their ranks. Puffing and pretension may win the ear of the outside public, and extort praise from the press, but inside the rooms of a Sotheby, a Puttick, or a Hodgson, these foolish persons count for nothing, and their names are seldom heard. Were an author to turn the pages of *Book Prices Current*, he could hardly fail, as he there read the names of famous men of old, to breathe the prayer, " May my books some day be found forming part of this great tidal wave of literature which is for ever breaking on Earth's human shores! " But the vanity of authors is endless, and their prayers are apt to be but empty things.

LIBRARIANS AT PLAY

1905

NO man of feeling will grudge the librarians of the universe their annual outing. Their pursuits are not indeed entirely sedentary, since at times they have to climb tall ladders, but of exercise they must always stand in need, and as for air, the exclusively bookish atmosphere is as bad for the lungs as it is for the intellectuals. In 1897 the Second International Library Conference met in London, attended several concerts, was entertained by the Marchioness of Bute and Lady Lubbock; visited Lambeth Palace and Stafford and Apsley Houses; witnessed a special performance of Irving's *Merchant of Venice*; were elected honorary members of the City Liberal, Junior Athenæum, National Liberal, and Savage Clubs; and, generally speaking, enjoyed themselves after the methods current during that period. They also read forty-six papers, which now alone remain a stately record of their proceedings.

I have lately spent a pleasant afternoon musing over these papers. Their variety is endless, and the dispositions of mind displayed by these librarians are wide as the poles asunder. Some of them babble like babies, others are evidently austere scholars; some are gravely bent on the best methods of classifying catalogues, economising space, and sorting borrowers' cards; others, scorning such mechanical details, bid us regard libraries, and consequently librarians, as the primary factors in human evolution. "Where," asks Mr. Ernest Cushing Richardson, the librarian of Princeton University, New Jersey, U.S.A., "lies the germ of the library?" He answers his own question after the following convincing fashion: "At the point where a definitely formed concept from another's mind is placed beside one's own idea for integration, the result being a definite new form, including the substance of both." The pointsman who presides over this junction is the librarian.

The young woman of whom Mr. Matthews, the well-known librarian of Bristol, tells us, who, being a candidate for the post of assistant librarian, boldly pronounced Rider Haggard to be the author of the *Idylls of the King*, Southey of *The Mill on the Floss*, and Mark Twain of *Modern Painters*, undoubtedly placed her own ideas at the service of Bristol alongside the preconceived conceptions of Mr. Matthews; but she was rejected all the same.

To speak seriously, who are librarians, and whence come they in such numbers? Of Bodley's librarian we have heard, and all the lettered world honours the name of Richard Garnett, late keeper of the printed books at the British Museum. But beyond these and half a dozen others a great darkness prevails. This ignorance is well illustrated by a pleasing anecdote told at the Conference by Mr. MacAlister:

Only the day before yesterday, on the Calais boat, I was introduced to a world-famed military officer who, when he understood I had some connection with the Library Association, exclaimed: "Why, you're just the man I want! I have been anxious of late about my man, old Atkins. You see the old boy, with a stoop, sheltering behind the funnel. Poor old beggar! quite past his work, but as faithful as a dog. It has just occurred to me that if you could shove him into some snug library in the country, I'd be awfully grateful to you. His one fault is a fondness for reading, and so a library would be just the thing.''

The usual titled lady also turned up at the Conference. This time she was recommending her late cook for the post of librarian, alleging on her behalf the same strange trait of character—her fondness for reading. Here, of course, one recalls Mark Pattison's famous dictum, " The librarian who reads is lost," about which there is much to be said, both *pro* and *con*; but we must not be put off our inquiry, which is: Who are these librarians, and whence come they? They are the custodians of the 70,000,000 printed books (be the numbers a little more or less) in the public libraries of the Western world, and they come from guarding their treasures. They deserve our friendliest consideration. If occasionally their enthusiasm provokes a smile, it is, or should be, of the kindliest. When you think of 70,000,000 books, instinctively you wish to wash your hands. Nobody knows what dust is who has not divided his time between the wine-cellar and the library. The work of classification, of indexing, of packing away, must be endless. Great men have arisen who have grappled with these huge problems. We read respectfully of Cutter's rules, which are to the librarian even as Kepler's laws to the astronomer. We have also heard of Poole's index. We bow our heads. Both Cutter and Poole are Americans. The parish of St. Pancras has just, by an overwhelming majority, declined to have a free library, and consequently a librarian. Brutish St. Pancras!

Libraries are obviously of two kinds: those intended for popular use and those meant for the scholar. The ordinary free library, in the sense of Mr. Ewart's Act of Parliament of 1850, is a popular library where a wearied population turns for distraction. Fiction plays a large part. In some libraries 80 per cent. of the books in circulation are novels. Hence Mr. Goldwin Smith's splenetic remark, " People have no more right to novels than to theatre-tickets out of the taxes." Quite true; no more they have—or to public gardens or to beautiful pictures or to anything save to peep through the railings and down the areas of Mr. Gradgrind's fine new house in Park Lane.

When we are considering popular libraries, it does not do to expect too much of tired human nature. This popular kind of library was well represented—perhaps a little over-represented, at the Conference. All our American cousins are not Cutters and Pooles. There was Mr. Crunden, who keeps the public library at St. Louis, U.S.A. He is all against dull text-books. As a boy he derived his inspiration from Sargent's *Standard Speaker*, and the interesting sketch he gives us of his education makes us wonder whether amidst his multitudinous reading he ever encountered Newman's marvellous description and handling of the young and over-read Mr. Brown, which is to be found under the heading " Elementary Studies " in *Lectures and Essays on University Subjects*.

I shuddered just a little on reading in Mr. Crunden's paper of the boy who, before he was nine, had read Bulfinch's *Age of Chivalry* and *Age of Charlemagne*, Bryant's *Translation of the " Iliad,"* a prose translation of the *Odyssey*, Malory's *King Arthur*, *and several other versions of the Arthurian legend*, Prescott's *Peru* and *Mexico*, Macaulay's *Lays*, Longfellow's *Hiawatha* and *Miles Standish*, the Jungle Books, and other books too numerous to mention. A famous list, but perilously long.

Mr. Crunden supports his case for varied reading by quotations from all quarters—Dr. William T. Harris, President Eliot, Professor Mackenzie, Charles Dudley Warner, Sir John Lubbock—but their scraps of wisdom or of folly do not remove my uneasiness about the digestion of the little boy who, before he was nine years old, had (not content with Malory) read several versions of the Arthurian legend!

Ladies make excellent librarians, and have tender hearts for children, and so we find a paper written by a lady librarian, entitled *Books that Children Like*. She quotes some interesting letters from children: " I like books about ancient history and books about knights, also stories of adventure, and mostly books with a deep plot and mystery about them." " I do not like *Gulliver's Travels*, because I think they are silly." " I read *Little Men*. I did not like this book." " I like *Ivanhoe*, by Scott, better than any." " My favourite books are *Tom Sawyer*, *Uncle Tom's Cabin*, and *Scudder's American History*. I like Tom Sawyer because he was so jolly, Uncle Tom because he was so faithful, and Nathan Hale because he was so brave." These are unbought verdicts no wise man will despise.

All this is popular enough. But the unpopular library must not be overlooked, for, after all, libraries are for the learned. We must not let the babes and sucklings, or the weary seamstress or badgered clerk, or even the working-man, ride rough-shod over Salmasius and Scaliger. In the papers of Mr. Garnett, Mr. Pollard, Mr. Dziatzko, Mr. Cutter, and others, the less popular and nobler side of the library is duly exhibited.

My anxiety about these librarians, who are beginning to be a profession by themselves, is how they are to be paid. That librarians must live is at least as obvious in their case as in that of any other class. They must also, if they are to be of any use, be educated. In 1878 the late Mr. Robert Harrison, who for many years led a grimy life in the London Library, advocated £250 as a minimum annual salary for a competent librarian. But, as Mr. Ogle, of Bootle, pertinently asked at the Conference, " Are his views yet accepted ? " We fear not. Mr. Ogle courageously proceeds:

The fear of a charge of trades unionism has long kept librarians silent, but this matter is one of public importance, and affects educational progress. A School-Board rate of 6d. or 1s. is willingly paid to teach our youth to read. Shall an additional 2d. be grudged to turn that reading talent into right and safe channels, where it may work for the public welfare and economy?

Festina lente, good Mr. Ogle, I beseech you. That way fierce controversy and, it may be, disaster lies. Do not stir the Philistine within us. The British nation is still savage under the skin. It has no real love for books, libraries, or librarians. In its hidden heart it deems them all superfluous. Anger it, and it may in a fit of temper sweep you all away. The loss of our free librarians would indeed be grievous. Never again could they meet in conference and read papers full of quaint things and odd memories. What, for example, can be more amusing than Mr. Cowell's reminiscences of forty years' library work in Liverpool, of the primitive days when a youthful Dicky Sam (for so do the inhabitants of that city call themselves) mistook the *Flora of Liverpool* for a book either about a ship or a heroine? He knows better now. And what shall we say of the Liverpool brush-maker who, at a meeting of the library committee, recited a poem in praise of woman, containing the following really magnificent line?—

> The heart that beats fondest is found in the stays.

There is nothing in Roscoe or Mrs. Hemans (local bards) one-half so fine. Long may librarians live and flourish! May their salaries increase, if not by leaps and bounds, yet in steady proportions. Yet will they do well to remember that books are not everything.

LAWYERS AT PLAY

1905

THAT dreary morass, that Serbonian bog, the Bacon-Shakespeare controversy, has been lately lit up as by the flickering light of a will-o'-the-wisp, by the almost simultaneous publication of an imaginary charge delivered to an equally imaginary jury by a judge of no less eminence than the late Lord Penzance (that tough Erastian) and of the still bolder *jeu d'esprit*, *A Report of the Trial of an Issue in Westminster Hall, June 20th*, 1627, which is the work of the unbridled fancy of His Honour Judge Willis, late Treasurer of the Inner Temple, and a man most intimately acquainted with the literature of the seventeenth century.

Neither production of these playful lawyers, clothed though they be in the garb of judicial procedure, is in the least likely to impress the lay mind with that sense of " impartiality " or " indifference " which is supposed to be an attribute of justice, or, indeed, with anything save the unfitness of the machinery of an action at law for the determination of any matter which invokes the canons of criticism and demands the arbitrament of a well-informed and lively taste.

Lord Penzance, who favours the Baconians, made no pretence of impartiality, and says outright in his preface that his readers " must not expect to find in these pages an equal and impartial leaning of the judge alternately to the case of both parties, as would, I hope, be found in any judicial summing-up of the evidence in a real judicial inquiry." And, he adds, " the form of a summing-up is only adopted for convenience, but it is in truth very little short of an argument for the plaintiffs, *i.e.*, the Baconians."

Why any man, judge or no judge, who wished to prepare an argument on one side of a question should think fit to cast that argument for convenience' sake in the form of a judicial summing-up of both sides is, and must remain, a puzzle.

Judge Willis, who is a Shakespearean, bold and unabashed, is not content with a mere summing-up, but, with a gravity and wealth of detail worthy of De Foe, has presented us with what purports to be a verbatim report of so much of the proceedings in a suit of Hall *v.* Russell as were concerned with the trial before a jury of the simple issue—whether William Shakespeare, of Stratford-upon-Avon, " the testator in the cause of *Hall v. Russell*," was the author of the plays in the Folio of 1623. We are favoured with the names of counsel employed, who snarl at one another with such startling verisimilitude, whilst the remarks that fall from the bench do so with such natural-ness, that it is perhaps not surprising, or any very severe reflection upon his literary *esprit*, that a member of the Bar, having heard Judge Willis deliver his lecture in the Inner Temple Hall, re-paired next day to the library to study at his leisure the hitherto unnoted case of *Hall v. Russell*. Ten witnesses are put in the box to prove the affirmative—that Shakespeare was the author of the plays. Mr. Blount and M. Jaggard, the publishers of the Folio, give a most satisfactory account of the somewhat crucial point—how they came by the manuscripts, with all the amendments and corrections, and pass lightly over the fact that those manuscripts had disappeared. " Rare Ben Jonson " in the witness-box is a masterpiece of dramatic invention; he demolishes Bacon's advocate with magnificent vitality. John Selden makes a stately witness, and Francis Meres a very useful one. Generally speaking, the weakest part in these interesting proceedings is the cross-examination. I have heard the learned judge do better in old days. No witnesses are called for the Baconians, though all the writings of the great philosopher were put in for what they were worth. The Lord Chief Justice, who seems to have been a friend of Shakespeare's, sums up dead in his favour, and the jury (with whose names we are not supplied, which is a pity—Bunyan or De Foe would have given them to us), after a short absence, a quarter of an hour, return a Shakespearean verdict, which of course ought by rights to make the whole question *res judicata.*

But it has done nothing of the kind. Could we really ask Blount and Jaggard how they came by the manuscripts, and who made the corrections, and did we believe their replies, why, then a stray Baconian here and there might reluctantly abandon his strange fancy; but as *Hall v. Russell* is Judge Willis's joke, it will convert no Baconians any more than Dean Sherlock's once celebrated *Trial of the Witnesses* compels belief in the Resurrection.

The question in reality is a compound one. Did Shakespeare write the plays ? If yes, the matter is at rest. If no—who did? If an author can be found—Bacon or anyone else—well and good. If no author can be found, Anon. wrote them—a conclusion which need terrify no one, since the plays would still remain within our reach, and William Shakespeare, apart from the plays, is very little to anybody who has not written his life.

But this is not the form the controversy has assumed. The anti-Shakespeareans are to a man Baconians, and fondly imagine that if only Will Shakespeare were put out of the way their man must step into the vacant throne. Lord Penzance in charging his jury told them that those of their number " who had studied the writings of Bacon " and were " keenly alive to his marvellous mental powers " would probably have " no difficulty," if once satisfied that the author they were seeking after was *not* Shakespeare, in finding as a fact that he *was* Bacon. But suppose James Spedding had been on that jury, and, rising in his place, had spoken as follows:

> My Lord,—If any man has ever studied the writings of Bacon, I have. For twenty-five years I have done little else. If any man is keenly alive to his marvellous mental powers, I am that man. I am also deeply read in the plays attributed to Shakespeare, and I think I am in a condition to say that, whoever was the real author, it was *not* Bacon.

That this is exactly what Spedding would have said we know from the letter he wrote on the subject to Mr. Holmes, reprinted in *Essays and Discussions*, and it completely upsets the whole scheme of arrangement of Lord Penzance's summing-up, which proceeds on the easy footing that the more difficulties you throw in Shakespeare's path the smoother becomes Bacon's.

That there are difficulties in Shakespeare's path, some things very hard to explain, must be admitted. Lord Penzance makes the most of these. It is, indeed, a most extraordinary thing that anybody should have had the mother-wit to write the plays traditionally assigned to Shakespeare. Where did he get it from? How on earth did the plays get themselves written? Where, when, and how did the author pick up his multifarious learnings? Lord Penzance, good, honest man, is simply staggered by the extent of the playwright's information. The plays, so he says, " teem with erudition," and can only have been written by someone who had the classics at his finger-ends, modern languages on the tip of his tongue—by someone who had travelled far and read deeply; and, above all, by a man who had spent at least a year in a conveyancer's chambers! And yet, when this has been said, would Lord Penzance have added that the style and character of the playwright is the style and character of a really learned man of his period! Can anything less like such a style be imagined? Once genius is granted, heaven-born genius, a mother-wit beyond the dreams of fancy, and then plain humdrum men, ordinary judicial intelligences, will do well to be on their guard against it. " Beware—beware! he is fooling thee." Shakespeare's genius has simply befooled Lord Penzance. Seafaring men, after reading *The Tempest*, are ready to maintain that its author must have been for at least a year before the mast. As for Shakespeare's law, which has taken in so many matter-of-fact practitioners, one can now refer to Ben Jonson's evidence in *Hall v. Russell*, where that

great dramatist has no difficulty in showing that
if none but a lawyer could have written Shakespeare's plays, a lawyer alone could have preached
Thomas Adams's sermons. Judge Willis's profound knowledge of sound old divinity has served
him here in good stead. The fact is it is simply
impossible to exaggerate the quick-wittedness and
light-heartedness of a great literary genius. The
absorbing power, the lightning-like faculty of apprehension, the instant recognition of the uses to
which any fact or fancy can be put, the infinite
number and delicacy of the mental feelers, thrust
out in all directions, which belong to the creative
brain and keep it in tremulous and restless activity,
are quite enough so to differentiate the possessor
of these endowments from his fellow mortals as
to make comparison impossible. Shakespeare the
actor was by the common consent of his enemies
one of the deftest fellows that ever made use of
other men's materials—" Convey, the wise it call."
I will again quote Spedding:

If Shakespeare was not trained as a scholar or a man of
science, neither do the works attributed to him show traces
of trained scholarship or scientific education. Given the
faculties, you will find that all the acquired knowledge, art,
and dexterity which the Shakespearean plays imply were
easily attainable by a man who was labouring in his vocation
and had nothing else to do.

I greatly prefer this cool judgment of a scholar
deeply read in Elizabethan lore to Lord Penzance's
heated and almost breathless admiration for the
" teeming erudition " of the plays.

Lord Penzance likewise displays a very creditable
non-acquaintance with the disposition of authors
one to another. He is quite shocked at the callous-
ness of Shakespeare's contemporaries to Shake-

speare if he were indeed the author of the Quartos which bore his name in his lifetime. But as it cannot be suggested that in, say, 1600 it was generally known that Shakespeare was not the author of these plays, it is hard to see how his contemporaries can be acquitted of indifference to his prodigious superiority over themselves. Authors, however, never take this view. Shakespeare's contemporaries thought him a mighty clever fellow and no more. Why, even Wordsworth was well persuaded he could write like Shakespeare had he been so minded. Mr. Arnold remained all his life honestly indifferent to and sceptical about the fame of both Tennyson and Browning. Great living lawyers and doctors do not invariably idolise each other, nor do the lawyers and doctors in a small way of business always speak well of those in a big way. The poets and learned critics of the seventeenth and eighteenth centuries—Dryden, Pope, Johnson —looked upon Shakespeare with an indulgent eye, as a great but irregular genius, after much the same fashion as did the old sea-dogs of Nelson's day regard the hero of Trafalgar. " Do not criticise him too harshly," said Lord St. Vincent; " there can only be one Nelson."

These are not the real difficulties, though they seem to have pressed somewhat heavily on Lord Penzance.

The circumstances attendant upon the publication of the Folio of 1623 are undoubtedly puzzling. Shakespeare died in 1616, leaving behind him more than forty plays circulating in London and more or less associated with his name. His will, a most elaborate document, does not contain a single reference to his literary life or labours. Seven years after his death the Folio appears, which contains twenty-six plays out of the forty just referred to, and ten extra plays which had never before been in print, and about six of which there is a very scanty Shakespearean tradition. Of the twenty-six old plays, seventeen had been printed in small Quartos, possibly surreptitiously, in Shakespeare's lifetime, but the Folio does not reprint from these Quartos, but from enlarged, amended, and enormously improved copies. Messrs. Heminge and Condell,[1] the editors of this priceless treasure, the First Folio, wrote a long-winded dedication to Lords Pembroke and Montgomery, which contains but one pertinent passage, in which they ask their readers to believe that it had been the office of the editors to collect and publish the author's " mere writings," he being dead, and to offer them, not " maimed and deformed," in surreptitious and stolen copies, but " cured and perfect of their limbs and all the rest, absolute in their numbers as he conceived them, who as he was a happie imitator of Nature was a most gentle expresser of it. His mind and hand went together, and what he thought, he uttered with that easiness, that we have scarce received from him a blot in his papers."

From whose custody did those " papers " come? Where had they been all the seven years? Of what did they consist? If in truth unblotted, all the seventeen Quartos as well as the new plays must have been printed from fair manuscript copies. From whom were these unblotted copies

---

[1] How many Londoners are aware that there is in their city a fine memorial outside a church of these two editors gazing at a bust of Shakespeare? Have " editors " ever been so honoured even in their own parish?

received, and what became of them? The silence of these players is irritating and perplexing,— though, possibly, the explanation of the mystery, were it forthcoming, would be, as often happens, of the simplest. It may be that these unblotted copies were in the theatre all the time.

Whether these interrogatories, now unanswerable, raise doubts in the mind of sufficient potency to destroy the tradition of centuries, and to prevent us from sharing the conviction of Milton, of Dryden, of Pope and Johnson that Shakespeare was the author of Shakespeare's plays, must be left for individual consideration. But, however destructive these doubts may prove, they do not go a yard of the way to let in Bacon.

One more I will quote Spedding, for he, of all the moderns, by virtue of his taste and devouring studies, is the best qualified to speak:

Aristotle was an extraordinary man. Plato was an extraordinary man. That two men each severally so extraordinary should have been living at the same time in the same place was a very extraordinary thing. But would it diminish the wonder to suppose the two to be one? So I say of Bacon and Shakespeare. That a human being possessed of the faculties necessary to make a Shakespeare should exist is extraordinary. That a human being possessed of the necessary faculties to make Bacon should exist is extraordinary. That two such human beings should have been living in London at the same time was more extraordinary still. But that one man should have existed possessing the faculties and opportunities necessary to make *both* would have been the most extraordinary thing of all. (Spedding's *Essays and Discussions*, 1879, pp. 371, 372.)

Great writers, especially being contemporary, have many features in common, but if they are really great writers they write naturally, and nature is always individual. I doubt whether there are five lines together to be found in Bacon which could be mistaken for Shakespeare, or five lines in Shakespeare which could be mistaken for Bacon, by one who was familiar with their several styles and practised in such observations. (*Ibid.*, p. 373.)

GOSSIP IN A LIBRARY

1905

THERE were no books in Eden, and there will be none in heaven; but between times —and it is of those I speak—it is otherwise. Mr. Thomas Greenwood, in a most meritorious work on Public Libraries, supplies figures which show that, without counting pamphlets (which are books gone wrong) or manuscripts (which are books *in terrorem*), there are at this present moment upwards of 71,000,000 printed books in bindings in the several public libraries of Europe and America. To estimate the number and extent of private libraries in those countries is impossible. In many large houses there are no books at all—which is to make ignorance visible; whilst in many small houses there are, or seem to be, nothing else— which is to make knowledge inconvenient; yet as there are upwards of 280,000,000 of inhabitants of Europe and America, I cannot greatly err if a passion for round numbers drives me to the assertion that there are at least 300,000,000 books in these countries, not counting bibles and prayer-books. It is a poor show! Russia is greatly to blame, her European population of 88,000,000 being so badly provided for that it brings down the average. Were Russia left out in the cold, we might, were our books to be divided amongst our population *per capita*, rely upon having two volumes apiece. This would not afford Mr. Gosse (the title of one of whose books I have stolen) much material for gossip, particularly as his two books might easily chance to be duplicates. There are no habits of man more alien to the doctrine of the Communist than those of the collector, and there is no collector, not even that basest of them all, the Belial of his tribe, the man who collects money, whose love of private property is intenser, whose sense of the joys of ownership is keener than the book-collector's. Mr. William Morris once hinted at a good time coming, when at almost every street corner there would be a public library, where beautiful and rare books will be kept for citizens to examine. The citizen will first wash his hands in a parochial basin, and then dry them on a parochial towel, after which ritual he will walk in and stand *en queue* until it comes to be his turn to feast his eye upon some triumph of modern or some miracle of old typography. He will then return to a bookless home proud and satisfied, tasting of the joy that is in widest commonalty spread.[1] Alas! he will do nothing of the kind, not, at least, if he is one of those in whom the old Adam of the bookstalls still breathes. A public library must always be an abomination. To enjoy a book, you must own it. " John Jones his book," that is the best book-plate. I have never admired the much-talked-of book-plate of Grolier, which, in addition to his own name, bore the ridiculous device *Et Amicorum*. Fudge! There is no evidence that Grolier ever lent any man a book

[1] On going through the proofs of this collected edition I am always coming across this Wordsworthian quotation, and have grown sick of its vain repetition; but I do not feel justified in striking it out even occasionally.

with his plate in it. His collection was dispersed after his death, and then sentimentalists fell a-weeping over his supposed generosity. It would be as reasonable to commend the hospitality of a dead man because you found amongst his papers a vast number of unposted invitations to dinner upon a date he long outlived. Sentiment is seldom in place, but on a book-plate it is peculiarly odious. To paste in each book an invitation to steal it, as Grolier seems to have done, is foolish; but so also is it to invoke, as some book-plates do, curses upon the heads of all subsequent possessors—as if any man who wanted to add a volume to his collection would be deterred by such braggadocio. But this is a digression. Public libraries can never satisfy the longings of book-collectors any more than can the private libraries of other people. Who ever really cared a snap of his fingers for the contents of another man's library, unless he is known to be dying? It is a humorous spectacle to watch one book-collector exhibiting his stores to another. If the owner is a gentleman, as he usually is, he affects indifference—" A poor thing," he seems to say, " yet mine own "; whilst the visitor, if human, as he always is, exhibits disgust. If the volume proffered for the visitor's examination is a genuine rarity, not in his own collection, he surlily inquires how it was come by; whilst if it is no great thing, he testily expresses his astonishment it should be thought worth keeping, and this although he has the very same edition at home.

On the other hand, though actual visits to other men's libraries rarely seem to give pleasure, the perusal of the catalogues of such libraries has always been a favourite pastime of collectors; but this can be accounted for without in any way aspersing the truth of the general statement that the only books a lover of them takes pleasure in are his own.

Mr. Gosse's recent volume, *Gossip in a Library*, is a very pleasing example of the pleasure taken by a book-hunter in his own books. Just as some men and more women assume your interest in the contents of their nurseries, so Mr. Gosse seeks to win our ears as he talks to us about some of the books on his shelves. He has secured my willing attention, and is not likely to be disappointed of a considerable audience.

We live in vocal times, when small birds make melody on every bough. The old book-collectors were a taciturn race—the Bindleys, the Sykeses, the Hebers. They made their vast collections in silence; their own tastes, fancies, predilections, they concealed. They never gossiped of their libraries; their names are only preserved to us by the prices given for their books after their deaths. Bindley's copy fetched £3 10s., Sykes' £4 15s. Thus is the buyer of to-day tempted to his doom, forgetful of the fact that these great names are only quoted when the prices realised at their sales were more than those now demanded.

But solacing as is the thought of those grave, silent times, indisposed as one often is for the chirpy familiarities of this present, it is, or it ought to be, a pious, and therefore pleasant, reflection that there never was a time when more people found delight in book-hunting, or were more willing to pay for and read about their pastime than now.

Rich people may, no doubt, still be met with who think it a serious matter to buy a book if it cost more than 3s. 9d. It was recently alleged in an affidavit made by a doctor in lunacy that for a well-to-do bachelor to go into the Strand, and in the course of the same morning spend £5 in the purchase of " old books," was a ground for belief in his insanity and for locking him up. These, however, are but vagaries, for it is certain that the number of people who will read a book like Mr. Gosse's steadily increases. This is its justification, and it is a complete one. It can never be wrong to give pleasure. To talk about books is better than to read about them, but, as a matter of hard fact, the opportunities life affords of talking about books are very few. The mood and the company seldom coincide; when they do, it is delightful, but they seldom do.

Mr. Gosse's book ought not to be read in a fierce, nagging spirit which demands, What is the good of this? or, Who cares for that? His talk, it must be admitted, is not of masterpieces. The books he takes down are—in some instances, at all events —sad trash. *Smart's Poems*, for example, in an edition of 1752, which does not contain the " David," is not a book which, viewed baldly and by itself, can be honestly described as worth reading. This remark is not prompted by jealousy, for I have the book myself, and seldom fail to find the list of subscribers interesting, for, among many other famous names, it contains those of " Mr. Gray, Peter's College, Cambridge," " Mr. Samuel Richardson, editor of *Clarissa*, two books," and " Mr. Voltaire, Historiographer of France." There

are various Johnsons among the subscribers, but
not Samuel, who apparently would liefer pray with
Kit Smart than buy his poetry, thereby showing
the doctor's usual piety and good sense.[1]

Although the nagging spirit before referred to is
to be deprecated, it is sometimes amusing to lose
your temper with your own hobby. If a book-
collector ever does this, he longs to silence whole
libraries of bad authors. " 'Tis an inglorious
acquist," says Joseph Glanvill in his famous *Vanity
of Dogmatizing*—I quote from the first edition,
1661, though the second is the rarer—" to have
our heads or volumes laden as were Cardinal
Campeius his mules, with old and useless luggage."
" 'Twas this vain idolizing of authors," Glanvill
had just before observed, " which gave birth to
that silly vanity of *impertinent citations*, and in-
ducing authority in things neither requiring nor
deserving it." In the same strain he proceeds,
" Methinks 'tis a pitiful piece of knowledge that can
be learnt from an *Index* and a poor ambition to be
rich in the inventory of another's Treasure. To
boast a *Memory* (the most that these pedants can
aim at) is but an humble ostentation. 'Tis better
to own a Judgment, though but with a *Curta
Supellex* of coherent notions, than a *Memory* like
a sepulchre furnished with a load of broken and dis-
carnate bones." Thus far the fascinating Glanvill,
whose mode of putting things is powerful.

There are times when the contemplation of huge
libraries wearies, and when even the names of
Bindley and Sykes fail to please. Dr. Johnson's

[1] " He insisted on people praying with him, and I'd as lief pray
with Kit Smart as with anyone else."

library sold at Christie's for £247 9s. Let those sneer who dare. It was Johnson, not Bindley, who wrote the *Lives of the Poets*.

But, of course, no sensible man ever really quarrels with his hobby. A little petulance every now and again variegates the monotony of routine. Mr. Gosse tells us in his book that he cannot resist Restoration comedies. The bulk of them he knows to be as bad as bad can be. He admits they are not literature—whatever that may mean—but he intends to go on collecting them all the same till the inevitable hour when Death collects him. This is the true spirit; herein lies happiness, which consists in being interested in something, it does not much matter what. In this spirit let me take up Mr. Gosse's book again, and read what he has to tell about *Pharamond ; or, the History of France. A Fam'd Romance. In Twelve Parts*, or about Mr. John Hopkins' collection of poems, printed by Thomas Warren for Bennett Bunbury at the Blue Anchor, in the Lower Walk of the New Exchange, 1700. The Romance is dull, and as it occupies more than 1100 folio pages may be pronounced tedious, and the poetry is bad, but as I do not seriously intend ever to read a line of either the Romance or the poetry, this is no great matter.

TOMKINS REDIVIVUS

BEING A FRAGMENT FROM A SPEECH "FOR THE
LIBERTY OF UNLICENSED PRINTING" MADE
BEFORE THE "WHITEFRIARS" ON DECEM-
BER 5TH, 1917.

IT has often given me a little needful relaxation whilst reading *Paradise Lost* to recall the fact that the first man on whom was cast the *duty* of reading this famous epic *all through* (for Ellwood read the manuscript in 1665 for pleasure and from friendship) was a clerical gentleman of the name of Tomkins—Thomas Tomkins, who in 1666–67 chanced to be Archbishop Sheldon's Chaplain and Deputy Licenser of Poetry, whether amatorious or majestical.

Oliver Cromwell, when he came into his own, abolished the twenty Presbyterians who in the early days of the Commonwealth had been constituted State Licensers; and against whom, therefore, the mighty shafts of the *Areopagitica* (November 1645) had been hurled with all the force and fury of a demigod ; but the Second, Charles, when restored, also restored the Censor not, we may be sure, in the interest of religion or morality, but for the sake of a quiet, sensible, easy life, and then proceeded to classify literature into subjects; and with that ironical humour of his which must have made Sir Charles Sedley (the only man in his Royal Master's expressed opinion fit to be " Apollo's Viceroy ") scream with laughter and roll on the floor, assigned poetry, in all its branches, to the Archbishop of Canterbury, who, in his turn, passed the job on to one of his chaplains.

Some of Milton's biographers, and like most great poets he has had too many, have thought it seemly to poke fun at Tomkins; and yet to be forced, as he was by virtue of his office, to be the first to give judgment upon the effect likely to be produced by the sudden appearance of such a poem as this of Milton's, in such a city as the City of London, in the year 1667, was no joke; and so Tomkins found out as he went on with his reading.

The Archbishop's Chaplain was a highly-educated man, being indeed a Fellow of All Souls, even as are to-day Lord Curzon, Sir John Simon, the Editor (by no means to be confused with the proprietor) of the *Times* newspaper, and many another living pundit, all notoriously of good taste. What is more, he was a poet on his own account; and as Sainte-Beuve observes: " Parler des poètes est toujours une chose bien délicate, et surtout quand on l'a été un peu soi-même." It is true that the verses of Tomkins are no longer on our lips, but we may be sure they were frequently on his, and this must, as indeed Sainte-Beuve in his exquisite French so delicately suggests, have made his task all the more difficult. I am confident that no better equipped man could be found to-day by any government, however well constructed, to consent to discharge the duty of a censor than was, in 1667, this accomplished Fellow of All Souls.

But consider for a moment the situation. On one side we discern the sublime author of the

Areopagitica, blind, baffled, poor, solitary, almost in hiding, in precarious health, and never at the best of times of the sweetest of tempers, feverishly anxious to see the poem he had been for so long composing by night and dictating by day, a poem which he knew, once published, must secure for him that immortality of fame on which he had set his heart since boyhood, well printed and off his mind, ere the " blind fury with abhorrèd shears " should enter his dark chamber and slit his " thin-spun life." On the other side we see Tomkins in his room in Lambeth House, with the ten books of *Paradise Lost* spread out before him, wondering what his duty was with regard to this puzzling poem, written by a man who, not so many years ago, had made all Europe resound with his " defences " of the murder of a King. Tomkins may have taken his time over the perusal of *Paradise Lost*; but do we not the same? The author shut up in his perpetual darkness in Artillery Walk, leading to those Bunhill Fields where the author of *The Pilgrim's Progress*, another troubled Nonconformist, was soon destined to lie, fretted and fumed, and employing the abusive vocabulary of a Carlyle, inflamed by the genuine passion of a Dante, cursed Tomkins day and night. The chaplain still read on, and the more he read the less he liked. I can well understand it. What made the Censor restive and uncomfortable was not so much a passage up and down, but the revelation in its entirety of the Miltonic spirit, which seemed to him, sitting there in Lambeth, to call up from the vasty deep of Revolution,

Gorgons, Hydras, and Chimæras dire.

Tomkins was the first to perceive, for I doubt whether the mild Quakerism of the youthful Ellwood saw it clearly, that the real hero of this epic was the Devil, the first of all rebels, and the most successful, for are not half the nations at this moment under his direct domination, and most men vassals of his will? No wonder the Fellow of All Souls was frightened. Why, Dr. Johnson, a century later, though he could stomach most things in Literature, disliked this Miltonic spirit; whilst after the passage of yet another century, Mr. Gladstone frankly abhorred it.

Returning to Tomkins; he doggedly went on reading a bit every day, and finally, with a groan, passed the book. A long-established tradition, and I am a firm believer in literary traditions, tells us that the lines which continued to trouble him up to the last moment were those famous ones occurring in the first book describing a solar eclipse:

> As when the sun, new risen,
> Looks through the horizontal, misty air,
> Shorn of its beams, or from behind the moon,
> In dim eclipse, disastrous twilight sheds
> On half the nations, and with fear of change
> Perplexes Monarchs.

There are still many who deem these lines to be truly glorious, and, for all we know, Tomkins may have done so, though that is perhaps unlikely, so diverse are they from his own. But Tomkins had nothing to do with glory; his job was Treason. "With fear of change perplexing Monarchs." What would Charles the Second, who had more intellectual curiosity than all our Monarchs put together, think of these lines? Charles feared neither God nor devil, but he was always des-

perately scared by the bare thought of Change.
He had lived, even as I have done, cheaply in
France. Nor could the Chaplain be expected to
forget himself. "How," he must have asked himself, "would change benefit me?" Were the King
to be turned out of Hampton Court, that loveliest
of palaces, what might not happen to Tomkins's
own snug quarters by the shores of the same ancient
river? The Chaplain bit his pen and, only half-
convinced, signed the "Imprimatur." So have I
seen the Chairman of Committees in the High
Court of Parliament, when sorely badgered over
an amendment, fling himself back, saying: "I
am still in doubt on the point of order, but I will
give the honourable Member the benefit of it, and
now call upon him to move his amendment."
After this fashion, and after no other, did *Paradise
Lost* appear in 1667 "licensed and entred according
to order."

Tomkins died young, in his thirty-seventh year,
only surviving by a twelvemonth the great poet
whose name alone has kept his alive. According
to the *D.N.B.*, he is buried in the chancel of a
parish church in Worcestershire. His portrait, if
one is extant, should certainly be hung up in the
Dining Hall of All Souls; and if no portrait is
procurable, it might be well, in order to keep his
memory green in his old college, to hang up one of
Milton's in its stead. I may observe, whilst passing
away from this branch of my subject, that the
manuscript of *Paradise Lost* has never been recovered. Would it be worth while looking for
it in the grave of Tomkins?

OLD PLEASURE GARDENS [1]

1905

T HIS is an honest book, disfigured by no
fine writing or woeful attempts to make us
dance round maypoles with our ancestors.
Terribly is our good language abused by the swell-
mob of stylists, for whom it is certainly not enough
that Chatham's language is their mother's tongue.
May the Devil fly away with these artists; though
no sooner had he done so than we should be " wae "
for auld Nicky-ben.   Mr. Wroth, of the British
Museum, and his brother, Mr. Arthur Wroth, are
above such vulgar pranks, and never strain after
the picturesque, but in the plain garb of honest
men carry us about to the sixty-four gardens where
the eighteenth-century Londoner, his wife and
family—the John Gilpins of the day—might take
their pleasure either sadly, as indeed best befits
our pilgrim state, or uproariously to deaden the
ear to the still small voice of conscience—the pangs
of slighted love, the law's delay, the sluggish step
of Fortune, the stealthy strides of approaching
poverty, or any other of the familiar incidents of
our mortal life.   The sixty-two illustrations which
adorn the book are as honest as the letterpress.
There is a most delightful Morland depicting a very
stout family indeed regaling itself *sub tegmine fagi*.

[1] *Pleasure Gardens of the Eighteenth Century* by Warwick Wroth,
F.S.A., assisted by Arthur Edgar Wroth.   London: Macmillan
and Co.

254

It is called a "Tea Party." A voluminous mother holds in her roomy lap a very fat baby, whose back and neck are full upon you as you stare into the picture. And what a jolly back and innocent neck it is! Enough to make every right-minded woman cry out with pleasure. Then there is the highly respectable father stirring his cup and watching with placid content a gentleman in lace and ruffles attending to the wife, whilst the two elder children play with a wheezy dog.

In these pages we can see for ourselves the British public—God rest its soul!—enjoying itself. This honest book is full of *la bourgeoisie*. The rips and the painted ladies occasionally, it is true, make their appearance, but they are reduced to their proper proportions. The Adam and Eve Tea Gardens, St. Pancras, have a somewhat rakish sound, calculated to arrest the jaded attention of the debauchee, but what has Mr. Wroth to tell us about them?

About the beginning of the present century it could still be described as an agreeable retreat, "with enchanting prospects"; and the gardens were laid out with arbours, flowers, and shrubs. Cows were kept for making syllabubs, and on summer afternoons a regular company met to play bowls and trap-ball in an adjacent field. One proprietor fitted out a mimic squadron of frigates in the garden, and the long room was used a good deal for beanfeasts and tea-drinking parties (p. 127).

What a pleasant place! Syllabubs! How sweet they sound! Nobody worried then about diphtheria; they only died of it. Mimic frigates, too! What patriotism! These gardens are as much lost as those of the Hesperides. A cemetery swallowed them up—the cemetery which adjoins the old St. Pancras churchyard. The Tavern, shorn of its amenities, a mere drink-shop, survived as far down the century as 1874, soon after which date it also disappeared. Hornsey Wood House has a name not unknown in the simple annals of tea-drinking. It is now part of Finsbury Park, but in the middle of the last century its long-room " on popular holydays, such as Whit Sunday, might be seen crowded as early as nine or ten in the morning with a motley assemblage eating rolls and butter and drinking tea at an extravagant price." " Hone remembered the old Hornsey Wood House as it stood embowered, and seeming a part of the wood. It was at that time kept by two sisters—Mrs. Lloyd and Mrs. Collier—and these aged dames were usually to be found before their door on a seat between two venerable oaks, wherein swarms of bees hived themselves."

What a picture is this of these vanished dames! Somewhere, I trust, they are at peace.

> And there, they say, two bright and aged snakes,
> Who once were Cadmus and Harmonia,
> Bask in the glens or on the warm sea-shore.

A more raffish place was the Dog and Duck in St. George's Fields, which boasted mineral springs, good for gout, stone, king's evil, sore eyes, and inveterate cancers. Considering its virtue, the water was a cheap liquor, for a dozen bottles could be had at the spa for a shilling. The Dog and Duck, though at last it exhibited depraved tastes, was at one time well conducted. Miss Talbot writes about it to Mrs. Carter, and Dr. Johnson advised his Thralia to try the waters. It was no mean place, but boasted a breakfast-room, a bowling-green, and a swimming-bath 200 feet long and 100 feet (nearly) broad. Mr. Wroth narrates the history of its fall with philosophical composure. In the hands of one Hedger the decencies were disregarded, and thieves made merry where once Miss Talbot sipped bohea. One of its frequenters, Charlotte Shaftoe, is said to have betrayed seven of her intimates to the gallows. Few visitors' lists could stand such a strain as Miss Shaftoe put upon hers. In 1799 the Dog and Duck was suppressed, and Bethlehem Hospital now reigns in its stead. "The Peerless Pool" has a Stevensonian sound. It was a dangerous pond behind Old Street, long known as "The Parlous or Perilous Pond" "because divers youth by swimming therein have been drowned." In 1743 a London jeweller called Kemp took it in hand, turned it into a pleasure bath, and renamed it, happily enough, "The Peerless Pool." It was a fine open-air bath, 170 feet long, more than 100 feet broad, and from 3 to 5 feet deep. "It was nearly surrounded by trees, and the descent was by marble steps to a fine gravel bottom, through which the springs that supplied the pool came bubbling up." Mr. Kemp likewise constructed a fish-pond. The enterprise met with success, and anglers, bathers, and at due seasons skaters, flocked to "The Peerless Pool." Hone describes how every Thursday and Saturday the boys from the Bluecoat School were wont to plunge into its depths. You ask its fate. It has been built over. Peerless Street, the second main turning on the left of the City Road just beyond Old Street in coming from the City, is all that is left to remind anyone of the once Parlous Pool, unless, indeed, it still occasionally creeps into a cellar and drowns cockroaches

instead of divers youths. The Three Hats, High-
bury Barn, Hampstead Wells, are not places to be
lightly passed over. In Mr. Wroth's book you
may read about them and trace their fortunes—
their fallen fortunes. After all, they have only
shared the fate of empires.

Of the most famous London gardens—Marylebone, Ranelagh, and, greatest of them all, Vauxhall
—Mr. Wroth writes at, of course, becoming
length. Marylebone Gardens, when at their largest,
comprised about eight acres. Beaumont Street,
part of Devonshire Street and of Devonshire Place
and Upper Wimpole Street, now occupy their site.
Music was the main feature of Marylebone. A band
played in the evening. Vocalists at different times
drew crowds. Masquerades and fireworks appeared
later in the history of the gardens, which usually
were open three nights of the week. Dr. Johnson's
turbulent behaviour, on the occasion of one of his
frequent visits, will easily be remembered. Marylebone, at no period, says Mr. Wroth, attained the
vogue of Ranelagh or the universal popularity of
Vauxhall. In 1776 the gardens were closed, and
two years later the builders began to lay out
streets. Ranelagh is, perhaps, the greatest achievement of the eighteenth century. Its Rotunda, built
in 1741, is compared by Mr. Wroth to the reading-
room of the British Museum. No need to give its
dimensions; only look at the print, and you will
understand what Johnson meant when he declared
that the *coup d'œil* of Ranelagh was the finest
thing he had ever seen. The ordinary charge for
admission was half-a-crown, which secured you tea
or coffee and bread-and-butter. The gardens were

usually open Mondays, Wednesdays, and Fridays,
and the amusements were music, tea-drinking,
walking, and talking. Mr. Wroth quotes a Frenchman, who, after visiting Ranelagh in 1800, calls it
" le plus insipide lieu d'amusement que l'on ait pu
imaginer," and even hints at Dante's Purgatory.
An earlier victim from Gaul thus records his experience of Ranelagh: "On s'ennuie avec de la
mauvaise musique, du thé et du beurre." So true
is it that the cheerfulness you find anywhere is the
cheerfulness you have brought with you. However,
despite the Frenchman, good music and singing
were at times to be heard at Ranelagh. The
nineteenth century would have nothing to do with
Ranelagh, and in 1805 it was pulled down. The
site now belongs to Chelsea Hospital. Cuper's
Gardens lacked the respectability of Marylebone
and the style of Ranelagh, but they had their
vogue during the same century. They were finely
situated on the south side of the Thames opposite
Somerset House. Cuper easily got altered into
Cupid; and when on the death of Ephraim Evans
in 1740 the business came to be carried on by his
widow, a comely dame who knew a thing or two,
it proved to be indeed a going concern. But the
new Licensing Bill of 1752 destroyed Cupid's
Garden, and Mrs. Evans was left lamenting and
wholly uncompensated. Of Vauxhall Mr. Wroth
treats at much length, and this part of his book is
especially rich in illustrations. Every lover of Old
London and old times and old prints should add
Mr. Wroth's book to his library.

OLD BOOKSELLERS

1905

THERE has just been a small flutter amongst those who used to be called stationers or text-writers in the good old days, before printing was, and when even Peers of the Realm (now so highly educated) could not sign their names, or, at all events, preferred not to do so—booksellers they are now styled—and the question which agitates them is discount. Having mentioned this, one naturally passes on.

No great trade has an obscurer history than the book trade. It seems to lie choked in mountains of dust which it would be suicidal to disturb. Men have lived from time to time of literary skill—Dr. Johnson was one of them—who had knowledge, extensive and peculiar, of the traditions and practices of " the trade," as it is proudly styled by its votaries; but nobody has ever thought it worth his while to make record of his knowledge, which accordingly perished with him, and is now irrecoverably lost.

In old days booksellers were also publishers, frequently printers, and sometimes paper-makers. Jacob Tonson not only owned Milton's *Paradise Lost*—for all time, as he fondly thought, for little did he dream of the fierce construction the House of Lords was to put upon the Copyright Act of Queen Anne—not only was Dryden's publisher, but also kept shop in Chancery Lane, and sold books across the counter. He allowed no discount, but, so we are told, " spoke his mind upon all occasions, and flattered no one," not even glorious John.

For a long time past the trades of bookselling and book-publishing have been carried on apart. This has doubtless rid booksellers of all the unpopularity which formerly belonged to them in their other capacity. This unpopularity is now heaped as a whole upon the publishers, who certainly need not dread the doom awaiting those of whom the world speaks well.

A tendency of the two trades to grow together again is perhaps noticeable. For my part, I wish they would. Some publishers are already booksellers, but the books they sell are usually only new books. Now it is obvious that the true bookseller sells books both old and new. Some booksellers are occasional publishers. May each usurp — or, rather, reassume — the business of the other whilst retaining his own!

The world, it must be admitted, owes a great deal of whatever information it possesses about the professions, trades, and occupations practised and carried on in its midst to those who have failed in them. Prosperous men talk " shop," but seldom write it. The book that tells us most about booksellers and bookselling in bygone days is the work of a crack-brained fellow who published and sold in the reigns of Queen Anne and George I., and died in 1733 in great poverty and obscurity. I refer to John Dunton, whose *Life and Errors* in the edition in two volumes edited by J. B. Nichols,

and published in 1818, is a common book enough
in the second-hand shops, and one which may be
safely recommended to everyone, except, indeed,
to the unfortunate man or woman who is not an
adept in the art, craft, or mystery of skipping.

The book will strangely remind the reader of
Amory's *Life of John Buncle*—those queer volumes
to which many a reader has been sent by Hazlitt's
intoxicating description of them in his *Round Table*,
and a few perhaps by a shy allusion contained
in one of the essays of Elia. The real John Dunton has not the boundless spirits of the fictitious
John Buncle; but in their religious fervour, their
passion for flirtation, their tireless egotism, and
their love of character-sketching, they greatly
resemble one another.

It is this last characteristic that imparts real
value to Dunton's book and makes it, despite
its verbiage and tortuosity, throb with human
interest. For example, he gives us a short sketch
of no less than 135 then living London booksellers
in this style:

Mr. Newton is full of kindness and good-nature. He is
affable and courteous in trade, and is none of those men of
forty whose religion is yet to chuse, for his mind (like his
looks) is serious and grave; and his neighbours tell me his
understanding does not improve too fast for his practice, for
he is not religious by start or sally, but is well fixed in the
faith and practice of a Church of England man—and has a
handsome wife into the bargain.

Most of the 135 booksellers were good men,
according to Dunton, but not all.

Mr. Lee in Lombard Street. Such a pirate, such a cor-
morant was never before. Copies, books, men, shops, all was
one. He held no propriety right or wrong, good or bad, till at
last he began to be known; and the booksellers, not enduring

so ill a man among them, spewed him out, and off he marched
to Ireland, where he acted as *felonious Lee* [1] as he did in London.
And as Lee lived a thief, so he died a hypocrite; for being
asked on his death-bed if he would forgive Mr. C. (that had
formerly wronged him), " Yes," said Lee, " if I die, I forgive
him; but if I happen to live, I am resolved to be revenged
on him."

The Act of Union destroyed the trade of these
pirates, but their felonious editions of eighteenth-
century authors still abound. Mr. Gladstone, I
need scarcely say, was careful in his Home Rule
Bill (which was denounced by thousands who never
read a line of it) to withdraw copyright from the
scope of action of his proposed Dublin Parliament.

There are nearly eleven hundred brief character-
sketches in Dunton's book of all sorts and kinds,
but with a preference for bookish people, divines,
both of the Establishment and out of it, printers
and authors. Sometimes, indeed, the description
is short enough, and tells one very little. To many
readers, references so curt to people of whom they
never heard, and whose names are recorded nowhere else, save on their mouldering grave-stones,
may seem tedious and trivial, but for others
they will have a strange fascination. Here are
a few examples:

Affable *Wiggins*.   His conversation is general but never
impertinent.

The kind and golden *Venables*. He is so good a man, and so
truly charitable, he that will write of him, must still write
more.

Mr. *Bury*—my old neighbour in Redcross Street. He is
a plain honest man, sells the best coffee in all the neighbourhood, and lives in this world like a spiritual stranger and
pilgrim in a foreign country.

Anabaptist (alias *Elephant*) *Smith*. He was a man of great
sincerity and happy contentment in all circumstances of life.

[1] This is Dunton's joke, not the printer's.

If an affection for passages of this kind be condemned as trivial, and akin to the sentimentalism of the man in Calverley's poem who wept over a box labelled " This side up," I will shelter myself behind Carlyle, who was evidently deeply moved, as his review of Boswell's Johnson proves, by the life-history of Mr. F. Lewis, " of whose birth, death, and whole terrestrial *res gestæ* this only, and, strange enough, this actually, survives—' Sir, he lived in London, and hung loose upon society. *Stat* PARVI *hominis umbra.*' " On that peg Carlyle's imagination hung a whole biography.

Dunton, who was the son of the Rector of Aston Clinton, was apprenticed, about 1675, to a London bookseller. He had from the beginning a great turn both for religion and love. He, to use his own phrase, " sat under the powerful ministry of Mr. Doolittle." " One Lord's day, and I remember it with sorrow, I was to hear the Rev. Mr. Doolittle, and it was then and there the beautiful Rachel Seaton gave me that fatal wound."

The first book Dunton ever printed was by the Rev. Mr. Doolittle, and was of an eminently religious character.

> One Lord's Day (and I am very sensible of the sin) I was strolling about just as my fancy led me, and, stepping into Dr. Annesley's meeting-place—where, instead of engaging my attention to what the Doctor said, I suffered both my mind and eyes to run at random—I soon singled out a young lady that almost charmed me dead; but, having made my inquiries, I found to my sorrow she was pre-engaged.

However, Dunton was content with the elder sister, one of the three daughters of Dr. Annesley. The one he first saw became the wife of the Reverend Samuel Wesley, and the mother of John and

Charles. The third daughter is said to have been married to Daniel Defoe.

As soon as he was out of his apprenticeship, Dunton set up business as a publisher and bookseller. He says grimly enough:

> A man should be well furnished with an honest policy if he intends to set out to the world nowadays. And this *is* no less necessary in a bookseller than in any other tradesman, for in that way there are plots and counter-plots, and a whole army of hackney authors that keep their grinders moving by the travail of their pens. These gormandizers will eat you the very life out of a *copy* so soon as ever it appears, for as the times go, *Original* and *Abridgement* are almost reckoned as necessary as man and wife.

The mischief to which Dunton refers was permitted by the stupidity of the judges, who refused to consider an abridgment of a book any interference with its copyright. Some learned judges have, indeed, held that an abridger is a benefactor, but as his benefactions are not his own, but another's, a shorter name might be found for him. The law on the subject is still uncertain.

Dunton proceeds:

> Printing was now the uppermost in my thoughts, and hackney authors began to ply me with *specimens* as earnestly and with as much passion and concern as the watermen do passengers with *Oars* and *Scullers*. I had some acquaintance with this generation in my apprenticeship, and had never any warm affection for them, in regard I always thought their great concern lay more in *how much a sheet*, than in any generous respect they bore to the *Commonwealth of Learning*; and indeed the learning itself of these gentlemen lies very often in as little room as their honesty, though they will pretend to have studied for six or seven years in the Bodleian Library, to have turned over the Fathers, and to have read and digested the whole compass both of human and ecclesiastic history, when, alas! they have never been able to understand a single page of St. Cyprian, and cannot tell you whether the Fathers lived before or after Christ.

Yet of one of this hateful tribe Dunton is able

to speak well. He declares Mr. Bradshaw to have
been the best accomplished hackney author he ever
met with. He pronounces his style incomparably
fine. He had quarrelled with him, but none the
less he writes:

> If Mr. Bradshaw is yet alive, I here declare to the world
> and to him that I freely forgive him what he owes, both in
> money and books, if he will only be so kind as to make me
> a visit. But I am afraid the worthy gentleman is dead, for
> he was wretchedly over-run with melancholy, and the very
> blackness of it reigned in his countenance. He had certainly
> performed wonders with his pen, had not his poverty pursued
> him and almost laid the necessity upon him to be unjust.

All hackney authors were not poor. Some of
the compilers and abridgers made what even now
would be considered by popular novelists large
sums. Scotsmen were very good at it. Gordon
and Campbell became wealthy men. If authors
had a turn for politics, Sir Robert Walpole was an
excellent paymaster. Arnall, who was bred an
attorney, is stated to have been paid £11,000 in
four years by the Government for his pamphlets.

> Come, then, I'll comply.
> Spirit of Arnall, aid me while I lie!

It cannot have been pleasant to read this, but
then Pope belonged to the opposition, and was a
friend of Lord Bolingbroke, and would consequently
say anything.

There is not a more interesting and artless autobiography to be read than William Hutton's, the
famous bookseller and historian of Birmingham.
Hutton has been somewhat absurdly called the
English Franklin. He is not in the least like
Franklin. He has none of Franklin's supreme
literary skill, and he was a loving, generous, and

tender-hearted man, which Franklin certainly was
not. Hutton's first visit to London was paid in
1749. He walked up from Nottingham, spent
three days in London, and then walked back to
Nottingham. The jaunt, if such an expression is
applicable, cost him eleven shillings less fourpence.
Yet he paid his way. The only money he spent
to gain admission to public places was a penny
to see Bedlam.

Interesting, however, as is Hutton's book, it
tells us next to nothing about bookselling, except
that in his hands it was a prosperous undertaking.

OUR GREAT MIDDLE CLASS

1905

THE republication of Mr. Arnold's *Friendship's Garland* after an interval of twenty-seven years may well set us all a-thinking. Here it is, in startling facsimile—the white covers, destined too soon to become black, the gilt device, the familiar motto. As we gazed upon it, we found ourselves exclaiming, so vividly did it recall the past:

It is we, it is we, who have changed.

Friendship's Garland was a very good joke seven-and-twenty years ago, and though some of its once luminous paint has been rubbed off, and a few of its jests have ceased to effervesce, it is a good joke still. Mr. Bottle's mind, *qua* mind; the rowdy Philistine Adolescens Leo, Esq.; Dr. Russell, of the *Times*, mounting his war-horse; the tale of how Lord Lumpington and the Rev. Esau Hittall got their degrees at Oxford; and many another ironic thrust which made the reader laugh " while the hair was yet brown on his head," may well make him laugh still, " though his scalp is almost hairless, and his figure's grown convex." Since 1871 we have learnt the answer to the sombre lesson, " What is it to grow old ? " But, thank God! we can laugh even yet.

The humour and high spirits of *Friendship's Garland* were, however, but the gilding of a pill,

268

the artificial sweetening of a nauseous draught. In
reality, and joking apart, the book is an indictment at the bar of *Geist* of the English people as
represented by its middle class and by its full-
voiced organ, the daily press. Mr. Arnold invented
Arminius to be the mouthpiece of this indictment,
the traducer of our " imperial race," because such
blasphemies could not artistically have been attributed to one of the number. He made Arminius
a Prussian because in those far-off days Prussia
stood for Von Humboldt and education and culture, and all the things Sir Thomas Bazley and
Mr. Miall were supposed to be without. Around
the central figure of Arminius the essentially playful fancy of Mr. Arnold grouped other figures,
including his own. What an old equity draughtsman would call " the charging parts " of the book
consist in the allegations that the Government of
England had been taken out of the hands of
an aristocracy grown barren of ideas and stupid
beyond words, and entrusted to a middle class
without noble traditions, wretchedly educated, full
of *Ungeist*, with a passion for clap-trap, only
wanting to be left alone to push trade and make
money; so ignorant as to believe that feudalism
can be abated without any heroic Stein, by pro-
viding that in one insignificant case out of a
hundred thousand land shall not follow the feudal
law of descent; without a single vital idea or sentiment or feeling for beauty or appropriateness; well
persuaded that if more trade is done in England
than anywhere else, if personal independence is
without a check, and newspaper publicity un-
bounded, that is, by the nature of things, to be

great; misled every morning by the magnificent *Times* or the "rowdy" *Telegraph*; desperately prone to preaching to other nations, proud of being able to say what it likes, whilst wholly indifferent to the fact that it has nothing whatever to say.

Such, in brief, is the substance of this most agreeable volume. Its message was lightly treated by the grave and reverend signors of the State. The magnificent *Times*, the rowdy *Telegraph*, continued to preach their gospels as before; but for all that, Mr. Arnold found an audience fit, though few, and, of course, he found it among the people he abused. The barbarians, as he called the aristocracy, were not likely to pay heed to a professor of poetry. Our working classes were not readers of the *Pall Mall Gazette* or purchasers of four-and-sixpenny tracts bound in white cloth. No; it was the middle class, to whom Mr. Arnold himself belonged, who took him to honest hearts, stuck his photograph upon their writing-tables, and sounded his praises so loudly that his fame even reached the United States of America, where he was promptly invited to lecture, an invitation he accepted. But for the middle classes Mr. Arnold would have had but a poor time of it. They did not mind being insulted; they overlooked exaggeration; they pardoned ignorance—in a word, they proved teachable. Yet, though meek in spirit, they have not yet inherited the earth; indeed, there are those who assert that their chances are gone, their sceptre for ever buried. It is all over with the middle class. Tuck up its muddled head! Tie up its chin!

A rabble of bad writers may now be noticed

pushing their vulgar way along, who, though born and bred in the middle classes, and disfigured by many of the very faults Mr. Arnold deplored, yet make it a test of their membership, an " open sesame " to their dull orgies, that all decent, sober-minded folk, who love virtue, and, on the whole, prefer delicate humour to sickly lubricity, should be labelled " middle class."

Politically, it cannot but be noticed that, for good or for ill, the old middle-class audience no longer exists in its integrity. The crowds that flocked to hear Cobden and Bright, that abhorred slavery, that cheered Kossuth, that hated the income-tax, are now watered down by a huge population who do not know, and do not want to know, what the income-tax is, but who do want to know what the Government is going to do for them in the matter of shorter hours, better wages, and constant employment. Will the rabble, we wonder, prove as teachable as the middle class? Will they consent to be told their faults as meekly? Will they buy the photograph of their physician, or heave half a brick at him? It remains to be seen. In the meantime it would be a mistake to assume that the middle class counts for nothing, even at an election. As to ideas, have we got any new ones since 1871? " To be consequent and powerful," says Arminius, " men must be bottomed on some vital idea or sentiment which lends strength and certainty to their action." There are those who tell us that we have at last found this vital idea in those conceptions of the British Empire which Mr. Chamberlain so vigorously trumpets. To trumpet a conception is hardly a happy phrase, but, as Mr. Chamberlain plays no other instrument, it is forced upon me. Would that we could revive Arminius to tell us what he thinks of our new Ariel girdling the earth with twenty Prime Ministers, each the choicest product of a self-governing and deeply-involved colony. Is it a vital or a vulgar idea? Is it merely a big theory or really a great one? Is it the ornate beginning of a Time, or but the tawdry ending of a period? At all events, it is an idea unknown to Arminius von Thunder-Ten-Tronckh, and we ought to be, and many are, thankful for it.

TAR AND WHITEWASH

1905

I AM, I confess it, hard to please. If a round dozen of Bad Women, all made in England too, does not satisfy me, what will? "What ails the fellow at them?" Yet was I at first dissatisfied, and am, therefore, glad to notice that whilst I was demurring and splitting hairs the great, generous public was buying the *Lives of Twelve Bad Women*, by Arthur Vincent, and putting it into a second edition. This is as it should be. When the excellent Dean Burgon dubbed his dozen biographies *Twelve Good Men*, it probably never occurred to him that the title suggested three companion volumes; but so it did, and two of them, *Twelve Bad Men* and *Twelve Bad Women*, have made their appearance. I still await, with great patience, *Twelve Good Women*. Twelve was the number of the Apostles. Had it not been, one might be tempted to ask, Why twelve? But as there must be some limit to bookmaking, there is no need to quarrel with an arithmetical limit.

My criticism upon the Dean's dozen was that they were not by any means, all of them, conspicuously good men; for, to name one only, who would call old Dr. Routh, the President of Magdalen, a particularly good man? In a sense, all Presidents, Provosts, Principals, and Masters of Colleges are good men—in fact, they must be so by the statutes—but to few of them are given the special notes of goodness. Dr. Routh was a remarkable man, a learned man, perhaps a pious man—undeniably, when he came to die, an old man—but he was no better than his colleagues. This weakness of classification has run all through the series, and it is my real quarrel with it. I do not understand the principle of selection. I did not understand the Dean's test of goodness, nor do I understand Mr. Seccombe's or Mr. Vincent's test of badness. What do we mean by a good man or a bad one, a good woman or a bad one? Most people, like the young man in the song, are "not very good, nor yet very bad." We move about the pastures of life in huge herds, and all do the same things, at the same times, and for the same reasons. "Forty feeding like one." Are we mean? Well, we have done some mean things in our time. Are we generous? Occasionally we are. Were we good sons or dutiful daughters? We have both honoured and dishonoured our parents, who, in their turn, had done the same by theirs. Do we melt at the sight of misery? Indeed we do. Do we forget all about it when we have turned the corner? Frequently that is so. Do we expect to be put to open shame at the Great Day of Judgment? We should be terribly frightened of this did we not cling to the hope that amidst the shocking revelations then for the first time made public our little affairs may fail to attract much notice. Judged by the standards of humanity, few people are either good or bad. "I have not been a great sinner," said the dying Nelson; nor had he—he had only been made a great fool of by a woman. Mankind is all tarred with the same brush, though some who chance to be operated upon when the brush is fresh from the barrel get more than their share of the tar. The biography of a celebrated man usually reminds me of the outside of a coastguardsman's cottage — all tar and whitewash. These are the two condiments of human life—tar and whitewash—the faults and the excuses for the faults, the passions and pettinesses that make us occasionally drop on all fours, and the generous aspirations that at times enable us, if not to stand upright, at least to adopt the attitude of the kangaroo. It is rather tiresome, this perpetual game of French and English going on inside one. True goodness and real badness escape it altogether. A good man does not spend his life wrestling with the Powers of Darkness. He is victor in the fray, and the most he is called upon to do is every now and again to hit his prostrate foe a blow over the costard just to keep him in his place. Thus rid of a perpetual anxiety, the good man has time to grow in goodness, to expand pleasantly, to take his ease on Zion. You can see in his face that he is at peace with himself—that he is no longer at war with his elements. His society, if you are fond of goodness, is both agreeable and medicinal; but if you are a bad man it is hateful, and you cry out with Mr. Love-lust in Bunyan's Vanity Fair: "Away with him. I cannot endure him; he is for ever condemning my way."

Not many of Dean Burgon's biographies reached this standard. The explanation, perhaps, is that the Dean chiefly moved in clerical circles where excellence is more frequently to be met with than goodness.

In the same way a really bad man is one who has frankly said, " Evil, be thou my good." Like the good man, though for a very different reason, the bad one has ceased to make war with the devil. Finding a conspiracy against goodness going on, the bad man joins it, and thus, like the good man, is at peace with himself. The bad man is bent upon his own way, to get what he wants, no matter at what cost. Human lives! What do they matter? A woman's honour! What does that matter? Truth and fidelity! What are they? To know what you want, and not to mind what you pay for it, is the straight path to fame, fortune, and hell-fire. Careers, of course, vary; to dominate a continent or to open a corner shop as a pork-butcher's, plenty of devilry may go to either ambi-tion. Also, genius is a rare gift. It by no means follows that because you are a bad man you will become a great one; but to be bad, and at the same time unsuccessful, is a hard fate. It casts a little doubt upon a man's badness if he does not, at least, make a little money. It is a poor business accompanying badness on to a common scaffold, or to see it die in a wretched garret. That was one of my complaints with Mr. Seccombe's Twelve Bad Men. Most of them came to violent ends. They were all failures.

But I have kept these twelve ladies waiting a most unconscionable time. Who are they? There are amongst them four courtesans: Alice Perrers, one of King Edward III.'s misses; Barbara Villiers, one of King Charles II.'s; Mrs. Mary Anne Clarke, who had to be content with a royal Duke; and Mrs. Con Phillips. Six members of the criminal class: Alice Arden, Moll Cutpurse, Jenny Diver, Elizabeth Brownrigg, Elizabeth Canning, and Mary Bateman; and only two ladies of title, Frances Howard, Countess of Somerset, and Elizabeth Chudleigh, Duchess of Kingston. Of these twelve bad women one-third were executed, Alice Arden being burnt at Canterbury, Jenny Diver and Elizabeth Brownrigg being hung at Tyburn, and Mary Bateman suffering the same fate at Leeds. Elizabeth Canning was sentenced to seven years' transportation, and, indeed, if their biographers are to be believed, all the other ladies made miserable ends. There is nothing triumphant about their badness. Even from the point of view of this world they had better have been good. In fact, squalor is the badge of the whole tribe. Some of them, probably—Elizabeth Brownrigg, for example—were mad. This last-named poor creature bore sixteen children to a house-painter and plasterer, and then became a parish midwife, and only finally a baby-farmer. Her cruelty to her apprentices had madness in every detail. To include her in this volume was wholly unnecessary. She lives but in George Canning's famous parody on Southey's lines to the regicide Marten.

With those sentimentalists who maintain that all bad people are mad I will have no dealings. It is sheer nonsense; lives of great men all remind us it is sheer nonsense. Some of our greatest men have been infernal scoundrels—pre-eminently bad men—with nothing mad about them, unless it be mad to get on in the world and knock people about in it.

Twelve Bad Women contains much interesting

matter, but, on the whole, it is depressing. It seems very dull to be bad. Perhaps the editor desired to create this impression; if so, he has succeeded. Hannah More had fifty times more fun in her life than all these courtesans and criminals put together. The note of jollity is entirely absent. It was no primrose path these unhappy women traversed, though that it led to the everlasting bonfire it were unchristian to doubt. The dissatisfaction I confessed to at the beginning returns upon me as a cloud at the end; but, for all that, I rejoice the book is in a second edition, and I hope soon to hear it is in a third, for it has a moral tendency.

EPITAPHS

PITAPHS, if in rhyme, are the real literature of the masses. They need no commendation and are beyond all criticism. A Cambridge don, a London bus-driver, will own their charm in equal measure. Strange indeed is the fascination of rhyme. A commonplace hitched into verse instantly takes rank with Holy Scripture. This passion for poetry, as it is sometimes called, is manifested on every side; even tradesmen share it, and as the advertisements in our newspapers show, are willing to pay small sums to poets who commend their wares in verse. The widow bereft of her life's companion, the mother bending over an empty cradle, find solace in thinking what doleful little scrag of verse shall be graven on the tombstone of the dead. From the earliest times men have sought to squeeze their loves and joys, their sorrows and hatreds, into distichs and quatrains, and to inscribe them somewhere, on walls or windows, on sepulchral urns and gravestones, as memorials of their pleasure or their pain.

> Hark! how chimes the passing bell—
> There's no music to a knell;
> All the other sounds we hear
> Flatter and but cheat our ear.

So wrote Shirley the dramatist, and so does he truthfully explain the popularity of the epitaph as distinguished from the epigram. Who ever wearies of Martial's " Erotion " ?—

> Hic festinata requiescit Erotion umbra,
> Crimine quam fati sexta peremit hiems.
> Quisquis eris nostri post me regnator agelli
> Manibus exiguis annua justa dato.
> Sic lare perpetuo, sic turba sospite, solus
> Flebilis in terra sit lapis iste tua—

so prettily Englished by Leigh Hunt :

> Underneath this greedy stone
> Lies little sweet Erotion,
> Whom the Fates with hearts as cold
> Nipped away at six years old.
> Thou, whoever thou may'st be,
> That hast this small field after me,
> Let the yearly rites be paid
> To her little slender shade ;
> So shall no disease or jar
> Hurt thy house or chill thy Lar,
> But this tomb be here alone
> The only melancholy stone.

Our English epitaphs are to be found scattered up and down our country churchyards—" uncouth rhymes," as Gray calls them, yet full of the sombre philosophy of life. They are fast becoming illegible, worn out by the rain that raineth every day, and our prim, present-day parsons do not look with favour upon them, besides which—to use a clumsy phrase—besides which most of our churchyards are now closed against burials, and without texts there can be no sermons :

> I'll stay and read my sermon here,
> And skulls and bones shall be my text.
>
> .   .   .   .   .   .
>
> Here learn that glory and disgrace,
> Wisdom and Folly, pass away,
> That mirth hath its appointed space,
> That sorrow is but for a day ;

That all we love and all we hate,
That all we hope and all we fear,
Each mood of mind, each turn of fate,
Must end in dust and silence here.

The best epitaphs are the grim ones. Designed, as epitaphs are, to assist and hold in their momentary grasp the wandering attention and languid interest of the passer-by, they must hit him hard and at once, and this they can only do by striking some very responsive chord, and no chords are so immediately responsive as those which relate to death and, it may be, judgment to come.

Mr. Aubrey Stewart, in his interesting *Selection of English Epigrams and Epitaphs*, published by Chapman and Hall, quotes an epitaph from a Norfolk churchyard which I have seen in other parts of the country. The last time I saw it was in the Forest of Dean. It is admirably suited for the gravestone of any child of very tender years, say four:

When the Archangel's trump shall blow
And souls to bodies join,
Many will wish their lives below
Had been as short as mine.

It is uncouth, but it is warranted to grip.

Frequently, too, have I noticed how constantly the attention is arrested by Pope's well-known lines from his magnificent *Verses to the Memory of an Unfortunate Lady*, which are often to be found on tombstones:

So peaceful rests without a stone and name
What once had beauty, titles, wealth, and fame.
How loved, how honoured once avails thee not,
To whom related or by whom begot.
A heap of dust alone remains of thee;
'Tis all thou art and all the proud shall be.

I wish our modern poetasters who deny Pope's

claim to be a poet no worse fate than to lie under stones which have engraved upon them the lines just quoted, for they will then secure in death what in life was denied them—the ear of the public.

Next to the grim epitaph, I should be disposed to rank those which remind the passer-by of his transitory estate. In different parts of the country —in Cumberland and Cornwall, in Croyland Abbey, in Llangollen Churchyard, in Melton Mowbray— are to be found lines more or less resembling the following:

> Man's life is like unto a winter's day,
> Some break their fast and so depart away,
> Others stay dinner, then depart full-fed,
> The longest age but sups and goes to bed.
> O reader, there behold and see
> As we are now, so thou must be.

The complimentary epitaph seldom pleases. To lie like a tombstone has become a proverb. Pope's famous epitaph on Newton,

> Nature and Nature's laws lay hid in night;
> God said, Let Newton be! and all was light,

is hyperbolical and out of character with the great man it seeks to honour. It was intended for Westminster Abbey. I rejoice at the preference given to prose Latinity.

The tender and emotional epitaphs have a tendency to become either insipid or silly. But Herrick has shown us how to rival Martial:

Upon a Child that Died

> Here she lies, a pretty bud,
> Lately made of flesh and blood;
> Who as soon fell fast asleep
> As her little eyes did peep.
> Give her strewings, but not stir
> The earth that lightly covers her.

Mr. Dodd, the editor of the admirable volume called *The Epigrammatists*, published in Bohn's Standard Library, calls these lines a model of simplicity and elegance. So they are, but they are very vague. But then the child was very young. Erotion, one must remember, was six years old. Ben Jonson's beautiful epitaph on S. P., a child of Queen Elizabeth's Chapel, beginning,

> Weep with me all you that read
> This little story;
> And know for whom the tear you shed
> Death's self is sorry,

is fine poetry, but it is not life or death as plain people know those sober realities. The flippant epitaph is always abominable. Gay's, for example:

> Life is a jest, and all things show it.
> I thought so once, but now I know it.

But *does* he know it? Ay, there's the rub! The note of Christianity is seldom struck in epitaphs. There is a deep-rooted paganism in the English people which is for ever bubbling up and asserting itself in the oddest of ways. Coleridge's epitaph for himself is a striking exception:

> Stop, Christian passer-by! stop, child of God,
> And read with gentle breast. Beneath this sod
> A poet lies, or that which once seemed he.
> O lift one thought in prayer for S. T. C.,
> That he who many a year with toil of breath
> Found death in life, may here find life in death!
> Mercy for praise—to be forgiven for fame,
> He ask'd and hoped through Christ. Do thou the same.

"HANSARD"

1905

"MEN are we, and must mourn when e'en
the shade of that which once was great
has passed away." This quotation—
which, in obedience to the prevailing taste, I print
as prose—was forced upon me by reading in the
papers an account of some proceedings in a sale-
room in Chancery Lane last Tuesday,[1] when the
entire stock and copyright of *Hansard's Parliamentary History and Debates* were exposed for sale,
and, it must be added, to ridicule. Yet *Hansard*
was once a name to conjure with. To be in it was
an ambition—costly, troublesome, but animating;
to know it was, if not a liberal education, at all
events almost certain promotion; whilst to possess
it for your very own was the outward and visible
sign of serious statesmanship. No wonder that
unimaginative men still believed that *Hansard* was
a property with money in it. Is it not the counter-
part of Parliament, its dark and majestic shadow
thrown across the page of history? As the pious
Catholic studies his *Acta Sanctorum*, so should the
constitutionalist love to pore over the *ipsissima
verba* of Parliamentary gladiators, and read their
resolutions and their motions. Where else save in
the pages of *Hansard* can we make ourselves fully
acquainted with the history of the Mother of Free

[1] March 8th, 1902.

284

Institutions? It is, no doubt, dull, but with the
soberminded a large and spacious dulness like that
of *Hansard's Debates* is better than the incongruous
chirpings of the new " humorists." Besides, its
dulness is exaggerated. If a reader cannot extract
amusement from it the fault is his, not *Hansard's*.
But, indeed, this perpetual talk of dulness and
amusement ought not to pass unchallenged. Since
when has it become a crime to be dull? Our fathers
were not ashamed to be dull in a good cause. We
are ashamed, but without ceasing to be dull.

But it is idle to argue with the higgle of the
market. " Things are what they are," said Bishop
Butler in a passage which has lost its freshness;
that is to say, they are worth what they will fetch.
" Why, then, should we desire to be deceived? "
The test of truth remains undiscovered, but the
test of present value is the auction mart. Tried
by this test, it is plain that *Hansard* has fallen
upon evil days. The bottled dreariness of Parliament is falling, falling, falling. An Elizabethan
song-book, the original edition of Gray's *Elegy*,
or *Peregrine Pickle*, is worth more than the
458 volumes of *Hansard's Parliamentary Debates*.
Three complete sets were sold last Tuesday; one
brought £110, the other two but £70 each. And
yet it is not long ago since a *Hansard* was worth
three times as much. Where were our young
politicians? There are serious men on both sides
of the House. Men of their stamp twenty years
ago would not have been happy without a
Hansard to clothe their shelves with dignity
and their minds with quotations. But these
young men were not bidders.

As the sale proceeded, the discredit of *Hansard* became plainer and plainer. For the copyright, including, of course, the goodwill of the name— the right to call yourself " Hansard " for years to come—not a penny was offered, and yet, as the auctioneer feelingly observed, only eighteen months ago it was valued at £60,000. The cold douche of the auction mart may brace the mind, but is apt to lower the price of commodities of this kind. Then came incomplete and unbound sets, with doleful results. For forty copies of the " Indian Debates " for 1889 only a penny a copy was offered. It was rumoured that the bidder intended, had he been successful, to circulate the copies amongst the supporters of a National Council for India; but his purpose was frustrated by the auctioneer, who, mindful of the honour of the Empire, sorrowfully but firmly withdrew the lot, and proceeded to the next, amidst the jeers of a thoroughly demoralised audience. But this subject why pursue ? It is, for the reason already cited at the beginning, a painful one. The glory of *Hansard* has departed for ever. Like a new-fangled and sham religion, it began in pride and ended in a police-court, instead of beginning in a police-court and ending in pride, which is the now well-defined course of true religion.

The fact that nobody wants *Hansard* is not necessarily a rebuff to Parliamentary eloquence, yet these low prices jump with the times and undoubtedly indicate an impatience of oratory. We talk more than our ancestors, but we prove our good faith by doing it very badly. We have no Erskines at the Bar, but trials last longer than

ever. There are not half a dozen men in the House
of Commons who can make a speech, properly so
called, but the session is none the shorter on that
account. *Hansard's Debates* are said to be dull to
read, but there is a sterner fate than reading a dull
debate: you may be called upon to listen to one.
The statesmen of the time must be impervious to
dulness; they must crush the artist within them
to a powder. The new people who have come
bounding into politics and are now claiming their
share of the national inheritance are not orators
by nature, and will never become so by culture;
but they mean business, and that is well. Caleb
Garth and not George Canning should be the model
of the virtuous politician of the future.

5 EDWARD VII., CHAPTER 12

1905

THE appearance of this undebated Act of Parliament in the attenuated volume of the Statutes of 1905 almost forces upon sensitive minds an unwelcome inquiry as to what is the attitude proper to be assumed by an emancipated but trained intelligence towards a decision of the House of Lords, sitting judicially as the highest (because the last) Court of Appeal.

So far as the *parties* to the litigation are concerned, the decision, if of a final character, puts an end to the *lis*. Litigation must, so at least it has always been assumed, end somewhere, and in these realms it ends with the House of Lords. Higher you cannot go, however litigiously minded.

In the vast majority of appeal cases a final appeal not only ends the *lis*, but determines once for all the rights of the parties to the subject-matter. The successful litigant leaves the House of Lords quieted in his possession or restored to what he now knows to be his own, conscious of a victory, final and complete; whilst the unsuccessful litigant goes away exceeding sorrowful, knowing that his only possible revenge is to file his petition in bankruptcy.

This, however, is not always so.

In August 1904 the House of Lords decided in

a properly constituted *lis* that a particular ecclesiastical body in Scotland, somewhat reduced in numbers, but existent and militant, was entitled to certain property held in trust for the use and behoof of the Free Church of Scotland.

There is no other way of holding property than by a legal title. Sometimes that title has been created by an Act of Parliament, and sometimes it is a title recognised by the general laws and customs of the realm, but a legal title it has got to be. Titles are never matters of rhetoric, nor are they *jure divino*, or conferred in answer to prayer; they are strictly legal matters, and it is the very particular business of courts of law, when properly invoked, to recognise and enforce them.

In the case I have in mind there were two claimants to the subject-matter—the Free Church and the United Free Church—and the House of Lords, after a great argle-bargle, decided that the property in question belonged to the Free Church.

Thereupon the expected happened. A hubbub arose in Scotland and elsewhere, and in consequence of the hubbub an Act of Parliament has somewhat coyly made its appearance in the Statute Book (5 Edward VII., chapter 12) appointing and authorising Commissioners to take away from the successful litigant a certain portion of the property just declared to be his, and to give it to the unsuccessful litigant.

The reasons alleged for taking away by statute from the Free Church some of the property that belongs to it are that the Free Church is not big enough to administer satisfactorily all the property it possesses; and that the State may reasonably refuse to allow a religious body to have more property than it can in the opinion of State-appointed Commissioners usefully employ in the propagation of its religion. Let the reasons be well noted. They have made their appearance before in history. These were the reasons alleged by Henry VIII. for the suppression of the smaller monasteries.

The State, having made up its mind to take away from the Free Church so much of its property as the Commissioners may think it cannot usefully administer, then proceeds, by this undebated Act of Parliament, to give the overplus to the unsuccessful litigant, the United Free Church. Why to them? It will never do to answer this question by saying because it is always desirable to return lost property to its true owner, since so to reply would be to give the lie direct to a decision of the Final Court of Appeal on a question of property.

In the eye—I must not write the blind eye—of the law, this parliamentary gift to the United Free Church is not a *giving back* but an *original free gift* from the State by way of endowment to a particular denomination of Presbyterian dissenters. In theory the State could have done what it liked with so much of the property of the Free Church as that body is not big enough to spend upon itself. It might, for example, have divided it between Presbyterians generally, or it might have left it to the Free Church to say who was to be the disponee of its property.

As a matter of hard fact, the State had no choice in the matter. It could not select, or let the Free Church select, the object of its bounty.

The public sense (a vague term) demanded that the United Free Church should not be required to abide by the decision of the House of Lords, but should have given to it whatever property could, under any decent pretext of public policy and by Act of Parliament, be taken away from the Free Church.

If the pretext of the inability of the Free Church to administer its own estate had not been forthcoming, some other pretext must and would have been discovered.

Having regard, then, to 5 Edward VII., chapter 12, how ought one to feel towards the decision of the House of Lords in the Scottish Churches case? In public life you can usually huddle up anything, if only all parties, for reasons, however diverse, of their own, are agreed upon what is to be done. Like many another Act of Parliament, 5 Edward VII., chapter 12, was bought with a sum of money. Nobody, not even Lord Robertson, really wanted to debate or discuss it, least of all to discover the philosophy of it. But in an essay you can huddle up nothing. At all hazards, you must go on. This is why so many essayists have been burnt alive.

First.—Was the decision wrong? "Yes" or "No." If it was right——

Second.—Was the law in pursuance of which the decision was given so manifestly unjust as to demand, not the alteration of the law for the future, but the passage through Parliament, *ex post facto*, of an Act to prevent the decision from taking effect between the parties according to its tenor?

Third.—Supposing the decision to be right, and

the law it expounded just and reasonable in general, was there anything in the peculiar circumstances of the successful litigant, and in the sources from which a considerable portion of the property was derived, to justify Parliamentary interference and the provisions of 5 Edward VII., chapter 12?

Number Three, being the easiest way out of the difficulty, has been adopted. The *decision* remains untouched, the *law* it expounds remains unaltered —nothing has gone, except the *order* of the Final Court giving effect to the untouched decision and to the unaltered law. *That* has been tampered with for the reasons suggested in *Number Three*.

John Locke was fond of referring questions to something he called " the bulk of mankind "— an undefinable, undignified, unsalaried body, of small account at the beginning of controversies, but all-powerful at their close.

My own belief is that eventually " the bulk of mankind " will say bluntly that the House of Lords went wrong in these cases, and that the Act of Parliament was hastily patched up to avert wrong, and to do substantial justice between the parties.

If asked, What can " the bulk of mankind " know about law? I reply, with great cheerfulness, " Very little indeed." But suppose that the application of law to a particular *lis* requires precise and full knowledge of all that happened during an ecclesiastical contest, and, in addition, demands a grasp of the philosophy of religion, and the ascertainment of true views as to the innate authority of a church and the development of doctrine, would there be anything very surprising

if half a dozen authorities in our Courts of Law
and Equity were to go wrong?

Between a frank admission of an incomplete
consideration of a complicated and badly presented case and such blunt *ex post facto* legislation
as 5 Edward VII., chapter 12, I should have
preferred the former. The Act is what would
once have been called a dangerous precedent.
To-day precedents, good or bad, are not much
considered. If we want to do a thing, we do it,
precedent or no precedent. So far we have done
so very little that the question has hardly arisen.
If our Legislature ever reassumes activity under
new conditions, and in obedience to new impulses,
it may be discovered whether bad precedents are
dangerous or not.

CONTEMPT OF COURT

1905

THE late Mr. Carlyle has somewhere in his voluminous but well-indexed writings a highly humorous and characteristic passage in which he, with all his delightful gusto, dilates upon the oddity of the scene where a withered old sinner perched on a bench, quaintly attired in red turned up with ermine, addresses another sinner in a wooden pew, and bids him be taken away and hung by the neck until he is dead; and how the sinner in the pew, instead of indignantly remonstrating with the sinner on the bench, " Why, you cantankerous old absurdity, what are you about taking my life like that ? " usually exhibits signs of great depression, and meekly allows himself to be conducted to his cell, from whence in due course he is taken and throttled according to law.

This situation described by Carlyle is doubtless mighty full of humour; but, none the less, were any prisoner at the bar to adopt Craigenputtock's suggestion, he would only add to the peccadillo of murder the grave offence of contempt of court, which has been defined " as a disobedience to the court, an opposing or despising the authority, justice, and dignity thereof."

The whole subject of Contempt is an interesting and picturesque one, and has been treated after an interesting and picturesque yet accurate and learned fashion by a well-known lawyer, in a treatise which [1] well deserves to be read not merely by the legal practitioner, but by the student of constitutional law and the nice observer of our manners and customs.

An ill-disposed person may exhibit contempt of court in divers ways—for example, he may scandalise the court itself, which may be done not merely by the extreme measure of hurling missiles at the presiding judge, or loudly contemning his learning or authority, but by ostentatiously reading a newspaper in his presence, or laughing uproariously at a joke made by somebody else. Such contempts, committed as they are *in facie curiæ*, are criminal offences, and may be punished summarily by immediate imprisonment without the right of appeal. It speaks well both for the great good sense of the judges and for the deep-rooted legal instincts of our people that such offences are seldom heard of. It would be impossible nicely to define what measure of freedom of manners should be allowed in a court of justice, which, as we know, is neither a church nor a theatre, but, as a matter of practice, the happy mean between an awe-struck and unmanly silence and free-and-easy conversation is well preserved. The practising advocate, to avoid contempt and obtain, if instructed so to do, a hearing, must obey certain sumptuary laws, for not only must he don the horsehair wig, the gown, and bands of his profession, but his upper clothing

---

[1] *Contempt of Court, etc.* By J. F. Oswald, Q.C. London: William Clowes and Sons, Limited.

must be black, nor should his nether garment be otherwise than of sober hue. Mr. Oswald reports Mr. Justice Byles as having once observed to the late Lord Coleridge whilst at the Bar: " I always listen with little pleasure to the arguments of counsel whose legs are encased in light grey trousers." The junior Bar is growing somewhat lax in these matters. Dark grey coats are not unknown, and it was only the other day I observed a barrister duly robed sitting in court in a white waistcoat, apparently oblivious of the fact that whilst thus attired no judge could possibly have heard a word he said. However, as he had nothing to say, the question did not arise. It is doubtless the increasing Chamber practice of the judges which has occasioned this regrettable laxity. In Chambers a judge cannot summarily commit for contempt, nor is it necessary or customary for counsel to appear before him in robes. Some judges object to fancy waistcoats in Chambers, but others do not. The late Sir James Bacon, who was a great stickler for forensic propriety, and who, sitting in court, would not have allowed a counsel in a white waistcoat to say a word, habitually wore one himself when sitting as vacation judge in the summer.

It must not be supposed that there can be no contempt out of court. There can. To use bad language on being served with legal process is to treat the court from whence such process issued with contempt. None the less, considerable latitude of language on such occasions is allowed. How necessary it is to protect the humble officers of the law who serve writs and subpœnas is proved by the case of one Johns, who was very rightly committed to the Fleet in 1772, it appearing by affidavit that he had compelled the poor wretch who sought to serve him with a subpœna to devour both the parchment and the wax seal of the court, and had then, after kicking him so savagely as to make him insensible, ordered his body to be cast into the river. No amount of irritation could justify such conduct. It is no contempt to tear up the writ or subpœna in the presence of the officer of the court, because, the service once lawfully effected, the court is indifferent to the treatment of its stationery; but such behaviour, though lawful, is childish. To obstruct a witness on his way to give evidence, or to threaten him if he does give evidence, or to tamper with the jury, are all serious contempts. In short, there is a divinity which hedges a court of justice, and anybody who, by action or inaction, renders the course of justice more difficult or dilatory than it otherwise would be, incurs the penalty of contempt. Consider, for example, the case of documents and letters. Prior to the issue of a writ, the owner of documents and letters may destroy them, if he pleases—the fact of his having done so, if litigation should ensue on the subject to which the destroyed documents related, being only matter for comment—but the moment a writ is issued the destruction by a defendant of any document in his possession relating to the action is a grave contempt, for which a duchess was lately sent to prison. There is something majestic about this. No sooner is the aid of a court of law invoked than it assumes a seizin of every scrap of writing which will assist

it in its investigation of the matter at issue between
the parties, and to destroy any such paper is to
obstruct the court in its holy task, and therefore
a contempt.

To disobey a specific order of the court is, of
course, contempt. The old Court of Chancery had
a great experience in this aspect of the question.
It was accustomed to issue many peremptory
commands; it forbade manufacturers to foul
rivers, builders so to build as to obstruct ancient
lights, suitors to seek the hand in matrimony of
its female wards, Dissenting ministers from attempting to occupy the pulpits from which their
congregations had by vote ejected them, and so on
through almost all the business of this mortal life.
It was more ready to forbid than to command;
but it would do either if justice required it. And
if you persisted in doing what the Court of Chancery told you not to do, you were committed;
whilst if you refused to do what it had ordered
you to do, you were attached; and the difference between committal and attachment need not
concern the lay mind.

To pursue the subject further would be to plunge
into the morasses of the law where there is no
footing for the plain man; but just a word or two
may be added on the subject of punishment for
contempt. In old days persons who were guilty
of contempt *in facie curiæ* had their right hands
cut off, and Mr. Oswald prints as an appendix to
his book certain clauses of an Act of Parliament
of Henry VIII. which provide for the execution
of this barbarous sentence, and also (it must be
admitted) for the kindly after-treatment of the

victim, who was to have a surgeon at hand to sear
the stump, a sergeant of the poultry with a cock
ready for the surgeon to wrap about the stump,
a sergeant of the pantry with bread to eat, and
a sergeant of the cellar with a pot of red wine
to drink.

Nowadays the penalty for most contempts is
costs.   The guilty party in order to purge his
contempt has to pay all the costs of a motion to
commit and attach.   The amount is not always
inconsiderable, and when it is paid it would be
idle to apply to the other side for a pot of red
wine. They would only laugh at you. Our ancestors had a way of mitigating their atrocities which
robs the latter of more than half their barbarity.
Costs are an unmitigable atrocity.

THE IDEAL UNIVERSITY

DELIVERED AT UNIVERSITY COLLEGE, LONDON, JUNE 17TH, 1898

MY Lord President, Gentlemen of the University College Union, Ladies and Gentlemen,—Although this is but the second occasion of the delivery of an oration, or what may, I hope, in these days of slipshod public speaking, pass muster for such, appropriate to the commemoration of the foundation of this College, I nevertheless find myself approaching my task, feeling deeply injured and most injuriously affected by the brilliant discourse of my friend, colleague, and only predecessor, Professor Poore.

It is quite true that I cannot possibly have any quarrel with that learned professor because he was minded to choose for his theme the history of this College, but I do think that he might have selected for the subject of his discourse, following in that respect the precedent set him by our historical examiners, some period of our college history, say five years or five months, or in these times of illustrative detail, five minutes; instead of which he took the whole past as his *peculium*, and beginning our history in its early days continued it right down to the present time, in a series of brilliant and fascinating paragraphs or pictures.

Not content with giving us a full, true, and particular account, culled from what rare and recondite sources of history I know not, of the cave-men of our remote antiquity, Bentham and Brougham, he persisted in pursuing us down the stream of time, nor rested until he brought his oration to a conclusion with a well-deserved panegyric upon Sir Blundell Maple, who is (as you all know) our professor of philanthropy, the only one of my colleagues who is unpaid, and teaches by example.

Thus driven from the fastnesses of antiquity, and deprived by the reckless prodigality of my predecessor even of a " modern instance," I have no choice but to abandon the past altogether; and leaving the real behind, to follow the tender, the lovely, the charming, but the ever-fleeting and elusive form of the Ideal.

Ladies and Gentlemen, I approach this subject with trepidation of mind. Mr. Rashdall begins his delightful history of the Universities of Europe in the Middle Ages by quoting from a mediæval author, who attributes the well-being and health of the Christendom he knew, to the joint operation of three great powers or virtues, which he designated by the names *Sacerdotium, Imperium, et Studium*— the Priesthood, the Empire, the University. Three moving words, stirring words, words well fitted to dominate both a Continent and an age; words crammed full of association, of that true history, the only true history that is made up of the lives of men.

The rule of Saint Benedict, the monks of the West, Emperor and Pope, the crowded class-rooms of famous professors, the poor scholars wandering from hospice to hospice throughout the length and breadth of Europe in search of learning, and even of lectures, the public disputations, the courses of study, grammar, logic, rhetoric! What a crowd of ideas, what a host of pictures are summoned to the bar of memory by the mere utterance of these dominating words, *Sacerdotium, Imperium, et Studium Generale*!

Of course, we are told by Professor Gradgrind that we no longer live in the Middle Ages. I believe that to be a fact. But it is one upon which I neither tender you my congratulations, nor proffer you my regrets; for although we may select for the purposes of study periods of history, for the purposes of living, we have no choice. Indeed, this chopping up of history into periods and ages is apt to impinge not a little upon the absurd.

"We are all," as Shakespeare says—and though Shakespeare was not a professor he is still quoted—" strangely woven of one piece "; and the glowing tapestry which is destined I hope to immortalise our doings, is being turned out from the same loom that wrought the records of the Middle Ages.

These words—the Priesthood, the Empire, the University—are still, though we do not live in the Middle Ages, master-words among us.

The Priesthood.—Well, I pass the Priesthood. But I do so with the observation that a man must be both ill-informed and singularly unobservant, whether he lives a cloistered or a public life, who does not perceive connected with this word *Sacerdotium* symptoms of an activity which shows no signs of abatement. It would be surprising if it did, for is not the Priesthood one of the most ancient and most fruitful of human conceptions?

The Empire.—Here, indeed, is a golden field for orators, for politicians, for political economists, and for stockbrokers. I pass it by also, merely observing that it would be a thousand pities if such a subject were to be disregarded by the learned and the studious, and left entirely for the consideration of meetings of shareholders in the Cannon Street Hotel, or even for the bronzed gentlemen in white waistcoats who frequent the Imperial Institute, and cheer the Colonial Secretary.

It is with the third master-word I am alone concerned—*the University*. This word, I trust, has lost but little of its ancient significance; for never was there a time which more stood in need of the co-operation, along with the other forces that go to make a nation really great, of a University, than the time that is present. Nor can it be said that we are without the means to give effect to our wishes in this respect if only we wish sufficiently strenuously—indeed, in these days we lack nothing to enable us to do anything, unless, indeed, it be the inspiration.

An ideal University would be famous and great, and as a consequence of its fame and greatness, it would be rich. It would be either possessed of its own right, or by reason of its situation be supplied with complete libraries, scientifically arranged, and some day or another usefully indexed; with museums that should be at once treasure-houses of a ransacked antiquity and storehouses of modern inventiveness; of laboratories where Science's favourite sons could repeat for the benefit of their pupils the experiments that have added to the stock of human knowledge, and also patiently pursue those original investigations, which are destined to add to it in the future; with a printing-press from which there should occasionally issue works of true scholarship, which in the best and noblest sense of a good and noble word should be, and for ever remain, essentially unpopular; with hospitals where by the bedside of suffering mortals, men, women and children, both professor and pupil shall be stirred by the noblest of all impulses, that which teaches us to regard ourselves as the servants of humanity.

These are indeed fine things, noble things, some of them pleasant things, but they are not "the pulse of the machine." The cowl does not make the monk, or the trappings the University. The great business of the University is to teach. Not everything; that is the vulgarest of vulgar errors. The famous University of Salerno had but one faculty, that of medicine; but teach *something* it must, and the more numerous its faculties, the wider does a University cast its net. But whatever it teaches, it must do so with the greatest fullness of knowledge possible to the age. The teaching at the Ideal University is without equivocation and without compromise. Its notes are zeal, accuracy, fullness and authority. The education it essays to give will not teach you to outgabble your neighbour in the law courts, to unseat him in his constituency, or undersell him in the market-place. Gentlemen, let it be understood once and for all, these things do *not* require a University education. The Commonwealth may safely leave them to be performed by the co-operation of the three primary forces—ambition, necessity, and greed.

To teach is, then, the first business of a true University, but only in those faculties in which it can command the attention of its scholars, and defy the criticism of learned Europe.

There was a private coach I used to hear of when I was at Cambridge, who was prepared to teach anybody anything. This honest man bargained but for one thing in addition to his exceedingly moderate terminal charges. " You must give me," so he would engagingly say, " five minutes' start." It was never refused him, and supplied with it, he and his pupil would amble contentedly along until they reached their desired haven, which, after all, was only the ordinary B.A. degree; equipped with which sign or symbol of a truly liberal education, the pupil, after endowing his bedmaker with all his worldly goods, so far as they were represented by broken crockery, would leave Cambridge by rail, prepared manfully to face the problems of the age; whilst the coach hied him back to the academical market-place, there to bespeak fresh pupils on the same fair handicap terms.

But the functions of the coach and the University are not the same.

How is a University to teach in those faculties which it feels itself competent to undertake? By means, of course, of its professors and lecturers, its demonstrators and tutors. You cannot teach without teachers, nor can a University be really great and famous which has not among its staff great and famous teachers.

In those bygone ages to which, as I have already remarked, we do not belong, there was apt to be a fierce contention among the Universities for the bodily possession of the most famous professors, theologians, canonists, etc. Indeed, so fierce did this contention sometimes become, that in order to capture a famous professor, Universities have been known to release him from all obligations to lecture; a frank departure from the ideal, which proves the continuity of human nature.

Listen to a description Sir William Hamilton gives of the great University and School of Leyden:

The principles of its founder were those which ought to regulate the practice of all academical patrons. He knew that at the rate learning was seen prized by the State in the Academy, it would be valued by the nation at large. In his eyes a University was not merely a mouthpiece of necessary instruction, but at once a pattern of lofty erudition, and a stimulus to its attainment. He knew that professors wrought more by example and by influence than by teaching; that it was theirs to pitch high or low the standard of learning in a country. . . . With these views Douza proposed to concentrate in Leyden a complement of professors, all illustrious for their learning, and if the *most* transcendent erudition could not be procured for the University with the obligations of teaching, that it should still be secured to it without. For example, Lipsius, the " Prince of Latin Literature," had retired. Who was to succeed him ? Joseph Scaliger, the most learned man whom the world had ever seen, was then living a dependent in the family of Rochepozay. He, of all men, was, if possible, to be obtained. The celebrated Baudius, and Tuningius, professor of civil law, were commissioned to proceed as envoys to France with authority to tender the appointment, and to acquiesce in any terms the illustrious scholar might propose. Nor was this enough. Not only did the curators of the University and the municipality of Leyden write in the most flattering strain to " the Prince of the Literary Senate " urging his acquiescence, but also the States of Holland, and Maurice of Orange. Nay, the States and Stadtholder preferred likewise strong solicitations to the King of France to employ his influence on their behalf with the " Phœnix of Europe," which the great Henry cordially did. The negotiation succeeded. Leyden was illustrated; the general standard of learned acquirement in the country and the criterion of professorial competency were elevated to a lofty pitch; erudition was honoured above riches and power, in the person of her favourite son. . . . After the death of Scaliger, who never taught, the curators tried to induce Julius Pacius to accept a large salary to become a resident in Leyden. But the place of Scaliger was to be filled by the only man who may contest with him the supremacy of learning; and Salmasius, who had been invited to Padua, but under the obligations of lecturing, preferred the literary leisure of Leyden with the emoluments and honours which its curators and magistracy lavished on him; simply that, as his call declares, "he might improve by conversation and stimulate by example the learned of the place."

There is a full-mouthed magnificence about this which is captivating, but perhaps a little deceptive. A Scaliger who does not teach and a Salmasius who only talks are dubious and familiar professorial figures.

Indeed, from the few specimens that have come down to us of the table-talk of Salmasius, it would be uncharitable to believe that in sober truth Leyden was in the least improved by it.

In whom should be the patronage? O, woeful word! How it hurls us from the heights of the ideal we were together seeking to scale. One thing is certain, patronage will be abused if it is not criticised: If the community does not always greatly care, the patrons will soon come not to care at all.

The history of Oxford and Cambridge during the last century proves the result of national indifference.

I have known a profligate debauchee chosen Professor of Moral Philosophy, and a fellow who never looked upon the stars soberly in his life, Professor of Astronomy. We have had History Professors who never read anything to qualify them for it but *Tom Thumb, Jack the Giant Killer, Don Belianis*

of Greece, and such-like valuable records. We have had likewise numberless Professors of Greek, Hebrew, and Arabic
who scarce understood their mother-tongue, and not long ago
a famous gamester and stock-jobber was elected Margaret
Professor of Divinity (*Terræ Filius,* 48).

This scandalous record dates, I admit, from
1721, but readers of Porson's Life, and even of
Adam Sedgwick's Life, will be able to carry the
bad tradition down to our own day.

An ideal patron is perhaps a contradiction in
terms, but if it is to be found anywhere it will be,
I believe, in a small combination of men of high
character, reputation, and general learning, who
may be trusted to act independently and judiciously. The head of a political department, a
town or county council? *Retro me, Sathanas!*
These are patrons that stand self-condemned;
they have not the time, the temper, the disposition, or, indeed, any single one of the necessary
qualifications. The existing Professors of the
University, though they might well be represented on the Board of Selection, should not
have, in an ideal University, a predominant
influence upon it, and especially should the Board
be confined to one particular University, of whose
exclusive interests they should be fiery partisans,
and with whose future fortunes and reputation
they should be as closely as possible allied.

Having got its professors and teaching-staff, the
University has to set them at work in their several
faculties; and for this purpose, to settle and
resettle courses of study, to arrange classes, to
name books, and to establish the machinery intended to help the students through the mazy
paths of knowledge. Here, no doubt, difficulties

arise and ideals will get entangled. The huge lecture-hall of a Scottish professor, crowded with pupils, who, armed with note-books, follow their favourite through an animated discourse, has played a great part in the national education of a well-educated country. It is different in England.

I shall never forget the surprise with which my father, an old pupil of Chalmers, entered a room in Cambridge where a Professor of Divinity was lecturing a handful of candidates for Anglican Orders. It certainly was not an animating picture. It did not remind one of Abelard. There was no crowd, no feeling, and yet the lecturer was Light-foot. I remember telling my father if he really wanted to see high pressure at Cambridge he must seek admission into the parlour in the private house in which the famous Routh was then rattling his pupils, a small transfigured band of future wranglers, along the path of glory.

Dealing here with ideals, I am bound to say an ideal University will keep its teaching as much as possible in its own hands, though whether its classes be large or small must be allowed to depend partly upon the subject which is being taught, partly upon the method of teaching that is being employed, and partly upon the character and genius of the individual teacher. Wherever there is life there is growth, and each soil, we know, has its preference. If only a tree is great and mighty, with deep roots and spreading branches, leafy choirs where the birds may sing, it matters not whether it be oak, elm, or beech.

What, we next ask, are the educational exercises a University should employ to stimulate the zeal, to awaken the enthusiasm, and test the requirements of its scholars ? Two well-worn methods will at once occur to all your minds—examinations and degrees. Examinations do not stand quite where they did. Robert Lowe, like Queen Anne, is dead. Familiarity with their results has bred a certain measure of contempt for the process. Examiners themselves have turned Queen's evidence, and have held up their hideous vocation to public scorn. But let us beware of the reaction. Against what does the ideal University most fiercely strive ? Against presumption, against ignorance, against conceit, against cheapjacks, quacks, and impostors. Tests and trials, discipline and correction, cross-examination, conviction, sentence, are all necessary parts of a University training. We cannot dispense with examinations—with frequent examinations—though not necessarily or on all occasions public examinations. The most vigorous defence of examinations that I ever came across occurs in a treatise of the celebrated Melanchthon. I quote from a translation to be found on p. 768 of Sir William Hamilton's *Discussions*:

No academical exercise can be more useful than that of examination. It whets the desire of learning, it enhances the solitude of study, while it animates the attention to whatever is taught. Every student is alarmed, lest aught should escape him which it behoves him to observe. This anxiety incites him also to canvass everything with accuracy, knowing that he must fully and perspicuously explain his understanding of each several doctrine. In this fear is found the strongest stimulus to the labour of learning; without it study subsides into a cold, sleepy, lifeless formality. What we have only heard or read come to us like the shadows of a dream, and like the shadows of a dream depart, but all that we elaborate for ourselves become part and parcel of our intellectual possessions. But this elaboration is forced upon us by examination; examination, therefore, may be called the life of studies, without which reading, and even meditation, is dead. Against prejudice and error there is no surer antidote than examination; for by this the intellect is explored, its wants detected and supplied, its faults and failings corrected. Examination likewise fosters facility of expression, counteracts perturbation and confusion, inures to coolness and promptitude of thought. Not less useful is examination in restraining the course of juvenile study within legitimate boundaries. Nothing is more hurtful, as nothing is more common, than vain and tumultuary reading, which inflates with the persuasion without conferring the reality of erudition. Wherefore, if examination brought no other advantage than that it counteracts the two greatest pests of education, found, indeed, usually combined, *sloth* to wit, and *arrogance*, for this reason alone should examination be cherished in our universities. Against sloth there is no goad sharper or more efficacious than examination; and as to arrogance, examination is the very school of humility and improvement. By no other discipline is a soaring conceit so effectually taken down, and this is the reason why self-satisfied pretenders ever fly examination, whilst those who think less of the little that they know than of the much they know not, resort to it as the most efficacious means of improvement.

One form of examination to which great importance should, I think, be attached in the ideal University, is that of written composition. This kind of examination is no doubt best conducted in private, but I know of nothing more valuable for the young and ardent soul than to be obliged to submit his written composition to the criticism of a ripe scholar.

In looking back upon my own life at Cambridge, I remember with peculiar pleasure how on two or three occasions (unfortunately they were no more) Professor Seeley did me the kindness of correcting in my presence effusions which I had written for his class. I was abashed, but it is when you are abashed that you learn. It was the only teaching of the kind I got at Cambridge.

Then come the degrees. Degree day must always

be a red-letter day in the academical year. Bacon somewhere speaks of the necessity of a few ostentatious feathers. It is, of course, true that universities do not exist in order to bespatter their *Alumni* with letters of the alphabet. That is the function of a Queen's birthday. But man is a competitive animal, nor would history warrant the assertion that he loses any portion of the spirit of strife and contention whilst he wanders mid the groves of the Academy.

Universities are wise in holding out honours and rewards, both pudding and praise, to the most diligent and successful of their scholars; and so far no better means have been devised for discovering who these are than by public examinations preceding the conferring of degrees, and determining to some extent the order of merit.

In the University of Louvain, early and long famous for the value of its degrees, nobody was ever plucked. The name of every candidate appeared in the classified list. It was not, however, altogether humanity that prompted this catholicity of treatment. No! such was the interest and feeling prevalent in Louvain in these matters, that whilst those who stood high in the annual lists were accounted as heroes and offered free libations, those who stood low were not infrequently subjected to contumely and public insult.

By whom should these public examinations be conducted? The answer must be, by those best qualified to conduct them, after the fashion most calculated to discover knowledge, to discern intelligence, to detect cram, and to expose brawling ignorance. To reject the teachers as examiners is impossible, to wish to do so would be foolish. No

University has ever entertained so uneducated an idea. What is required is to make such a selection of examiners as shall be above suspicion. This is a task that rarely presents the least difficulty. Like the so-called religious difficulty in our primary schools, it is a bugbear of the street, of the platform, of Parliament, not of the class-room or the Senate-house.

The social side of our ideal University is not likely to be forgotten or neglected in this country, where, owing to the fascination exercised over all middle-aged men by Oxford and Cambridge memories, it has become too general to overlook the University in a congeries of colleges. To speak disrespectfully of a college is, in most Englishmen's eyes, as bad as insulting a mother. It is within the crumbling walls of colleges that mind meets with mind, that permanent friendships are formed, habits of early rising contracted, lofty ambitions stirred. It is indeed a great and a stirring tradition. Who does not recall the neat little banquets in the monastic cells? Which of us who is clad in the sober russet of middle life can gaze without emotion upon the old breakneck staircase in the corner of an ancient quadrangle, where once he kept, and where were housed for a too brief season the bright-coloured, long since abandoned garments of a youth apparently endless, and of hopes that knew no bounds?

In the ideal University there will be academical houses—the sweet community, the eager rivalries, I hope none of the deadly hatreds, of college life. But supreme above her boarding-houses will always tower the ideal University.

I will end where a more dexterous orator probably would have begun, with the site of my ideal University. Much has been written, much can still be written, on this golden theme. Had one the eye of an old Benedictine or Cistercian monk, seeking where to establish a religious house of his Order to the glory of God and the comfort of the brethren, one might enlarge upon soils and prospects, on water meadows and trout streams; dreams of Tintern and of Fountains, of Wye and Tweed might cross the inward eye—that is " the bliss of solitude "—but standing here where I do in

Streaming London's central roar,

amid the huge population of the mightiest and richest, though not the most beautiful or the most beauty-loving city the world has ever known, I have already found the object of my search. When all is said and done, what is more stimulating to the mind of man than the vast tide of population as it pours through the arteries of a great city? Where else in the wide world is there so powerful a magnet as London? Not a day passes but hundreds are drawn within her grasp. Where else are there, can there be, so many young creatures richly endowed with natural gifts capable of cultivation, astir with the uneasiness of youth, seeing " the vision of the world," feeling the " wild pulsation," hearing " their days before them and the tumult of their lives," and " yearning for the large excitement that the coming years may yield " ?

If ever there was a theatre for academical actors, it is London. If ever there was a people and an age that needed the Higher Education, we are that people, and we live in that age.

IS IT POSSIBLE TO TELL A GOOD BOOK FROM A BAD ONE?

AN ADDRESS DELIVERED AT EDINBURGH ON NOVEMBER 3RD, 1899

DURING the last few months a saying of Voltaire's has been sounding uncomfortably in my ears. It occurs in one of his amusing letters from England. He remarks: " The necessity of saying something, the perplexity of having nothing to say, and a desire of being witty are three circumstances which alone are capable of making even the greatest writer ridiculous." A hasty assent to an ill-considered request has placed me where I am to-night. The popularity of Lord Rosebery has filled this hall, and I feel the direful necessity of saying something, whilst, at the same time, a rigorously conducted self-examination has made plain to me what is the perplexity of having nothing to say. As for the desire of being witty, there was a time, I frankly confess, when I was consumed by it; I am so no longer. This desire of being witty, sneered at as it always is, has in most cases an honourable because a humane origin. It springs from pity for the audience. It is given but to half a dozen men in a century really to teach their grown-up contemporaries, whilst to inflame them by oratory is happily the

province of a very few, but to bore them well-nigh
to extinction is within the scope of most men's
powers. This desire to amuse just a little ought
not, therefore, to be so very contemptible, springing as it does from the pity that is akin to love.
But now, to me, at all events, it matters not to
whom this desire is related or by whom it was
begot. I have done with it. Ten years in the
House of Commons and on the political platform
have cured me of a weakness I now feel to be
unmanly; I no longer pity my audiences; I
punish them.

Having made this point clear, I pass on.

There is something truly audacious in my talking to Edinburgh people on a question of Taste;
indeed, it is not only an audacious, but an *eerie*
thing to do. I remember, Lord Rosebery, how
you were affected, so you have told us, the first
time you addressed the society of which you are
now president, by the air of old-world wisdom
that hung about Lord Colonsay. But, at all events,
that venerable lawyer was then in the flesh. To-
night I seem surrounded by ghosts in wigs, the
ghosts of Edinburgh men all famous in their day,
some famous for all days, who, at the very sound
of the word *Taste* uttered after all this lapse of
years in this hall, have hurried hither this wet
and stormy night, full of doubts and suspicions,
to hear how a theme once their very own may
come to be handled by a stranger at the end of a
century not their own.

> What else should tempt them back to taste our air,
> Except to see how their successors fare?

I shall say nothing to offend these courtly shades.

I am far too much in doubt about the Present, far too perturbed about the Future, to be otherwise than profoundly reverential towards the Past. Besides, as they cannot speak, it would be ill-bred even to poke a little fun at them. I wish it were otherwise. I wish—how I wish!—that Lord Rosebery could now call upon Dr. Blair to address you—the great Dr. Blair, whose *Lectures on Taste* may still be had of the Edinburgh secondhand booksellers for a sum it would be ungenerous to state in figures. After all, the best books are the cheapest. Mr. Home, the author of *Douglas*, would, I dare say, conquer the shyness that pursued him through life and say a few words in response to a call; " Jupiter " Carlyle would probably prefer to reserve till supper-time (the meal when mostly truth is spoken) his trenchant criticisms. It would be honouring the occasion too much to suppose that the great Adam Smith would care to attend, or a greater than Adam Smith, David Hume, a man who, though the twentieth century may slip his collar, has more than any other single thinker dominated the nineteenth, from its tremendous beginnings to its sombre close. David Hume is, of all others, the Edinburgh man I should most like to hear on the *Standard of Taste*. One hundred and fifty-seven years have gone by since he published an essay on this very subject, to which I shall refer in a minute.

I have raised the subject of taste and a standard of taste by asking the question, " Is it possible to tell a good book from a bad one ? " This almost involves an affirmative reply. A well-known Nonconformist divine wrote a short treatise which he entitled, *Is it Possible to make the Best of Both Worlds?* But this world, at all events, always persisted (much to the author's annoyance) in calling the book *How to make the Best of Both Worlds*, whilst in the trade the volume was always referred to (curtly enough) as *Binney's Best*.

The world is a vulgar place, but it has the knack, the vulgar knack, of hitting nails on the head. Unless, in the opinion of the author, it *was* possible to make the best of both worlds, there was small probability of a prosperous Protestant divine asking the question at all; and in the same way, unless I am prepared to answer my own query with a blunt negative and to sit down, it becomes necessary to drop a hint or two as to how a good book may be known from a bad one.

Firstly, it is a very difficult thing to do, but difficulty is no excuse. Are there not treatises extant which instruct their readers how to tell a good horse from a bad one, and even, so over-reaching is the ambition of man, how to boil a potato?—both feats of great skill and infrequent achievement.

Secondly, not only is the task difficult, but the necessity for mastering it is urgent. The matter really presses.

It is, I know, usual when a man like myself, far gone in middle life, finds himself addressing a company containing many young people, to profess great sorrow for his own plight and to heap congratulations on the youthful portion of his audience. I am in no mood to-night for any such polite foolery. When I think of the ever-increasing activity of the press, home, foreign and colonial—the rush of money into the magazine market, the growth of what is called education, the extension of the copyright laws, and the spread of what Goethe somewhere calls " the noxious mist, the dropping poison of half-culture " —so far from congratulating those of you who are likely to be alive fifty years hence, I feel far more disposed to offer these unlucky youths and maidens my sincerest condolences, and to reserve all my congratulations for myself.

The output of books is astounding. Their numbers destroy their reputation. A great crowd of books is as destructive of the literary instinct, which is a highly delicate thing, as is a London evening party of the social instinct. Novel succeeds novel, speculative treatise speculative treatise, in breathless haste, each treading upon the heels of its predecessor, and followed by a noisy crowd of critics bellowing and shouting praise or blame. Newspaper paragraphs about the books that are to be rub the bloom off these peaches long before they lie upon our tables. The other day I read this announcement: " The Memoir of Dr. Berry, of Wolverhampton, will bear the *simple* title, *Life of the Rev. C. A. Berry, D.D.*" Heavens! what other title could it bear? These paragraphs are usually inspired by the publisher, for nowhere is competition more fierce than among publishers, who puff their own productions and extol the often secret charms of their kept authors with an impetuosity almost indelicate. In the wake of the publisher and the critic there sidles by a subtler shape, the literary interviewer, one of the choicest products of the age, who, playing with deft fingers on that most responsive of all instruments, human vanity, supplies the newspapers with columns of confessions taken down from the lips of authors themselves, who seem to be glad to tell us how they came to be the great creatures advertisement has made them, how their first books got themselves written, and which of their creations they themselves love the best. Let us never be tempted to underrate the labours of the interviewer. There is apt to be far more of that delicious compound human nature in the writings of the interviewer than in the works of the interviewed. If authors only knew it, by far their most interesting character is their own.

But not only is the output enormous, and what may be called the undergrowth rank, but the treatment is too frequently crude. Penmen, as bookwriters are now pleasingly called, in their great haste to carry their goods early to market, are too apt to gobble up what they take to be the results of scientific investigation; and stripping them bare of the conditions and qualifications properly belonging to scientific methods, to present them to the world as staple truths, fit matter for æsthetic treatment. There is something half comic, half tragic in the almost headlong apprehension of half-born truths by half-educated minds. Whilst the serious investigator is carefully " sounding his dim and perilous way," making good his ground as he goes,

Till captive Science yields her last retreat,

these half-inspired dabblers, these ready-reckoners, are already hawking the discovery about the streets, making it the *motif* of their jejune stage-plays and the text of their blatant discourses.

To stay this Niagara, to limit this output, is, of course, impossible. Nothing can stop it. Agricultural depression did not hit it. Declining trade never affected it. It is confidently anticipated that the millionaires of the future will be the writers of really successful shilling shockers and farces that take the town. *Charley's Aunt* has made more money than would be represented by the entire fortunes of Sir Walter Scott, Thackeray, and Dickens all added together.

Our concern to-night is with none of these fine folks. I, for one, am always ready to prostrate myself at the feet of Genius. Nothing will ever induce me to quarrel with genius. Without it there would be no rapture in reading, and small joy in life. Talent must be a very delightful thing both to possess and to exercise. Learning is for ever honourable; industry is always respectable. To be a successful impostor, a really fraudulent author, to live in luxury by the bad taste of your contemporaries, to splash with the mud from the wheels of your fast-driven curricle the blind Miltons and angry Carlyles of your own day as they painfully pedestrianise the pavement, must have an element of fun about it—but it is not for us. I am assuming that we do not belong to the many who write, or to the many who criticise in print what is written, but to the few who read. How are *we* to tell a good book from a bad one? Not for the purpose of making money out of the process, but for the solace of our own souls, for the education of our own powers, for the increase of our own powers, for the multiplication of our own joys. It is done by the exercise of a discriminative faculty called Taste. If you ask that amusing figment the man in the street what Taste is, the only answers you are likely to get are that "Tastes differ," or "What is one man's meat is another man's poison," or "All is grist that comes to my mill," or "*De gustibus non est disputandum*"; most discouraging replies every one of them. Nor would it be wise to attempt to minimise these differences of Taste; they are most real. Hume, in the Essay I promised to quote from, says only too truthfully:

Every voice is united in applauding elegance, propriety, simplicity, spirit in writing; and in blaming fustian, affectation, coldness, and a false brilliancy. But when critics come to particulars this seeming unanimity vanishes, and it is found they had affixed a very different meaning to their expressions. In all matters of opinion in science the case is opposite. The difference among men is there oftener found to lie in generals than in particulars, and to be less in reality than in appearance. An explanation of the terms commonly ends the controversy, and the disputants are surprised to find that they had been quarrelling while, at bottom, they agreed in their judgment.

The truth of this is obvious. We all hate fustian and affectation; but were I to have such bad taste as to inquire whether that popular novelist Mr. A. B. ever writes anything but fustian, or whether the exquisite style of Mr. C. D. has not a strong savour of affectation about it, I should excite angry passions.

But as it is Hume's contention that there is a standard of Taste, he necessarily proceeds to say, "that though this axiom (namely, that tastes differ), by passing into a proverb, seems to have attained the sanction of common-sense, there is certainly a species of common-sense which opposes it." Having said this, Hume determined to give his readers an illustration of this standard, and in order to do so, he adopted the common and useful device of selecting extreme instances. He took two authors so good that all, he thought, must acknowledge their goodness, and two authors so bad that all, he thought, must acknowledge their badness. "Whoever," he writes, "would assert an equality of genius and elegance between Ogilby and Milton, or Bunyan and Addison, would be thought to defend no less an extravagance than if he had maintained a molehill to be as high as Teneriffe or a pond as extensive as the ocean. Though there may be found persons who give the preference to the former authors, no one pays attention to such a taste, and we pronounce without scruple the sentiment of these pretended critics to be absurd and ridiculous."

Hume's first illustration will pass muster. In the case of Ogilby v. Milton, the pursuer has long since been dismissed with expenses; but otherwise with Bunyan v. Addison, for dearly as we may love Sir Roger de Coverley, and fond though we may be of taking a turn among the tombs in Westminster Abbey with Mr. Spectator, Bunyan's Christian and Faithful, his Mr. Worldly-Wiseman, Giant Despair, Vanity Fair, and Interpreter's House have established for themselves a homestead in the minds and memories of the English-speaking race, from which they can only be evicted along with Moses in the Bulrushes, Daniel in the Lions' Den, the Canterbury Pilgrims, Rosalind in the Forest of Arden, and Jeannie Deans in the

Robber's Cave, near Gunnersley Hill in Lincolnshire. So difficult is it to be a critic! The good-natured ghost of St. David will pardon a reference only made for the purpose of remarking how, if he made a bad shot in 1742, it is more than probable—nay, it is certain—that the critics of 1899 do not always hit the target.

The fact is, and we may as well recognise it frankly, all critical judgments are and must ever remain liable to two sources of variation, to both of which Hume refers. The one is the different humours of particular men, the other is the particular manners and opinions of our age and country. There is no escaping from these, and this being so, it is idle to expect the abolition of differences of opinion in matters of taste. How Hume came to go wrong—for I assume he did go wrong—about John Bunyan we can see from his use of the word *elegance* in conjunction with *genius*; " an equality of genius and elegance," he wrote. Elegance was one of the catch-words of the eighteenth century. It was, at all events, a sensible catch-word, though, like all catch-words, sure occasionally to mislead.

The upshot of all this is depressing and discouraging to the very last degree. In the realm of morals we may believe with the great Bishop Butler that there is in every man a superior principle of reflection or conscience which passes judgment upon himself, which, without being consulted, without being advised with, magisterially exerts itself and approves or condemns accordingly. In the region of the exact sciences, among a thousand different opinions which different men may entertain of the same subject, there is one, and but one, that is just and true. But who will dare so to lay down the law about the life of a book, or the future of a picture, or the reputation of a building; and yet who can doubt that in the realm of beauty there is a reign of law, a superior principle of reflection, passing judgment and magisterially asserting itself on every fit occasion?

Butler's theory of the conscience has been called "the pope in your bosom theory." What happiness to have an æsthetic pope, a prisoner in the Vatican of your own breast!

Speaking for myself, I could wish for nothing better, apart from moral worth, than to be the owner of a taste at once manly, refined and unaffected, which should enable me to appreciate real excellence in literature and art, and to depreciate bad intentions and feeble execution wherever I saw them. To be for ever alive to merit in poem or in picture, in statue or in bust; to be able to distinguish between the grand, the grandiose, and the merely bumptious; to perceive the boundary between the simplicity which is divine and that which is ridiculous, between gorgeous rhetoric and vulgar ornamentation, between pure and manly English meant to be spoken or read, and sugared phrases, which seem intended, like lollipops, for suction; to feel yourself going out in joyful admiration for whatever is noble and permanent, and freezing inwardly against whatever is pretentious, wire-drawn and temporary—this, indeed, is to taste of the fruit of the tree, once forbidden, of the knowledge of good and evil.

But this is simply to extol what has not yet

been proved to be attainable. What is "good taste"? My kingdom for a definition. I think the best is Burke's, given by him in that treatise on the *Sublime and Beautiful*, which he wrote before he handed over to Lord Rockingham and the Duke of Richmond and Lord John Cavendish what was meant for mankind.

I mean by the word taste no more than that faculty or those faculties of the mind which are affected with or form a judgment of the works of imagination and the elegant arts. The cause of a wrong taste is a defect of judgment, and this may arise from a natural weakness of the understanding, or, which is much more commonly the case, it may arise from a want of proper and well-directed exercise which alone can make it strong and ready. . . . It is known that the taste is improved, exactly as we improve our judgment, by extending our knowledge, by a steady attention to our object, and by frequent exercise; they who have not taken these methods, if their taste decides quickly, it is always uncertainly, and their quickness is owing to their presumption and rashness, and not to any sudden irradiation that in a moment dispels all darkness from their minds.

"The cause of a wrong taste," says Burke, "is a defect of judgment"; and here I must add on my own account that nobody comes into this world with a ripe judgment. You are as likely to be born with a silk hat on your head as with good taste implanted in your breast. To go wrong is natural, to go right is discipline. Generation after generation of boys go to schools and universities to be taught to play cricket, to row, and nowadays how to play golf. Each generation reproduces with startling fidelity to the type the same old, familiar, deep-rooted faults. No generation escapes them, but each in its turn has painfully to be taught to leave undone the things that naturally they would do, and do those things which, if left to themselves, they would most certainly leave undone. With oaths and revilings are they adjured to abandon nature and to practise art, to dig up the faults they were born with, and to adopt in their place methods which time has approved and discipline established. Success is very partial, but sometimes it does happen that a patient teacher finds an apt scholar, and then, when, after weary months, it may be years of practice, something like perfection is attained, and we see before us a finished oarsman, a faultless bat, a brilliant golfer, we exclaim with admiration as we watch the movements so graceful, so easy, so effective, of this careful product of artifice, " How naturally he does it! "

Gentlemen, if you want to find the natural man at work, you must look for him in the bunkers of life. There you will find crowds of them trying to get out and upbraiding the ill-luck that (as they think) got them in. Their actions are animated, their language is strong, but neither actions nor language are in good taste.

If, then, we would possess good taste we must take pains about it. We must study models, we must follow examples, we must compare methods, and (above anything else) we must crucify the natural man. If there is one thing to be dreaded in these matters, it is what is called the unaided intelligence of the masses. A crudely-coloured oleograph of the Albert Memorial may give pleasure to an unaided intelligence, but is that pleasure to be compared in depth of satisfaction with that which is afforded when the educated eye feasts upon the nature-interpreting canvas of a great artist?

All, I think, are agreed about the study of the models; of the things which are attested, the things which, as St. Augustine says, " sana mens omnium hominum attestatur." The elegant Addison agrees. " Literary taste," says he, " is the faculty which discerns the beauties of an author with pleasure and the imperfections with dislike. If a man would know whether he is possessed of this faculty I would have him read over the celebrated works of antiquity, which have stood the test of so many different ages and countries." Hume says the same thing. So does Goethe, who said to Eckermann, " Taste is only to be educated by contemplation not of the tolerably good, but of the truly excellent. I therefore show you only the best works, and when you are *grounded* in these you will have a standard for the rest, which you will know how to value without overrating them. And I show you the best in each class, that you may perceive that no class is to be despised, but that each gives delight when a man of genius attains the highest point." Mr. Matthew Arnold strongly held the same view, and recommended us all to carry in our heads scraps of Homer and Virgil, of Dante and Shakespeare, of Milton and Keats, and whenever we are required, as we so often are, to admire the worthless and extol the commonplace, to murmur these passages under our breath as a kind of taste-tonic. Somewhat in the same way the excellent John Howard used in his prison visitations to secrete small weighing scales about his person, and after asking to see a prisoner's ration of food would whip out his machine and convict the gaoler before his face

of trying to palm off one pound for two.   Mr.
Arnold's pocket scales for testing poets have been
ridiculed, but I recommend their use unhesitatingly.

We may then, I think, assume that the best
way of telling a good book from a bad one is to
make yourself as well acquainted as you can with
some of the great literary models.   Do not be
frightened of them.   They afford the widest choice;
they are not for all moods.   There is no need to like
them all alike.   The language difficulty presses
heavily upon some, but, as we are seeking only
our own good and not aspiring to instruct the
world, we need not postpone our own critical
education until we can read Sophocles for fun.
No doubt it would be well if we all could, but just
as it is better to spend three days in Rome or
three hours in Athens than never to see those
cities, so it is better to read the *Antigone* in the
translation of Mr. Jebb than not to read it at all.
It is all very well for scholars to turn up their
noses at translations, but plain Britons, whose
greatest book is a translation by divers hands,
and whose daily prayers have been done into
English for them from the Latin, may be well
content, if they do not happen to be masters of
the languages of antiquity, or of all the tongues
of the modern world, to gain through the medium
of the best translations some insight into the ways
of thought and modes of expression of the sove-
reigns of literature, the lords of human smiles and
tears.   But, indeed, with the *Golden Treasury of
Songs and Lyrics* in your pocket, and such volumes
as *Chambers's Encyclopædia of Literature* on your
shelf, the man who has only his own English at

command has ample room and verge enough
within which to cultivate a taste which ought to
be sufficiently sound to prevent him from wallow-
ing among the potsherds, or, decked out with
vulgar fairings, from following some charlatan in
his twenty-eighth edition.

We begin, then, with tradition—with tradition,
which plays so great a part in religion, in law, in
life. Genius may occasionally flout it, but I am
assuming we have no genius. We shall do well to
pay tradition reverence. It would be a nice
inquiry whether it is better for a man's morale to
be a rebel or a slave; but I am not concerned with
it to-night. Veneration for the models does not
involve servility.

It is a tremendous saying of Landor's, "We
admire by tradition and we criticise by caprice."

To admire by tradition is a poor thing. Far
better really to admire Miss Gabblegoose's novels
than pretend to admire Miss Austen's. Nothing
is more alien to the spirit of pure enjoyment
than simulated rapture, borrowed emotion. If
after giving a classic a fair chance you really
cannot abide him, or remain hermetically sealed
against his charm, it is perhaps wisest to say
nothing about it, though if you do pluck up heart
of grace and hit him a critical rap over his classical
costard it will not hurt him, and it may do you
good. But let the rap succeed and not precede a
careful study, for depend upon it it is no easy
matter to become a classic. A thousand snares
beset the path to immortality, as we are pleased
to call a few centuries of fame. Rocks, snows,
avalanches, bogs—you may climb too high for

your head, you may sink too low for your soul;
you may be too clever by half or too dull for
endurance, you may be too fashionable or too
outrageous; there are a hundred ways to the pit
of oblivion.   Therefore, when a writer has by
general consent escaped his age, when he has
survived his environment, it is madness and folly
for us, the children of a brief hour, to despise the
great literary tradition which has put him where
he is. But, I repeat, to respect tradition is not to
admire traditionally.

Tradition is the most trustworthy advertisement
and the wisest advice. Ah, advertisement! there,
indeed, is a word to make one blush. Ruskin has
somewhere told us that we are not to buy our
books by advertisement, but by advice. It is very
difficult nowadays to distinguish between the two.
Into how many homes has the *Times* succeeded
in thrusting the *Encyclopædia Britannica* and the
Century Dictionary ? The *Daily News* has its
own edition of Dickens, whilst the *Standard* daily
trumpets the astounding merits of an Anglo-
American compound which compresses into twenty
volumes the best of everything. These newspapers
advise us in their advertisement columns to buy
books in the sale of which their proprietors are
personally interested. Is their advice advertisement, or is their advertisement advice?

The advice given you by literary tradition is,
at all events, absolutely independent. I therefore
say, be shy of quarrelling with tradition, but by
all means seek to satisfy yourselves that the particular tradition is sound. We criticise by caprice;
this is the other half of Landor's saying.   The

history of criticism is a melancholy one. What are we to say to the blank indifference of our fathers to *Sartor Resartus*, to *Bells and Pomegranates*, to the early poems of Tennyson and Matthew Arnold and William Morris, to *The Ordeal of Richard Feverel*? Are we likely to be wiser than our fathers? All we can do is to keep hard at it crucifying the natural man. This is best done, as Burke said, by *extending our knowledge, by a steady attention to our object, and by frequent exercise.*

In extending our knowledge we must keep our eye on the models, be they books or pictures, marbles or bricks. We must, as far as possible, widen our horizons, and be always exercising our wits by constant comparisons. Above all must we ever be on our guard against prejudice, nor should we allow paradox to go about unchained.

I go back to Hume. " Strong sense united to delicate sentiment, improved by practice, perfected by comparison, and cleared of all prejudice, can alone entitle critics to be judges of the fine arts "; and again he says, " It is rare to meet with a man who has a just taste without a sound understanding."

Go get thee understanding, become possessed of strong sense, if thou wouldst know how to tell a good book from a bad one. You may have— though it is not likely—Homer by heart, Virgil at your fingers' ends, all the great models of dignity, propriety and splendour may be on your shelves, and yet if you are without understanding, without the happy mixture of strong sense and delicacy of sentiment, you will fail to discern amid the crowd and crush of authors the difference between the good and the bad; you will belong to the class who preferred Cleveland to Milton, Montgomery to Keats, Moore to Wordsworth, Tupper to Tennyson.

Understanding may be got. By taking thought we can add to our intellectual stature. Delicacy may be acquired. Good taste is worth striving after, it adds to the joy of the world.

> For most men in a brazen prison live,
> Where in the sun's hot eye,
> With heads bent o'er their toil, they languidly
> Their lives to some unmeaning task-work give,
> Dreaming of nought beyond their prison wall;
> And as year after year
> Fresh products of their barren labour fall
> From their tired hands, and rest
> Never yet comes more near,
> Gloom settles slowly down over their breast,
> And while they try to stem
> The waves of mournful thought by which they are prest,
> Death in their prison reaches them,
> Unfreed, having seen nothing, still unblest.

From this brazen prison, from this barren toil, from this deadly gloom, who would not make his escape if he could ? A cultivated taste, an educated eye, a pure enthusiasm for literature, are keys which may let us out if we like. But even here one must be on one's guard against mere *connoisseurship*. "Taste," said Carlyle—and I am glad to quote that great name before I have done— "if it means anything but a paltry connoisseurship, must mean a general susceptibility to truth and nobleness, a sense to discern and a heart to love and reverence all beauty, order and goodness, wheresoever or in whatsoever forms and accomplishments they are to be seen."

Wordsworth's shepherd, Michael, who

> had been alone
> Amid the heart of many thousand mists
> That came to him and left him on the heights,

had doubtless a greater susceptibility to truth and nobleness than many an *Edinburgh* or *Quarterly* reviewer; but his love, as Wordsworth tells us, was a blind love, and his books, other than his Bible, were the green valleys and the streams and brooks.

There is no harm in talking about books, still less in reading them, but it is folly to pretend to worship them.

> Deign on the passing world to turn your eyes,
> And pause awhile from letters to be wise.

To tell a good book from a bad one is, then, a troublesome job, demanding, *first*, a strong understanding; *second*, knowledge, the result of study and comparison; *third*, a delicate sentiment. If you have some measure of these gifts, which, though in part the gift of the gods, may also be acquired, and can always be improved, and can avoid *prejudice*—political prejudice, social prejudice, religious prejudice, irreligious prejudice, the prejudices of the place where you could not help being born, the prejudices of the university whither chance sent you, all the prejudices that came to you by way of inheritance, and all the prejudices you have picked up on your own account as you went along—if you can give all these the slip and manage to live just a little above the clouds and mists of your own generation, why then, with luck, you may be right nine times out of ten in your judgment of a dead author, and ought not to be wrong more frequently than perhaps three times out of seven in the case of a living author; for it is, I repeat, a very difficult thing to tell a good book from a bad one.

THE HOUSE OF COMMONS

A LECTURE DELIVERED AT THE COWDENBEATH (FIFESHIRE) LITERARY SOCIETY ON OCT. 15TH, 1896

THERE is a story told of an ancient dandy in London who, taking, one sunny afternoon, his accustomed stroll down Bond Street, met an acquaintance hurrying in the direction of Westminster. " Whither away so fast this hot day? " murmured the dandy. " To the House of Commons," cried his strenuous friend, brushing past him. " What! " said the dandy, with a yawn, " does that go on still? " Yes; the House of Commons still goes on, still attracts an enormous, some think an inordinate, amount of public attention. What are called " politics " occupy in Great Britain a curiously prominent place. Literature, art, science, are avenues to a fame more enduring, more agreeable, more personally attractive than that which awaits at the end of his career the once prominent party politician. Yet with us a party leader looms more largely in the public mind, excites more curiosity, than almost any other description of mortal. He often appears where he would not seem to have any particular business. If a bust is to be unveiled of a man of letters, if a public eulogium is to be pronounced on a man of science, if the health is to be proposed of a painter or

an actor, or if some distinguished foreigner is to
be feasted, the astute managers of the function,
anxious to draw a crowd, and to make the thing
a success, try, in the first instance, at all events,
to secure the presence of Mr. Balfour, or Lord
Rosebery, or Lord Salisbury, or Mr. Chamberlain,
rather than of Lord Kelvin or Mr. Leslie Stephen.
The fact is that politicians, and particularly the
heroes of the House of Commons, the gladiators
of politics, share in the country some of the
popularity which naturally belongs to famous
jockeys, which once belonged to the heroes of
the prize ring. It is more difficult to explain this
than to understand it. Our party strife, our
Parliamentary contests, have long presented many
of the features of a sport. When Mr. Gladstone
declared in the House of Commons, with an
irresistible twinkle of the eye, that he was an
" old Parliamentary hand," the House was con-
vulsed with laughter, and the next morning the
whole country chuckled with delight. We all
liked to think that our leading statesman was
not only full of enthusiasm and zeal, but also a
wily old fellow, who knew a thing or two better
than his neighbours. I have always thought the
instantaneous popularity of this remark of Mr.
Gladstone's illustrates very well the curiously
mixed feelings we entertain towards those great
Parliamentary chieftains who have made their
reputations on the floor of the House of Commons.
There is nothing noble or exalted in the history
of the House of Commons. Indeed, a devil's
advocate, had he the requisite talent, could
easily deliver an oration as long and as eloquent

as any of Burke's or Sheridan's, taking as his subject the stupidity, cowardice, and, until quite recent times, the corruption of the House of Commons. I confess I cannot call to mind a single occasion in its long and remarkable history when the House of Commons, as a whole, played a part either obviously heroic or conspicuously wise; but we all of us can recall hundreds of occasions when, heroism and wisdom being greatly needed, the House of Commons exhibited either selfish indifference, crass ignorance, or the vulgarest passion. Nor can it honestly be said that our Parliamentary heroes have been the noblest of our race. Among great Ministers, Sir Robert Walpole had good sense; Lord North, a kind heart; the elder Pitt, a high spirit; his son, a lofty nature; Peel, a sense of duty; Lord John Russell, a dauntless courage; Disraeli, patience to wait; but for no one of these distinguished men is it possible to have any very warm personal regard. If you turn to men who have never been powerful Ministers, the language of eulogy is perhaps a little easier. Edmund Burke, alone of Parliamentary orators, lives on in his speeches, full as they are of wisdom and humanity; through the too fierce argumentations of Charles James Fox, that great man with a marred career, there always glowed a furious something which warms my heart to its innermost depth. John Bright is a great Parliamentary figure, though many of his speeches lack a " gracious somewhat." Richard Cobden's oratory possessed one unique quality: it almost persuaded his political opponents that he was right and they were wrong. Among the many brilliant lawyers who have, like birds of passage, flitted through the House of Commons, usually on their way to what they thought to be better things, I know but one of whom I could honestly say, "May my soul be with his!" I refer to Sir Samuel Romilly, the very perfection in my eyes of a lawyer, a gentleman, and a member of Parliament, whose pure figure stands out in the frieze of our Parliamentary history like the figure of Apollo amongst a herd of satyrs and goats. And he, in a fit of depression, made an end of himself.

No, the charm—the undeniable charm; the strength—the unquestioned strength; the utility —of the House of Commons do not depend upon the nobility of the characters of either its leaders or its rank and file; nor on its insight into affairs —its capacity to read the signs of the times, its moral force, still less its spiritual depth; but because it has always somehow or other, both before Reform Bills and after Reform Bills, represented truthfully and forcefully, not the best sense of the wisest people, not the loftiest aspirations of the noblest people, but the primary instincts, the rooted habits of a mixed race of men and women destined in the strange providence of God to play a great part in the history of the world. A zealous philanthropy may well turn pale at the history of the House of Commons which, all through the eighteenth century, tolerated with fearful composure the infamies of the slave trade, the horrors of our gaols, the barbarity of our criminal code, the savagery of the press-gang, the heathenism of the multitude, the condition of things in our mines. The eager reformer must blush as he reads of our

Parliamentary representation—of rotten boroughs, of deserted villages with two members, and of Manchester with none. The financial purist must shudder as he studies the Civil List, and ponders over the pensions and sinecures which spread corruption broadcast through the land. It is true enough, and yet the fact remains, that all this time the British nation was stumbling and groaning along the path which has floated the Union Jack in every quarter of the globe. I do not know that it can be said the House of Commons did much to assist the action of this drama; but, at all events, it did not succeed in frustrating it.

However, my object to-night is to say something about the House of Commons as it exists at present, and as it strikes the humble individual who has sat in it for seven years as your representative. Well, first of all I am a Scottish member, and as a Scottish member one's attitude to the House of Commons is not a little that of an outsider. Scotland has nothing to do with the early history of the English Parliament. Until 1707 you had a Parliament of your own, with Lords and Commons sitting all together cheek by jowl. A great economy of time, for, as Andrew Fairservice in *Rob Roy* puts it, there was no need then for Lords and Commons to have their havers twice over. There is no need to be ashamed of the old Scots Parliament. It passed laws of unrivalled brevity and perfect intelligibility, a now lost art. Scotland owes more to its old Parliament than it yet does to the United Parliament. If you seek a record of its labours you will find one in an essay penned sixty years ago by a Scotch Tory, the very man who wrote a history of Europe in twenty volumes, to prove that Heaven was always on the side of the Tories.[1]

The old Scots Parliament met for the last time on March 25th, 1707. Unions are never popular. The Union of England and Scotland was undoubtedly most unpopular. One member for Fifeshire voted for it, and two against it. I wonder which way I should have voted. Cupar, Burntisland, Kinghorn, Dunfermline, Inverkeithing, and Queensferry voted Aye; but St. Andrews, Dysart, Kirkcaldy, Pittenweem, voted No. The first article of the Treaty for Union, which involved the rest, was carried by 116 votes against 83; and then, as Lord Seafield said, "There was the end of an auld sang"; but some day—who knows? —the auld sang may be set to a new tune. But this much is certain—the new tune will in no way affect the loyalty of Scotsmen to the Union of the two countries. But for that Union Scotland would not stand where she does in the eyes of the world. What Scotland wanted, what Scotland standing alone could never have had, was a theatre wide enough for the energy of her sons. A country so small, so barren, could never have supplied such a theatre. Scotsmen must have taken service abroad, and spent their lives fighting other men's battles, or building up other men's fortunes. United with South Britain she has been able to play a glorious part both at home and abroad, and this she has done without losing either her Scottish character or her Scottish accent. Still, the fact remains that the seventy-two members

---

[1] Alison's *Essays,* vol. i.

from Scotland preserve a character of their own among the 590 representatives from England, Wales, and Ireland. This must be so. Scotch law is very different from English law. We have in Scotland our own laws and our own judicature. A Scotsman cannot be sued in an English court unless he is snapped with a writ whilst sojourning in that strange land. Scotland has her own religion; for, though I am far from saying that traces of a common Christianity may not be found lurking both in Presbyterianism and Episcopacy, still, speaking as a Parliament man, the religions of the two countries may be considered as distinct. In England, those who do not believe in the Divine authority of Episcopacy, who deny either the validity of the orders of the Episcopalian clergy or that there are such things as Holy orders at all, who repudiate the Sacramentarian system, and hate the pretensions of a priesthood, are engaged in a daily, bitter strife with the Church party, with which Scotland has as yet no concern. The educational system is different. Here you have universal School Boards, and pay an allegiance—sometimes real, sometimes formal—to a Catechism which, though often supposed to be the most Scotch thing in existence, was, as a matter of fact, compiled in England by Englishmen. In England School Boards are far from universal, and clerically conducted schools provide the education of half the school-going population. The Scottish system of local government is different in important respects from the English. For example, your Parish Councils administer the Poor Law; in England they do not. Your rating system is different. Here the rate is divided between the owner and the occupier; in England the occupier pays the whole rate. All these differences invite different treatment—there have to be English Bills and Scotch Bills; and though some Scotch members may honestly try to understand English Bills, I never knew an English member, unless he was by birth a Scotsman, who ever took, or pretended to take, the least trouble to understand a Scotch Bill. They vote if they happen to be in the House whilst Scotch business is being discussed, but they vote as they are told by their party managers. It follows, as I say, from this that a Scotch member surveys the House of Commons somewhat as an outsider.

The great characteristic of the House of Commons is that it is a deliberative and consultative chamber, meeting together for the purposes of framing laws (if it considers any new laws necessary) which are to bind the whole nation, and of criticising the Executive. It does not meet for the purpose of oratory, or to strengthen party organisation, but to frame laws of universal obligation and to find fault with or support Ministers. This at once gets rid of the platform orator, and establishes the difference between public meetings and the House of Commons. It is no discredit to the public meeting or to the House of Commons to say that what will find favour with the one excites the disgust of the other, for the two have little in common. The object of a speaker at a public meeting is to excite enthusiasm and to spread his faith; but in the House of Commons his object is to remove objections, to state propositions in a way least likely to make reply easy, to show that a scheme is practicable and free from particular injustices, to handle figures with dexterity, and to avoid empty phraseology. There is nothing the House of Commons hates more than to be reminded of the purgatorial flames through which each member has had to pass in order to take his seat by the side of the Speaker; and therefore it is that the utterance in all innocence, by some new member of either party, of the cries and watchwords with which he was accustomed to enliven his electioneering speeches never fails to excite the angry groans of his opponents and the sarcastic smiles of his friends. Nor is there anything dishonest in this. There is a time for all things, and the House of Commons is before everything a deliberative and consultative assembly. Another marked characteristic of the House of Commons is its total indifference to outside reputations or great fortunes. Local magnates, manufacturers whose chimneys blacken a whole countryside, merchants whose ships plough the broad and narrow seas, speculators in cotton and in sugar, mayors and provosts whose portraits adorn town halls, whose names are household words in their own districts, lawyers so eminent that they will not open their mouths in the courts for less than a hundred guineas, need not hope to be received by the House of Commons otherwise than with languid indifference. If they prove to be bores, so much the worse; if they prove not to be bores, so much the better. If they push themselves to the front, it will be by Parliamentary methods; if they remain insignificant, it is only what was to be expected. Never was an assembly so free from all taint of mercenariness as the House of Commons. It does not care a snap of its finger whether the income of a new member is £100,000 a year or £3 a week—whether his father was a duke or a blacksmith; its only concern with him is that, if he has anything to say, he may say it, and that if he has nothing to say, he will say nothing.

The House of Commons is often said to be a place of great good-fellowship. Within certain necessarily restricted limits it is. It is difficult to maintain aloofness. You may find yourself serving on a Committee alongside someone whose public utterances or party intrigues you have always regarded with aversion; but it may easily be that you agree with him, not, it may be, as to the Government of Ireland or the sacred principles of Free Trade, but as to the prudence or folly of a particular line of railway, or the necessity of a new water-supply for some large town. You hob-a-nob at luncheon, you grumble together over your dinner, you lament the spread of football clubs and brass bands in your respective constituencies; you criticise your leaders, and are soon quite at home in the society of the very man you thought you detested. There is nothing like a common topic to break the ice, and two members of Parliament have always something to talk about. But farther than this it is hard to go. The House is too large. Amongst an assembly of 670 men well on in life the hand of Death is always busy. Vacancies occur with startling regularity. The only uncertainty is, who is to drop out of the ranks.

"Death of a Member of Parliament" is a common announcement on the placards of the evening papers; and then the thriftiest of Scotch members fumbles for his bawbee, buys the paper, stops under the next lamp-post to see who it is who has gone, whose figure will no more be seen in the Tea-room and the Lobby. Whoever it is, big man or little, a silent member or a talkative one, a wise man or a fool, his place will soon be filled up, and his party Whip will be heard moving for a new writ to issue for the Borough of Small-Talk in the place of Jeremiah Jones, deceased. "Poor Jones!" we all say; "not a bad fellow, Jones; I suppose Brown will get the seat this time."

I know no place where the great truth that no man is necessary is brought home to the mind so remorselessly, and yet so refreshingly, as the House of Commons. Over even the greatest reputations it closes with barely a bubble. And yet the vanity of politicians is enormous. Lord Melbourne, you will remember, when asked his opinion of men, replied, with his accustomed expletive, which I omit as unfit for the polite ear of Cowdenbeath, "Good fellows, very good fellows, but vain, very vain."

There is a great deal of vanity, both expressed and concealed, in the House of Commons. I often wonder why, for I cannot imagine a place where men so habitually disregard each other's feelings, so openly trample on each other's egotisms. You rise to address the House. The Speaker calls on you by name. You begin your speech. Hardly are you through with the first sentence when your oldest friend, your college chum, the man you have appointed guardian of your infant children, rises in his place, gives you a stony stare, and, seizing his hat in his hand, ostentatiously walks out of the House, as much as to say, " I can stand many things, but not this."

Whilst speaking in the House I have never failed to notice one man, at all events, who was paying me the compliment of the closest attention, who never took his eyes off me, who hung upon my words, on whom everything I was saying seemed to be making the greatest impression. In my early days I used to address myself to this man, and try my best to make my discourse worthy of his attention; but sad experience has taught me that this solitary auditor is not in the least interested either in me or in my speech, and that the only reason why he listens so intently and eyes me so closely is because he has made up his mind to follow me, and is eager to leap to his feet, in the hope of catching the Speaker's eye, the very moment I sit down. Yet, for all this, vanity thrives in the House— though what it feeds on I cannot say. We are all anxious to exaggerate our own importance, and desperately anxious to make reputations for our- selves and to have our names associated with some subject—to pose as its patron and friend. On great Parliamentary nights these vanities, from which even our leaders are not wholly exempt, are very conspicuous. On such occasions the House of Commons has reminded me of a great drying- ground, where all the clothes of a neighbourhood may be seen fluttering in a gale of wind. There are night-gowns and shirts and petticoats so distended and distorted by the breeze as to seem the garments of a race of giants, rather than of poor mortal man; even the stockings of some slim maiden, when puffed out by the lawless wind, assume dropsical proportions. But the wind sinks, having done its task, and then the matter-of-fact washerwoman unpegs the garments, sprinkles them with water, and ruthlessly passes over them her flat-irons, and, lo and behold! these giants' robes are reduced to their familiar, domestic, and insignificant proportions.

A marked characteristic of the House of Commons is its generosity. We have heard far too much lately of contending jealousies. The only thing the House is really jealous of is its own reputation. If a member, no matter who he is, or where he sits, or what he says, makes a good speech and creates a powerful impression, nobody is more delighted, more expansively and effusively delighted, than Sir William Harcourt. On such occasions he glows with generosity. And this is equally true of Mr. Balfour, and indeed of the whole House, which invariably welcomes talent and rejoices over growing reputations.

Members of Parliament may be divided into two classes: Front Bench men and Back Bench men. The former are those who fill or have filled posts in an Administration, and they sit either on the Government Bench or on the Front Opposition Bench. These personages enjoy certain privileges, and the most obvious of these privileges is that they speak with a table in front of them, whereby they are enabled cunningly to conceal their notes. Now, the private or Back Bench member has no place in which to conceal his notes, save his hat, a structure ill-fitted for the purpose. Another of the privileges of a Front Bench man is that he has, or is supposed to have, a right of intervention in debate just when he chooses. This is an enormous advantage. Just consider the unhappy fate of a private member who is anxious to speak during an important debate. He prepares his speech, and comes down to the House with it concealed about his person. He bides his time; an excellent opportunity occurs; nobody has as yet said what he is going to say; he rises in his place; but, alas! fifteen other members with fifteen other speeches in their pockets rise too, and the Speaker calls on one of them, and down falls our unhappy member, to wait another opportunity. This may happen frequently, and often does happen fifteen or sixteen times. He has to sit still and hear other men mangle his arguments, quote his quotations. Night follows night, and the speech remains undelivered, festering in his brain, polluting his mind. At last he gets his chance—the Speaker calls out his name; but by this time he has got sick of the subject—it has grown weary, stale, flat, and unprofitable. He has lost his interest, and soon loses the thread of his discourse; he flounders and flops, has recourse to his hat, repeats himself, grows hot and uncomfortable, forgets his best points, and finally sits down dejected, discouraged, disappointed. And all the time his wife is in the Ladies' Gallery gnashing her teeth at the poor figure he is cutting! No wonder he hates the Front Bench man. But there are gradations in the Front Bench. Between the leaders of the House, who bag all the best moments, and the humble Under Secretary or Civil Lord there is a great gulf fixed. These latter gentry are not allowed to speak at all, except on matters relating to their departments, or when they are told off to speak by the leader. Nothing is more amusing than to notice the entire eclipse of some notorious chatterbox who has been given some minor post in an Administration. Before he took office he was chirping on every bough; hardly a night passed but his sweet voice was to be heard. After he has taken office he frequently has to hold his tongue for a whole session. Poor fellow! he will sometimes buttonhole you in the Lobby, and almost tearfully complain of the irksomeness of office, and tell you how he longs for the hour of emancipation, when once more his voice, like that of the turtle, shall be heard in the land. If you gently remind him of the salary he draws, and hint that it may be some consolation even for silence, ten to one he walks away in a huff, and attributes your innocent remarks to jealousy. Between the Front Bench and the Back Bench there has always been a feud. Front Bench men of the first rank are too apt, so it is said, to regard the House of Commons as a show run for their benefit, to look upon themselves as a race of actor-managers who arrange the playbill, and divide all the best parts among themselves. The traditions of Parliament foster this idea. But the Back Bench men are not always in the mood to submit to be for ever either the audience or the supernumeraries, and whenever they get the chance of asserting themselves against their leaders they take it. But in public they seldom get the chance, so they have to content themselves with being as disagreeable in private as they possibly can. What I think is a just complaint, frequently made by Back Benchers, relates to the habit Parliamentary leaders of late have greatly indulged in, of occupying an enormous amount of time abusing one another for past inconsistencies of conduct. These amenities, sometimes called *tu quoques*, or " You are another," are infinitely wearisome, and proceed upon the mistaken assumption that the House of Commons greatly concerns itself with the political reputation of its leaders. It does nothing of the sort. What it wants is leaders who can make business go, who will show sport, and lead their hounds across a good line of country.

As a Back Bench man, the only real complaint I have to make is of the woeful waste of time. One goes down to the House every day—Saturdays and Wednesdays excepted—at 4 o'clock, and you are supposed to remain there till midnight. On Wednesdays the House meets at 12 and adjourns at 5.30. What do we do all this time? To be interested in everything that is going on is flatly impossible. A quantity of the business is of a local character, dealing with places and schemes of which we know and can know nothing. Then there are terribly protracted debates on the second readings of Bills, occasionally interesting, but necessarily full of repetitions. I do not well see how this is to be prevented; but it is a shocking infliction. The Committee stage of a Bill you have really mastered is interesting and instructive, but even this stage is too protracted; and then comes a later stage— the report stage—when a great deal is said all over again; and even this is frequently followed by a debate on the third reading. Of course, you are not in the House all the time. There is the Library, the Tea-room, and the Smoking-room, where you may play chess and draughts, but no other game whatsoever. But nobody does anything vehemently. An air of languor pervades the whole place. Listlessness abounds. Members stroll from one room to another, turn over the newspapers, and yawn in each other's faces. In the summer months, the Terrace by the riverside has been recently converted into a kind of watering-place. From five o'clock to seven it is crowded with fine ladies and country cousins, drinking tea and devouring strawberries. Occasionally some Parliamentary person of importance will choose to stalk by, and even—such is the affability of true greatness—have a cup of tea with a party of friends. A poorer way of killing time has not, I think, yet been discovered; but it is a convincing proof of the *ennui* of Parliamentary life.

The great problem of Ministers is the reform of the rules of the House of Commons—how to make the House at once a deliberative and yet a business-like assembly.

And yet men do not willingly strike off the chains of this slavery. A private member of Parliament nowadays gets nothing, neither pudding nor praise, in exchange for his time and his money. Patronage he has absolutely none—not a single place, even in the Post-Office, to give away. Nor has he a single privilege that I am aware of. His routine duties on committees are onerous, nor are his opportunities of making speeches, if he wishes to do so, otherwise than few and far between. His leaders treat him with frigid civility, and nobody cares for a letter from him unless it encloses a postal order for at least ten shillings. And yet the labour of winning a seat and of retaining a seat is very great; nor is the expense insignificant.

When one thinks of all the different ways of spending £700, a Parliamentary election does not obviously strike you as being one of the most delightful. It may be said you have the opportunity of legislating on your own account. You may bring in a Bill of your own, and have the satisfaction of hearing it read a third time. Hardly is this true. In former days some of the most useful laws in the Statute Book were pioneered through the House by private members. But now, so greedy have Governments become, that they take nearly all the time available for legislative purposes, and, unless the private member gets the first place in the ballot, he has not a chance of carrying any measure through if it excites the least opposition. But when all is said and done, the House of Commons is a fascinating place. It has one great passion, one genuine feeling, and that is to represent and give practical expression to the mind of the whole nation. It has no prejudices in this matter, for it has no existence independent of its creators. It has nothing to do with the choice of its component parts. The constituencies may send up whom they choose, but these persons, when they do come up, must not expect to be hailed as " Saviours of Society." No; they must be content to be parts of a whole, to give and take, to hear their pet creeds, faiths, and fancies rudely questioned, tested, and weighed. A great nation will never consent to be dominated either by a sect or by an interest. And yet, if the House of Commons has a leaning to any particular class of member—which by rights it ought not to have—it is for an increased direct representation of the wage-earning community. I hope such representatives may be forthcoming in greater numbers as time goes on. But if they are to do any good in the House of Commons, they must go there, not as conquering heroes to whom the unknown future belongs, but as Britons anxious to contribute out of their special knowledge, from their hived experience, to the collective wisdom of the nation; they must be willing to learn as well as to teach, to increase the stock of their information, to acknowledge mistakes, to widen their views; and, above all, must they recognise that the mighty river of our national existence, if it is to continue to flow as triumphantly as before, must continue to be fed by many tributary streams.

There are, I know, those who affect to believe that representative assemblies do not stand where they did, and that the day of their doom is not far distant. I see no reason to believe anything of the kind, for, scan the horizon as you may, you cannot discover what there is to take their place. We have no mind for military despotisms, even if we had a military hero. Nor are we disposed to believe in the superior wisdom of that so-called statesmanship which is manufactured in Government offices. Better by far the occasional mistakes of a free people and a popular assembly than the deadly and persistent errors of diplomatists and hereditary statesmen. The House of Commons will, I cannot doubt, be still going on when the twentieth century breathes its last. Change it will know, and reform; but, founded as it is upon a rational and manly system of representation, why should it not always continue to reflect, cautiously but truthfully, the mind and will of the British people?

ON A DICTUM OF MR. DISRAELI'S AND OTHER MATTERS

1912

TO an historically-minded person like myself, in whose ears resound the

Murmur of living,
Stir of existence,

and whose imagination, " a poor, ill-favoured thing, but mine own," is always attempting to paint some picture of the storied past, it is no light matter to stand before you at this uncomfortably early hour of the morning, encumbered—I dare not add adorned — with the robes of my office as Lord Rector of this famous University.[1] I cannot forget that I am, for the hour, the last in a long line, which travels back to a time when, as Macaulay reminded you sixty-three years ago, the Moslems were plundering the Christian churches and palaces of Constantinople. Could I, following a distinguished example elsewhere, pluck but one of my more ancient predecessors from his cranny in the wall of Time, and tell you what manner of man he actually was, and what he really did think about the Universe, whenever he thought about it at all, I might be able to light up some of those dim years which belong to the Past, and therefore ought to belong to us, but do not.

[1] Glasgow Rectorial Address, December 5th, 1912.

356

I cannot do these things, having neither the accumulated knowledge of the scholar, the audacity of the historical novelist, nor the *afflatus* of the orator; besides, in addition to these disqualifications, I am convinced of nothing half so clearly as of this: that of all the hidden, and unfathomable things in this unintelligible world, the deepest hidden, and the least fathomable, is the mind of man.

Most reluctantly, therefore, I leave my predecessors alone, and stand before you, not only a sad, but a solitary figure.

It is, however, never wise to make much fuss about anything personal to yourself. You know as well, perhaps even better than I do, how I come to be here. I do not—you will take my word for this—drop from, the sky. I was elected, after a contest, vigorously conducted, on party lines. I am sometimes credited by my enemies with knowing a good deal about such occurrences, although, in truth, few public men are as innocent as I. Elections—and I would bid you young men and women to keep this well in mind—do not stand where once they did. Representative Government is, we know, the great discovery of modern democracy, its one gift to an exceedingly ill-governed world; and Democracy, having been lately taught to read, write, and cipher at the expense of the rates, is beginning to do her own sums, to verify her *formulæ* for herself, and to examine, with an eye of critical discontent, the mechanical instrument which hitherto has been supposed to serve her turn and to secure for her that complete representation which she demands: the problem being, How is Democracy to see her own stern lineaments reflected as in a flawless mirror, without the omission or the distortion of a single feature?

Thus tested, elections, even popular elections, vigorously conducted and on party lines, are failing to give satisfaction. They have, however, and I thank heaven for it, at all events lasted my time, and I now desire to thank from the bottom of my heart all the odd men and women—I speak arithmetically and in no sense descriptively—whose votes have, to my honour, and your momentary distress, placed me where I now stand.

Ladies and gentlemen, for the last few weeks, those of you who are entranced by the drama of life, not the life of the individual, but that larger life which sweeps along with its social organisations, institutions, principalities and powers, have been living under the sway and domination of great events.

It is considerably more than forty years ago since I read for the first time, with an excitement and " a hurry of the spirit " no book need now hope to arouse in my aged breast, Disraeli's famous novel, *Coningsby*; and there I encountered the following observation: " What wonderful things are events! The least are of greater importance than the most sublime and comprehensive speculations." I remember how greatly I was startled, and from that time forward the words have lain on the very top of my memory. For good or for ill, I have done my best, with what success I know not, to keep them in constant circulation. I have printed them and quoted them again and again, and here I am, in the evening of my days, under the starry influences of the hour, the magic of this vain world, quoting them once more, probably for the last time.

I will not inquire, What did Disraeli mean? that is a question which has been asked so often; but I will inquire, What do *we* mean, when we own to the fascination of great events? Things that happen in the world of action. Blows instead of books. It must, I think, be because we are glad to recognise in the happening of great events, the outcome and the realisation, in some more or less permanent form, of what was honestly due to real effort, and to that Might, that superiority of Strength, which comes from hard discipline and sternly maintained purpose.

Then we think of some of the benefits that follow in the train of great events. Words accumulate, phrases multiply and are handed about from mouth to mouth, from one leading article to another, from one Foreign Office to another, until they become as greasy as a bundle of Scotch one-pound notes in the slimy pocket-book of a Highland drover. Acres of rubbishy talk, forests of futile palaver, obscuring the heavens, obstructing the path—then, suddenly, something really happens, one of Disraeli's great events, and away it goes, and is heard of no more; and we all begin again, and at once, chattering as busily as ever, but afresh; covering the empty sites, replanting the cleared forests, handing about new one-pound notes, until, in the fullness of time, another great event reverberates through the World, and once again what has by that time become rubbish is shot into limbo.

It must always be a melancholy reflection to Christian and Humanitarian alike that Wars and the fortunes of War are still, after the Passion of well-nigh two thousand years, the great disponers—and still make, or seem to make, the stablest foundations on which to build new States or to reconstitute old ones.

This is to me, I confess, a gloomy, a bewildering, a perturbing reflection. It was not so in other generations, perhaps more God-fearing than our own.

Nearly a hundred years ago, the 18th of January, 1816, was chosen in Great Britain as a day of general thanksgiving on which to celebrate the close of a long series of great events, beginning with the French Revolution, and ending on the field of Waterloo; and William Wordsworth, of the Lakes, a true poet, a fervent patriot, and, in the opinion of many of his sworn admirers, a good Christian, sat himself down to compose an ode for that occasion.

Like too much of Wordsworth's poetry, the ode he produced is of unequal merit; the author of *The Excursion* not being one of the mighty masters of song; still, it contains some tremendous lines:

> But Thy most dreaded instrument
> In working out a pure intent
> Is man—arrayed for mutual slaughter—
> Yea—Carnage is Thy daughter.

It seemed natural to Wordsworth in 1816 to write like this, nor did the lines I have just quoted, and others in the same sense, disappear from his editions until some late date in his long life.

For reasons, or for what pass for such, we no longer use or much care to hear used such language.

We no longer take pleasure in proclaiming God
Almighty as guiding the pestilence, as the author
of the consuming drought and the tainting mildew,
as putting the earthquake " on her still design,"
or directing the tornado to destroy the ships of
our enemies; and yet, when we worship events
and rejoice over great occurrences, *what* is it
we are worshipping and over *what* do we rejoice? We do not worship brute force, I hope,
or rejoice over blind fate. To do that would be
to dethrone conscience, to deny justice, which
resides between the endless jar of right and wrong,[1]
and to deride human effort. A rabbit caught in
a trap would then indeed be the fittest emblem
of history and the completest epitome of man.

Carried away though I was forty years ago
by the Disraelian dictum about the Majesty of
Great Events, even then I was taken aback by
the audacity of the subsequent statement that,
in comparison with them, the most sublime and
comprehensive speculations sink into insignificance.

Years do not always bring the philosophic mind,
that must depend upon how they have been spent,
but they can hardly fail to infuse into one's being
a melancholy pensiveness; and in this mood to-day
I pluck up courage flatly to deny this statement,
made though it was by a man who lived to become
Lord Rector of this University. Lord Rectors, like
auctioneers, sometimes talk wild.[2] What event that
ever happened can compare in lasting significance
with a sublime and comprehensive speculation!

---

[1] *Troilus and Cressida*, Act I. Sc. 3.
[2] See *Middlemarch,* Chapter xxxii.: " ' Auctioneers talk wild,'
said Solomon. ' Not but what Trumbull has made money.' "

Great events adorn for a time the pages of history, stirring men's blood; deeds inflame us, exciting our imagination, but save and in so far as they prove to be the outward and visible signs of men's subsequent thoughts, and thus indicate the direction of men's philosophy, eventually they fade away from memory like the baseless fabric of a dream. Oblivion must have swallowed whole Iliads of great events. Has a great comprehensive speculation ever wholly disappeared? Whatever endures must rest on a thought-basis, and must continue to be conceivable, credible, in accord with our mentality. So far, then, and not one inch further, as *words* are the vestments of *thoughts*, it is words and not deeds that mark the true epochs. Some books—not many, I dare say—have been more decisive than any battles, and some hypotheses and some canons of critical and scientific investigation have got quit of more irrelevant nonsense, of more darkening counsel, of more greasy, meaningless phrases, thereby unclogging the machinery of mind, than all the Alexanders and Akbars of history put together.

It is not so much what are called events, as the way we set about our thinking, that marks the passage of time and separates us from our predecessors. Man remains the same, it is his thinking that differs.

Ever since, in this western world, we emerged from the savage state, there has been noticeable about us a great uniformity. " The same heart beats in every human breast." [1] The Five Senses (those most inadequate avenues of sensation);

[1] Matthew Arnold, *The Buried Life.*

the Four Seasons, in a word, the Weather; the Certainty of Death; Pain and Pleasure; Mirth and Melancholy; the eternal contrast between the Greatness and the Littleness of human life; the Joys of perfect bodily health, and the Languor of disease, have so wrought upon us, have so turned and twisted us and shaped us, that what Shakespeare says is no more than the plain truth: "All are woven so strangely in one piece."[1]

But though the material may be the same, how different are the instruments of thought, or at any rate, the methods of thinking! The orthodox theologian of to-day and a Christian Father of the fourth century; their documents are the same, their creed is professedly the same, their humanity is the same, everything else is different. Pass in rapid review the lawyers, the historians, the natural philosophers, say even of the seventeenth century, and compare them with our own corresponding pundits. The men are much the same, their subject-matter is the same, but their methods have been so revolutionised by speculative thought, that Hannibal crossing the Alps on his elephant is not too antiquated a figure to be used by way of a metaphorical comparison. The world's great poets are the glorious exceptions. "Time writes no wrinkle on their azure brows," if I may be allowed a slight misquotation. But of them I must not speak to-day, though it is never easy to keep them out of any human discourse.

If we survey the field of speculation from close at hand, and watch the fighting that always is going on between contending ideas and rival

[1] *Henry VIII.*, Act IV. Sc. I.

schools—the old ideas, and if you will, old schools, but very differently armed—those of us who feel we have no gifts for exact thinking, and who prefer a poet to either a philosopher or a divine, may sometimes be tempted to run for shelter once again behind Disraeli's gaberdine, and in our haste to cry out with him, " Give us great events, something that really happens under our noses, and not this endless flux and reflux of wordy speculation." But we should do wrong to do anything of the kind.

I number, I am glad to say, among my friends, two or three—at the most it is three—philosophers of repute:

> Dread openers of the mysterious doors
> Leading to universal knowledge.[1]

stout men whose conceptions dodge " the very bourne of Heaven." [2]

These friends, not being of the kind so detested by the poet Cowper, who would " needlessly set foot upon a worm " like me, occasionally, out of sheer kindness, and of their compassion for the limited range of my studies, tell me of a philosophical or quasi-philosophical work—it is usually I fear the latter—which they think I might partially understand. Lately, noticing perhaps that I was somewhat harassed, they have recommended to me the writings of Professor Eucken, of the University of Jena. Always docile, I procured a volume, and in the intervals of other business, began to read it. The first thing Eucken has told me is that I am living in a transitional period, face to face with a crisis, moral and intellectual.

---

[1] Keats's *Endymion*.   [2] *Ibid.*

This was no news to me, who before I had read *Coningsby* had been initiated into that glorious art, craft and mystery, the style of Thomas Carlyle. That same Thomas of Ecclefechan and Craigenputtock—" God be with his soul, he was a merry man "[1]—had long years before I was born, to wit in 1829 and 1831, scattered broadcast through the heartless, callous and sterile pages of the *Edinburgh Review*, where they still may be found, glowing like red embers in an otherwise raked-out grate, two famous articles, called " Signs of the Times " and " Characteristics," which took as their text this very same transitional period and an almost identical crisis. In 1829 this aspect of affairs may, I dare say, have been somewhat of a novelty, but its sudden promulgation, in what was then a new language, in the pages of the *Blue and Buff*, momentarily united in the bonds of a common detestation, two of your Lord Rectors, who otherwise hated each other as only Lord Rectors can, Brougham and Macaulay. How, indeed, it came about that Carlyle obtained, even for a short time, a right of entry into these great Whig preserves must have remained inexplicable unto this day, had we not been permitted to learn, through the delightful tell-tale channels of autobiography, that it was attributable to an Editorial flirtation with the *femme incomprise* of the distinguished contributor.

Anyhow, from 1829 onward, every ingenuous young soul in these islands was free to know that he lived in a transitional period, face to face with a crisis. So it has long continued. In 1861, John

[1] *Romeo and Juliet*, Act I. Sc. 3.

Stuart Mill pressed home the very same thing that stared me in the face when, at the bidding of my philosophers, I took up Eucken. Mill, in 1861, wrote: "When the philosophic minds of the world can no longer believe its religion, or can only believe in it with modifications amounting to an essential change of its character, a transitional period commences of weak convictions, paralysed intellects, and growing laxity of opinions."[1] This is but a pale echo of the articles of 1829 and 1831, and now in 1912 a highly-recommended voice from Jena says the same thing.

A transitional period, involving a crisis which lasts a century, suggests a misnomer. Was there ever, I wonder, a perfectly stable equilibrium in men's belief? Did Religion ever wholly chime with all human experiences? St. Augustine, no less than Thomas Arnold, had to stifle his doubts. In the later Middle Ages, though Aristotle, imprisoned by St. Thomas Aquinas, may have regulated, perhaps usefully, all university studies, he did not dominate university life. The Latin poems attributed to Walter Mapes (the friend of that Giraldus Cambrensis who has suddenly been aroused from his slumbers to be bandied across the floor of the House of Commons) and the Merry Verses called *Carmina Burana* always seem to me to carry along with them more than a savour of my own transitional period, and to suggest very emphatically a real crisis.

Between 1829 and 1912, however, one change is very noticeable. In 1829 we find Carlyle writing cautiously: "To what extent theological unbelief,

[1] *Autobiography*, p. 239.

we mean intellectual dissent from the Church in her view of Holy Writ, prevails at this day, would be a highly important, were it not in any circumstances an almost impossible enquiry."

This reticence, this circumspection, this timidity, so noticeable all through the last century, has in 1912 wholly disappeared. I find my new friend Eucken saying, "There is probably more antipathy against religion to-day, and a more widespread and popular denial of it, than ever has been the case before."[1]

But if the real change is that people now speak out who formerly held their peace, it may well be that the Professor is mistaken.

A Cambridge scholar, and a most devout Christian and High Churchman, Dr. Figgis, is, however, of the same opinion as the German professor, and lately told an audience of Bostonians that in his opinion there are no longer grounds for believing that the Western World is Christian in any sense in which it was not in the period immediately preceding Constantine the Great. We no more live in a Christian world, he says, than was done in the time of Tertullian. The atmosphere in literature and art, in novels and dramas, in newspapers and reviews, is not only no longer, so Dr. Figgis declares, Christian, but is largely anti-Christian, even on the ethical side. He goes on to ask, " If you inquired of the most highly educated society in the West whether it is Christian, I think the answer is not doubtful. Would there be any large proportion of Christians at any meeting

[1] See *Main Currents of Modern Thought* (T. Fisher Unwin, 1912), p. 46.

of scholars or scientific men? Is there, in any real
sense, at the Universities?"[1]

These are searching questions to be asked by
anyone, at any time and in any place. You must
answer them for yourselves.

Our moods vary, and sometimes, whilst we
contemplate this "curious, restless, clamorous,
panting life of man" (the words are Dr. Newman's), it might seem as if the great mass of
people, busily occupied as they necessarily are with
their own affairs, hard put to it to survive from
week to week, must live outside all thought and
speculation. What can it matter, then, what they
think, and, after all, do we ourselves differ greatly
from the bulk of mankind?

But it does matter enormously. Everyone in
the world has a stand of his own; some bases of
thought, however conventional; some foundations, however seemingly insecure, which just
manage to keep him from going down on all fours.

Therefore, I say to you (I have no right to do
more): Do your thinking seriously, and never allow
yourselves in these coming days to sneer at the
convictions of other people, however remote from
reality those convictions may appear to you to be.

A great University like yours, founded by a
Papal Bull, and where for centuries there has been
a *Studium Generale*, and where you have to-day
learned professors illustrating all the faculties,
and crowded lecture-halls and class-rooms, is the
very last place for either an unwarrantable dog-
matism or an uneducated exclusiveness. It is,

[1] See *Civilisation at the Cross-roads*. By J. N. Figgis. (Longmans,
1912, pp. 29–64.)

for example, as contrary to the spirit of true learning for a man of scientific pursuits to sneer at the study — the living study, not the mere professional, tied-house study—of theology as it would be absurd for a theologian to imagine that he can keep the scientific spirit and historical criticism outside his curriculum.

Widely different as men's conclusions may still be, the thoughts, the conceptions, the conditions out of which they are now all fashioned belong to a common stock. Toleration, that master-word, which, so far from being a synonym for indifference, as some would still have us believe, is, in the long run, the only guarantee for honesty, has finally broken down the barbed-wire fencing which once kept nations, churches, sects, towns, and even streets apart. This community, this contagion of thought, though not in the least interfering with the intensity of our convictions once obtained, does undoubtedly greatly widen, for all of us, the areas of choice. The beliefs of members of the same household are often as wide apart as will be their graves. This freedom, whilst increasing personal responsibility, heightens interest and makes for sincerity.

Candid biography is, almost for the first time, beginning to play a significant part in the records, still too scanty, of mental experience. In the last few years the interested English reader has been presented with three remarkable biographies, two of Cardinals of Rome and one, just published, of a late member of the great Society of Jesus. Avoiding all controversy, no one will deny that, true as it may well be that Authority resides somewhere, these biographies have exposed one particular reputed place of residence to a searching criticism; and when we get, as we may surely hope to get, equally candid biographies of men of science and philosophy, we shall be the gainers.

I really want, for my own sake at least as much as for yours, to get if I can a little light upon this troublesome, transitional period of " weak convictions, paralysed intellects, and growing laxity of opinions," into which I was born and in which I must apparently die.

If a period can go on being transitional for one or two centuries, or possibly even three centuries, the truth I am searching after seems to be no more than our very familiar friend—the most familiar tag of all the tags with which men have ever loved to garnish their speech—" *Tempora mutantur, nos et mutamur in illis.*"

To be brought bolt up against either a platitude or a paradox is a very common incident in the life of the humble seeker after truth.

Looking back, we find far more celebrated persons than ourselves—I mean quite historical people like Petrarch and Boccaccio—spending all their days in the most famous and one of the longest transitional periods that ever was—I mean the Renaissance, which began in Petrarch's time, when the scholars of Italy, who for seven long centuries had known no Greek and only such meagre scraps of Greek literature as existed in Latin translations, first found themselves reading, in recently discovered manuscripts, Homer and Plato.

These were indeed not only transitional but exciting times. The quest throughout Europe and Asia Minor of old Greek manuscripts; the rediscovery of the imperishable (for now, thanks to the mechanical arts, they are imperishable) masters of thought and expression; the re-reading of what

> The lofty grave Tragedians taught
> In Chorus or Iambic—Teachers best
> Of Moral Prudence, with delight received
> In brief sententious precepts, while they treat
> Of fate, and chance, and change in human life; [1]

the discovery, I say, of these things hidden among the mountains in out-of-the-way monasteries and in the muniment chests of cathedral churches, in the days of Petrarch and Boccaccio, of Salutati and Poggio, of Aurispa and Filelfo, makes all our boasted book-hunting appear a sport not much more dignified than the murderous trivialities of a Sparrow Club.

In Sir John Sandys' fascinating *History of Classical Scholarship*,[2] you may read for yourselves —I could not do so without undue emotion—of the *bonnes fortunes* of the Sicilian scholar, Aurispa, a mighty hunter in his day. Sophocles, Euripides, Thucydides, the Homeric Hymns, Pindar, Aristophanes, nearly all Demosthenes, Plato, Xenophon —these were but a few of his MSS., for when he came to Venice in 1423, he brought with him two hundred and thirty-eight, almost entirely consisting of the Greek Classics. As sometimes happens with great collectors, he did not make much use of his treasures, nor, when he came to die in Ferrara in 1459, was there any great " Aurispa Sale," such as nowadays proclaims the demise, or

---

[1] *Paradise Regained*, Book IV. ll. 261–5.
[2] Published at the University Press, Cambridge. 3 vols. 1908.

the bankruptcy, or the change of taste of some rich book-collector of New York or Philadelphia!

I must, however, beware of speaking of this wonderful revival of learning as if it were a virtuoso's whim. It was a mighty movement lasting two hundred years, which wrought havoc upon the mediæval mind and introduced the note of modernity into our Cosmos.

Petrarch, an impressionable, vain man, slightly constructed, it may be, but of genius, felt himself, so he has told us, to be standing between two great sets of people—those behind him and those in front—on a great divide between two ages.

The Renaissance, which historians date as from the birth of Petrarch in 1304 to the Sack of Rome in 1527, was followed by another almost equally famous transitional period, the Reformation of Religion; which in its turn had to give way to what we call, so conveniently and compendiously, the Revolution.

Great epochs indeed. You cannot read a European book of the least note for five minutes without being able to place it as having been composed before or after the revival of the ancient learning, before or after the reformation of religion, before or after the Revolution.

The immediate force of these great movements is now spent. They still swell the current, but the waters are so intermingled that no one of us can point,

> As with a wand, and say
> This portion of the river of my mind
> Came from yon fountain.[1]

[1] *The Prelude*, Bk. II.

The great achievements of these periods in art, in letters, in theology, no longer dominate. We have emerged from beneath their shadows, and can and do and will criticise their several productions with the freedom which only belongs to those who live outside a jurisdiction.

To sum all this up, if I can. Were I once again young, I should not dwell as much as I was early led to do by my reading, upon the transitional character of the period of time in which I found myself, nor upon any particular crisis I was supposed to be facing; but I should try to be content, without compassionating myself, or frequent takings of my moral temperature, to lead the life of my own time, sharing to the full its thoughts and speculations without recklessness, levity, or cowardice; not, as were the mediævalists, intimidated by the fear of death, yet with a Johnsonian gravity befitting its ever-nearing approach.

I say to you, therefore: Think seriously, for the times we live in are serious, and as men think so will they live; and it is the lives of men, and not blind fate, that weave the destiny of the human race.

SPEECH AT THE LUNCHEON AT GLASGOW UNIVERSITY AFTER THE RECTORIAL ADDRESS, DEC. 5TH, 1912

M R. PRINCIPAL, my Lords and Gentlemen,—Listening as I have just done with emotion, not unmingled with surprise, to the very kindly observations of the Principal, I could not but think what would I not have given forty years ago to have had such a *testamur* from any of my professors. Everything, they say, comes to the man who knows how to wait, and I have had to wait for forty long years for any such expression of professorial and learned approval. However, I accept it. Although late, I hope it may throw a tinge of melancholy joy over the evening of my days. I should like to have had it a little earlier, but, never mind, it has come at last. I can only assure you all that I regard this happy connection of mine with your University, which, as the Principal has so kindly reminded you—I did not need to be reminded of it—was also my father's, as one of the happiest incidents in my life. I shall never forget it, and never can forget it, and I feel it very deeply. I always think that politicians, although politics are coldly received sometimes, get far more than their deserts, and if I could live life over again and exercise more influence than ever I have been able to do in public assemblies, I would say: Beware of too much honour upon

politicians! Try other sources. Look for your
Lord Rectors elsewhere, because although I accept
with sincerity what has been indicated, apparently
with some approval, that when you chose me you
were not thinking at all of politics—you were
simply thinking of your goddess Letters, and you
looked about to find some modest, retiring, quiet
essayist, some humble denizen of his own study,
and then you were going to come to him with
your golden crown and say to him: " None of your
politics for us; we do not care for those dreary
partisans. We bring to you this great honour
fresh from academic hearts; we select a man of
letters; and we give the contemptuous go-by to
the chatterboxes in the House of Commons."

If that is so, all I can say is I think you are
beginning after some centuries of bad habit to see
where you should carry your great honours. But
I am afraid sometimes you like a politician, not
because you think he is a wise man, but because
you think he will be able to carry through somehow, whereas the modest man of letters might
break down. In St. Andrew's Hall, you think,
he might not be able to face, I must not say the
mob, but the learned populace. I cannot help
surmising that that is the reason why, notwithstanding the way you lightly disclaim politics,
you are at all events glad to find your man of
letters has been corrupted to that extent by communication with that bad practice as to be the sort
of Lord Rector you best desire. But I assure you,
if in future you wish to avoid politicians altogether
and select a quiet and reposeful man of letters,
nothing will give me greater pleasure than to appear

on the platform by his side to play the part of
Aaron to his Moses and hold up one of his hands.
Gentlemen, I desire to thank you very much,
because it enables me to do what is always a pleasure to me, to assert myself a Scotsman. Nobody
believes me. Nobody ever has believed me, but I
assure you if blood or feeling has anything to do
with it there is no better Scotsman than myself,
because, although born in Liverpool and educated
in England, after all I was born none the less in
a Scottish home, and I can assure you, what with
my father and mother and my nurse—who came
from Dysart and never could be got to believe that
my father's birthplace of Kirkcaldy was worth
mentioning—the atmosphere of that home was
just as likely to make me a good Scotsman as if it
had been in the Kingdom of Fife or the city of
Glasgow. I was brought up perhaps somewhat
narrowly in the Scottish faith. I remember quite
honestly believing that the birth of Christ and
the Hegira of Mahomet found an event of almost
equal importance in the Disruption of the Scottish
Church in 1843 — and although bound to admit
that subsequent study and such moments of reflection that have been allowed me in a crowded
life have induced me somewhat to alter the per-
spective, nevertheless I remain choke-full of honest
Scottish prejudices. My grandfather, my mother's
father, Dr. Henry Grey, was one of the leaders
of that Disruption, and succeeded Dr. Chalmers
as Moderator of the Free Kirk, and his bust adorns
the Free Church Hall in Edinburgh. I mention
these things because nobody else will.

But there was something else besides and beyond

the Disruption. There was the glorious atmosphere
of Sir Walter Scott which dominated the whole of
my boyhood, and my earliest and most tender
associations are connected with my mother's voice
reading, and sometimes breaking down in, passages
of those novels which at all events moved her to
tears. Then other favourite novels in our household were the Scottish novels, quite as Scottish,
perhaps even more Scottish than Sir Walter Scott's
novels—I mean John Galt's novels, the *Annals
of the Parish* and *The Provost*. I knew *The Provost*
almost by heart when a boy, and I attribute to
my knowledge of it the astonishing good terms
on which I have been with all Provosts, whether
of the numerous towns which adorn the Kingdom
of Fife—a portion of which I once represented—
or the Provosts of even greater and more important
cities. Everybody who knows Galt, knows his
Provost to the centre of his soul—and it is no mean
acquisition to possess that knowledge—and I was
made free of it almost from my childhood. Therefore I do not feel out of place in a Scottish University, and I thank you most cordially for the very
kind reception you have given me. I recommend
what the Principal has said about me to your
careful consideration. Let it sink into your hearts
if critically you find room for it, but I beg you also
to listen to what I have said, and to remember
that whatever happens to your Lord Rector, he
will die, as he has lived, a good Scotsman. And
now the honour devolves upon me, having got rid
of that speech, to propose the health of this great
University, and I do so, I need scarcely say, feeling
that it is a toast which, in this assembly, needs no

recommendation. The University of Glasgow is known throughout the world. It has its graduates in every civilised quarter. It has its recollections therefore, and its old friendships striking an electrical chord throughout the whole world. Wherever Glasgow people forgather, their University has a proud place in their recollections, and nothing gives me greater happiness than to see how closely the University is here connected with your great city. You are no alien plant living exterritorially, as it were, on Glasgow soil. You are all one together, each proud of the other, each contributing to the welfare, to the endowment, and to the greatness of each other. The union of the University and the city now exists on the happiest terms, and I pray it may long abide. I ask you to drink prosperity to the future of the University of Glasgow.

A BIBLIOGRAPHICAL NOTE

(November 1922)

In this edition are included *all* the Essays first collected in the six volumes named below. An asterisk is attached (in the Table of Contents) to those Essays and Addresses which hitherto have not been collected.

(1) OBITER DICTA.   London, Elliot Stock, 1884.

> Carlyle
> On the Alleged Obscurity of Mr. Browning's
>   Poetry
> Truth-hunting
> Actors
> A Rogue's Memoirs
> The Via Media
> Falstaff

(2) OBITER DICTA (Second Series). London, Elliot Stock, 1887.

> John Milton
> Pope
> Dr. Johnson
> Burke
> The Muse of History
> Charles Lamb
> Emerson
> The Office of Literature
> Worn-out Types
> Cambridge and the Poets
> Book-buying

(3) RES JUDICATÆ. London, Elliot Stock, 1892.

> Samuel Richardson
> Edward Gibbon
> William Cowper
> George Borrow
> Cardinal Newman
> Matthew Arnold
> William Hazlitt
> The Letters of Charles Lamb
> Authors in Court
> Nationality
> The Reformation
> Sainte-Beuve

(4) MEN, WOMEN AND BOOKS. London, Elliot Stock, 1894.

> Dean Swift
> Lord Bolingbroke
> Sterne
> The Gospel according to Dr. Johnson
> Richard Cumberland
> Alexander Knox and Thomas De Quincey
> Hannah More
> Marie Bashkirtseff
> Sir John Vanbrugh
> John Gay
> Roger North's Autobiography
> Books Old and New
> Book-binding
> Poets Laureate
> Parliamentary Candidates
> The *Bonâ-fide* Traveller
> " Hours in a Library "
> Americanisms and Briticisms
> Authors and Critics

(5) MISCELLANIES. London, Elliot Stock, 1902.

> John Wesley
> What happened at the Reformation?

Christian Evidences
Ideal of a University
Walter Bagehot
J. A. Froude
Robert Browning
Is it possible to tell a good Book from a bad one ?
The House of Commons
Sir Robert Peel

(6) IN THE NAME OF THE BODLEIAN.   London, Elliot
Stock, 1905.
" In the Name of the Bodleian "
Bookworms
Confirmed Readers
First Editions
Gossip in a Library
Librarians at Play
Lawyers at Play
The Non-Jurors
Lord Chesterfield
The Johnsonian Legend
Boswell as Biographer
Old Pleasure Gardens
Old Booksellers
A Few Words about Copyright in Books
Hannah More once More
Arthur Young
Thomas Paine
Charles Bradlaugh
Disraeli *ex relatione* Sir William Fraser
A Connoisseur
Our Great Middle Class
Tar and Whitewash
Itineraries
Epitaphs
" Hansard "
Contempt of Court
5 Edward VII., chapter 12